South America To-Day

CHAPTER I
THE OUTWARD VOYAGE

The *Regina Elena* is in harbour. A great white boat vomits volumes of black smoke from its two funnels, whilst the siren sounds the familiar farewell. Two gangways, on which luggage and passengers are jostling desperately, present the peculiar spectacle of departing crowds. On a dais of multi-coloured sunshades, the wide hats of beautiful Genoese women offer their good wishes to the little veiled toques of the travellers. People stop in the narrowest part of the gangway to laugh and cry together. Vainly the human flood tries to break through the obstacle. The current, according to its strength, carries the living mass of feathers and ribbons back to the landing-place or pushes it on to the deck, where, in a perfect maze of movement and exclamations, it continues to stop the traffic.

Not far away, heavily laden with nondescript burdens, the silent emigrant forces his way to the lower deck, dragging old parents and young children after him. Do not imagine the emigrant leaving Italy for the Argentine to be the miserable human specimen one generally sees. He is neither more nor less than a workman moving from one hemisphere to another. We shall meet him again on board. Strongly attached to family life, his peculiarity is to move about with his wife and progeny. The difference in seasons allows him, after cutting corn on the Pampas, to return to Italy for the harvest. Often he settles down in the Argentine under the conditions which I shall explain later, and takes strong root there. Often, again, the love of his native land speaks louder than his love of adventure, and the steamship companies are glad to profit by the circumstance.

The siren has blown its last authoritative blast; the last visitors have returned to land; the huge monster glides gently out to sea. One sees nothing but waving handkerchiefs and hears nothing but parting words. We are off. "Good-bye." The grand amphitheatre of white marble and sunburnt stones glides slowly past us, dazzling in the warm light. Already our eyes were looking with curiosity and hopefulness towards the liquid plain. Are we flying from Europe, or is Europe flying from us? From this moment we shall look to see America surge up from the horizon on the day ordained.

The first impressions of the boat are excellent: it is admirably fitted up; clean as a new pin, with good attendance. We are welcomed in a most charming manner by the Captain, de Benedetti, a *galant 'uomo*, who advertises his French sympathies by flying a French flag. A fortnight in a handsome moving prison, with floods of salt air to fill one's lungs, and the marvellous panorama of sky and sea, shot with luminous arrows. Our daily promenades are those of prisoners condemned to walk in an eternal circle. As long as land is in sight, our eyes linger on the blue line of mountains, which speaks to us of the country which, in spite of the revolving screw, our hearts refuse to leave.

The Ligurian coast, crowned by Alpine heights; Provence, rich in memories, blue mountains darkened by the dying day; grey spots, which represent Toulon and Marseilles. A choppy, rather rough sea, complicated by a ground swell, as we cross the Bay of Lyons, tries the ladies, who had hitherto been very lively. They retire to their cabins, whence issue sinister sounds.

But let us pass on. To-morrow's sun will illumine the joyous hospitality of Barcelona.

Never did land look so fascinating to me. I have crossed the Atlantic eight times without ever feeling that kind of anticipated regret for the old Continent. Youth longs for the Unknown, but age learns to fear it.

The passengers lunched on shore. Then came a visit to the *Rambla*, sad and deserted under the grey sky. We linger over our first letters home, which can neither be called letters from abroad nor letters of farewell. A cab carries us about in a haphazard way, past modern houses which are a disgrace to Spain and our epoch, and past façades of convents burnt down in the last revolution. Finally, we are driven back to the quay, where, since morning, a crowd of fruit-sellers, picturesquely attired in red and yellow, have been selling their wares to the emigrants, forbidden by the regulations to land at the ports of call. Nets attached to long poles, filled with provisions of all sorts, are offered to the passengers on the lower decks and held at a safe distance until the sum, which has been volubly disputed, falls into the outstretched apron below.

But the signal is given. The teeming market disappears, and, without more ado, we put out to sea. In the dusk of the evening we discern the white summits of the Sierra Nevada, in whose shadow lie Granada and the Alhambra. We shall pass Gibraltar in the night, and at dawn to-morrow we shall have only the blue monotony of the infinite sea.

It is five days' steam to St. Vincent, in the Cape Verde Islands. The passengers shake down, grouping themselves according to national or professional affinities. Stretched on arm-chairs of excessive size—which turn the daily walk into a steeplechase—fair ladies, wrapped in shawls and gauzes, and profoundly indifferent to the comfort of others, try to read, but only succeed in yawning. They chatter aimlessly without real conversation. The cries of the children create a diversion, and a badly-trained dog is a fruitful topic for discussion. The men sit down to bridge, or smoke innumerable pipes in the Winter Garden. I catch scraps of business talk around me.

The boldest foot it on the deck, but their enterprise does not please the gentler passengers, who are in quiet possession of the only space available for exercise. Soon, under the guise of sops to the ravenous ocean appetite, piles of plates, glasses, and decanters, complicated with stools and travelling rugs, encumber the passageway. As the soft roll of the ship causes a certain disturbance of the crockery, the pedestrian, young or old, has always a chance of breaking his leg—a contingency to which the ladies appear to be perfectly indifferent. The piano suffers cruelly from sharp raps administered by knotty juvenile fingers. An Italian lady sings, and one of my own countrywomen sketches a group of emigrants.

In the primitive setting of the steerage everybody is already at home and appears happy. Attentive fathers walk and play with their offspring and occasionally smack them by way of showing them the right path. Mothers are nursing their babies or washing clothes. I am told that there are no fewer than twenty-six nursing mothers out of a total of six hundred third-class passengers on board. Amid the Italian swarm, brightly coloured groups of Syrians stand out. The women, tattooed, painted, and clad in light-coloured draperies, sometimes covered with silver ornaments, fall naturally into the dignified and statuesque pose of the Oriental. A few are really handsome, with a sort of passive sensuality of bearing. It is said that the Syrians are the licensed pedlars of the Pampas.

A visit between decks shows that the ventilation is good and that cleanliness is insured by incessant application of brush and hose. The sick bay is well kept. One or two patients are in the maternity ward awaiting an interesting event before the Equator can be reached. The food is wholesome and abundant. The Italian Government keeps a permanent official on board who is independent of the officers of the ship, and sees that the regulations concerning hygiene and safety for this class of passengers are rigorously carried out. Frightful abuses in former days necessitated these measures, which are now entirely efficacious.

We are looking forward to calling at St. Vincent as a welcome break in the monotony of our days. However, thanks to wireless telegraphy, we are no longer cut off from the world on this highly perfected raft which balances our fortunes between heaven and sea. One cannot help feeling surprised when presented with an envelope bearing the word "Telegram." Some one has sent me his good wishes for the voyage from France by way of Dakar. Then by the same mysterious medium the passengers of a ship we shall meet to-morrow wave their hats to us in advance. On several occasions I have had the pleasure of receiving messages of this sort; they are incidents in a day. From time to time we can read the despatches of the news agencies posted in the saloon. I leave you to imagine how, with our abundant leisure, we discuss the news. From St. Vincent to the island of Fernando de Noronha, the advanced post of Brazil, I do not think we were ever more than two days out of range of wireless telegraphy. When it is compulsory to have a wireless installation on board all ships, collisions at sea can never occur. I visit the telegraph office situated forward on the upper deck. It is a small cabin where an employee sits all day striking sparks from his machine as messages arrive from all parts of the horizon; the sound reminds me of the crackling of a distant mitrailleuse. Here one must not allow the mind to wander even with the smoke of one's cigarette. Through a technical blunder our unfortunate telegraphist, without knowing it, sent the information to Montevideo that we were in danger. In consequence, we learnt from the newspapers on our arrival that the Government was sending a State ship to our help. We thus experienced the sweet sensation of peril without danger, whilst the employee guilty of the error found himself discharged.

We shall not profit by the call at St. Vincent, since we arrive in the night. It is in vain that they tell us that the Cape Verde Islands are nothing but a series of arid, yellow rocks; that St. Vincent can only show commonplace houses and cabins with the inevitable cocoanut-trees; that the "town" is only inhabited by negroes who pick up a living from the ships that put in here to coal; whilst the English coal importers and real masters of this Portuguese possession live up in the hills. Nevertheless, we are disappointed of an opportunity to stroll on shore towards a clump of trees, apparently planted there with the object of justifying the name of the place, which is in reality the most barren spot.

On our way we had passed the denuded rocks which somebody tells us are called the Canaries. St. Vincent, it seems, is a second edition of the Canaries —only more sterile. We have no difficulty in believing it when at nightfall the *Regina Elena* stops at the bottom of a deep black hole dotted with distant lights, of which some are fixed to the bows of small craft or tugboats drawing coal lighters, which dance up to us on the waves.

Suddenly, as in the third act of *L'Africaine*, under the orders of an invisible Nelusko, we are invaded on the starboard and port side by a dual horde of savages. They are fearful-looking blacks, with grinning masks, clothed in coal-dust, who swarm like monkeys up the shrouds and fall on deck with the laugh of cannibals. We are assured that our lives are not in danger, and, in fact, they are no sooner amongst us than, attacked with sudden shyness, they offer in a low voice and in a language in which French and English are strangely mixed, an assortment of cocoanuts, bananas, and bags made of melon seeds, to which they seem to attach great importance.

Once more we fall back on the small events of our daily life on board, of which the principal is to find the point in the southern horizon by which the speed of the ship can be calculated, under given conditions of wind and tide. On the New York crossing, the Americans make of this detail an excuse for a daily bet. I notice that the South Americans are less addicted to this form of sport. The first impression made upon me by these South American families with whom I am thrown in daily contact is eminently favourable. Simplicity, dignity, and graciousness are what I see: I find none of the extravagance ascribed to them by rumour. Only on one point am I led to make a criticism: their children seem to enjoy the utmost license of speech and action.

Henceforth our only subject of conversation is the probable date on which we shall cross the Equator. The *Regina Elena*, with a displacement of 10,000 tons, did 17 knots on her trials. If she makes 14 or 15 now, we are satisfied. The sea is calm: not a stomach protests. In these latitudes the storms of the North Atlantic are unknown. We shall make the crossing from Barcelona to Buenos Ayres in fifteen or sixteen days. A long rest for any one leaving or seeking a life of excitement.

We amuse ourselves by watching troops of dolphins, divine creatures, passing from the joys of the air to those of the sea with a facile grace. What legends have been created about these mammals! From the most ancient times they have been the friends of the seafarer! They save the shipwrecked, and surrender to the charms of music. According to Homeric song, it was from the dolphin that Apollo borrowed the disguise in which he led the Cretan fishermen to the shores of Delphi, where later his temple was built. How true to life is the undulating line of the bas-reliefs on the monument of Lysicrates, in which the Tyrrhenian pirates, transformed into dolphins, fling themselves into the ocean, as though in feverish haste to try a new life! Souvenirs of this old tale surge in my brain until I hear a voice saying harshly: "All these filthy beasts ought to be killed with dynamite, for they destroy the nets of the fishermen." Good-bye to poetic legend! Friendship between man and the dolphin ends in utilitarian holocausts!

Civilisation has not yet stamped out the flying-fish. It is still left to us to enjoy the spectacle of the great sea-locusts in flight, rising in flocks into the air to escape from their greedy comrades in the water, and dappling the wide blue plain with their winged whiteness. They remind me of the story of the traveller who was readily believed when he declared he had found at the bottom of the Red Sea a horseshoe belonging to the cavalry of Pharaoh swallowed up in their pursuit of the Hebrews. But when he talked of flying-fish, he found no credence anywhere! It is true men have told so many tales that it is not easy to know when it is safe to show surprise.

A daily increasing and heavy heat meets us as we draw near the Line. Light flannel suits are brought into requisition, and breathing becomes difficult to redundant flesh. We are in the *Black Pot*—skies low, heavy with iron-grey clouds; an intermittent, fine rain which cools nothing; a glassy sea; no breeze stirring. It feels like the interior of a baker's oven. We take refuge in the dangerous electric fan which is unequalled for adding a bad cold to the disagreeable sensation of suffocation.

Nothing remains of the famous ceremony of christening the passenger who crosses the Line for the first time. The innocent performance is now converted into a ball, with a subscription for the crew. Passengers on the lower deck waltz every evening with far less ceremony, to the strains of an accordion, varying the entertainment by playing at *Morra*, the national game. They stand up in couples and aim terrific blows at each other's faces, accompanying the movement with savage cries. If you watch carefully you will find that in this game of fisticuffs the closed hand is stopped just in time and, at the same moment, a certain number of fingers are shot out. Simultaneously a voice cries a number, always less than ten; and the game consists in trying to announce beforehand how many fingers have been pointed by the two partners. This sport, which has the advantage of requiring none but Nature's implements, is a great favourite with the Italians. Often, in the early morning, from my berth, I used to hear an alarming barking in the direction of the bows, which seemed to be the beginning of a deadly quarrel, but was in reality merely the fun of the *Morra*.

Brazilian territory is now in sight—Fernando de Noronha. It is a volcanic island three days off Rio de Janeiro. Successive streams of lava have given strangely jagged outlines to the peaks. A wide opening in the mountain lets in a view of the shining sea on the other side of the island. Three lofty poles of wireless telegraphy stand out among the foliage. They say that these posts were set there by Frenchmen. Goodluck to them!

Captain de Benedetti pays me the compliment of celebrating the Fourteenth of July. The Queen's portrait is framed in the flags of the two nations. In the evening we have champagne and drink healths. An Italian senator, Admiral de Brochetti, expresses, in well-chosen language, his appreciation of the friendship of France and I echo his good wishes for the sister nation.

Is there any better relief from the exhaustion of a sleepless night in the tropics than a solitary walk beneath the starry firmament of the Southern Hemisphere? Naturally, I sought the Southern Cross as soon as it had risen above the horizon. It was another disillusionment caused by an inflated reputation. Where are ye, O Great Bear and Pleiades, and where the Belt of

Orion? On the other hand, words fail to describe the Alpha of Argo. Every morning, between three and four o'clock, I see on the port side a sort of huge blue diamond which appears to lean out of the celestial vault towards the black gulf of the restless sea as if to illumine its abysses. I receive the most powerful sensation of living light that the firmament has ever given to me. If there is in any part of infinite space a prodigious altar of celestial fire, that focus must be Canopus. It was assuredly there that Prometheus stole the heavenly spark with which he kindled in us the light of life. There, too, Vesta watches over the eternal hearth of sacred fire in which is concentrated a more divine splendour than even that of a tropical sun.

But now the earth calls us back to herself, or, rather, it is the stormy ocean that rouses us, for as we approach the immense estuary of La Plata a tempest of icy wind blows suddenly upon us from the south. This is the *pampero*, the south wind, the wind from the Pampas, which blows straight from the frozen tops of the Andes. A heavy swell makes the *Regina Elena* roll in the great yellow waves, for already the clay of the Rio de la Plata is perceptible in the sea and gives it the aspect of a vast ocean of mud. To-morrow morning we shall be in Montevideo.

CHAPTER II
MONTEVIDEO AND BUENOS AYRES

Through the vaporous atmosphere of the sky-line appear the serrated edges of Montevideo, the capital of Uruguay, which was formerly a province of the Argentine, but is to-day an independent republic. In the current language of Buenos Ayres, Uruguay is known simply as "the Oriental Band," and when you hear it said of any one that "he is an Oriental," know that by this term is not meant a Turk or a Levantine, but the inhabitant of the smallest republic in South America, hemmed in between the left bank of the Uruguay, Brazil, and the sea.

Quite apart from the question of size, the Argentine and Uruguay have too much in common not to be jealous of each other. The Argentinos would appear to think that the prodigious development of their country must ultimately have the effect of bringing back Uruguay to the fold. This may be so; but it is also quite possible that the "Oriental Band" in her pride will continue to cherish her independence. Meantime, while leaving to the future the solution of the question, there is a little friction between them. Uruguay's revolutionary shocks usually originate in Argentine territory, across the river. The Argentine Government is certainly averse to any leniency towards those who incite to civil war, but it is not always able to exact obedience. South American ways! It is hardly necessary to add that the leaders of an unsuccessful party are wont to take refuge in Buenos Ayres—ten hours distant by the fine boats on the estuary—and that the natural magnet of commercial prosperity enlarges this political nucleus by the powerful factor of trade. There are no less than fifty thousand Orientals [1] in the Argentine capital, and the daily traffic between the two cities may be judged by the crowd assembled morning and evening on board the *Piroscafi*.

A brisk walk round the city to obtain a first impression of South America was the most I could do in a stop of a few hours. The landing was somewhat laborious owing to a heavy sea. The President of the Republic was obliging enough to send me a greeting by one of his aides-de-camp, and placed at my disposal the most comfortable of boats, which, after dancing gaily for a while on the waves, finally landed us without too much trouble. The docks, constructed by a French firm, are nearly approaching completion. The great European vessels could here, as at Rio, moor alongside the quays. Why should the *Regina Elena* lie off outside? A question of red-tape, such as I found later at Rio de Janeiro, exposes travellers to the annoyance of transhipping when every accommodation exists for mooring inside the harbour. Thus on these Latin shores I found a familiar feature of my own bureaucratic land.

Beside the French Minister, who is a friend, numerous journalists of pen and kodak came to offer a cordial welcome to their *confrère*. M. Sillard, an eminent engineer from the "Central" School at the head of the French colony here, is in charge of the harbour works. He has succeeded in winning for our country the esteem of every class of the population. The motor-cars start off. The first visit is to the Post-office where I am greeted by a cordial Montevidean whom I do not recognise but whose first word reveals an *habitué* of Paris. I have travelled by a long road to find out here the boulevard atmosphere!

There can be no two opinions about Montevideo. It is a big, cheerful town, with handsome avenues well laid out. Some fine monuments denote a capital city. Streets animated but not too noisy; sumptuous villas in the suburbs; subtropical vegetation in gardens and parks; a pleasant promenade amid the palm-trees by the sea. The dwelling-houses are for the most part of the colonial type. A very lofty ground-floor, with door and windows too often surcharged with ornament resembling the sugar-icing of the Italian pastry-cook, and calculated to convey to these sunny lands an idea of cheap art. The unexpected thing is that the first floor stops short at its balconies as if sudden ruin had overtaken the builder. I found this feature repeated *ad infinitum* wherever I went. The most modest of citizens, as soon as he can turn his back on his primitive cabin of corrugated iron, makes a point of arousing the admiration of the public with the decorative balcony of a first floor that will never be built. Roofs flat and without chimneys: the climate allows of this. Occasionally a balustrade that almost gives the illusion of a finished building, but that the balcony, cut off short at a height of from two to three feet, leaves you again in doubt as to its object. The drawing-room windows are naturally in the front of the house, and here ladies in their indoor dress have no objection to showing themselves for the delectation of passers-by.

But let us say at once that in these countries where the blood is hot misconduct is rare. Men marry young, and the demands of a civilisation as yet untouched by decadence leaves little energy for pleasure that must be sought elsewhere than on the strait path. I will not say but what the great attraction of Paris for many South Americans is precisely the pleasure of the novelty it offers in this respect. It is sufficient for me to set down what came under my notice: happy homes and regular habits; a tranquil enjoyment of a life of virtue. The living-rooms are always grouped around a *patio* with its colonnade bright with trees and flowers, and here their occupants enjoy the utmost privacy with an absence of street noises.

These are the impressions gathered in a hasty walk, since my first visit was necessarily for the President of the Republic and my time was strictly limited. The Presidential palace was a modest-looking house, distinguished only by its guard. Many of the soldiers show strong signs of mixed blood. Curiously enough the sentry is posted not on the pavement but out in the street, opposite the palace. As traffic increases, this rule will need to be changed. The President was not in his office. I was cordially received, however, by the Minister of Foreign Affairs, who was like the most obliging of Parisians. A few steps from the palace I met the President of the Republic, with a small crowd round him, and easily recognisable by his high hat. I was careful not to interrupt him. He is going to do me the honour of receiving me when I return to the capital of Uruguay.

Señor Williman is a compatriot, the son of a Frenchman, of Alsatian origin. Before his election he was professor of physics, and he has not thought it necessary to allow his political duties to interfere with his educational work; twice a week he lectures in the college, where he becomes again the happy schoolmaster whose pupils have not yet developed their powers of contradiction. This charming democratic simplicity is in curious contrast with our own persistent efforts to save as much of the ancient autocratic machinery as possible from the revolutionary shipwreck. It is agreeable to be able to testify to the great personal influence that M. Williman wields in this land of Latin dissension.

We must get back to the ship, which is announcing its departure. With what pleasure shall I revisit Montevideo! There is perhaps more of a French atmosphere about the capital of Uruguay than any other South American city, and it has just enough exotic charm to quicken our pleasure at finding French sympathies in these foreign hearts. We get a view from the deck of the *Regina Elena,* as we pass, of the *Cerro,* which is something like the Mont-Valérien of Paris, and which in this land of flat alluvial soil assumes a very great importance. Like its prototype, it is crowned with a bristling line of fortifications, and Uruguay is so proud of this phenomenon that it has placed the *Cerro* in the national arms, where it figures in the form of a green sugar-loaf; no good Oriental omits to tell you that there is nothing like it in the Argentine.

Under the stinging breeze of the persistent *pampero,* our "screw" began to turn again in the heavy, clayey waters, with a slow, regular rhythm. To-morrow at daybreak we shall be looking through our glasses at the port of Buenos Ayres.

The estuary of the Rio de la Plata (Silver River [2]) that we have now entered is a veritable sea. Though this immense sheet of water is practically landlocked, there is no trace of land on the horizon. It is said to be as wide as the Lake of Geneva is long, not far short of thirty miles, spreading to nearly five times these dimensions at its mouth, after a course of 350 kilometres.

The area covered by the estuary is larger than Holland. Two big rivers, the Uruguay and the Parana, pour their waters into this enormous *cul de sac,* which is often ruffled by an unpleasant sea, as at this moment, and, after their junction at the small town of Nueva Palmira, in Uruguay, they project into the Atlantic a huge volume of water drawn from a vast watershed representing one quarter of South America. The tide is felt nearly a hundred miles above the confluence. Montevideo, 200 kilometres from Buenos Ayres, seems to guard the entrance of this inner sea, whilst the Argentine capital, situated on the opposite shore, is almost at the extremity of the bay. Clay deposits, silted down by a relatively weak current, clog the estuary and require constant dredging to keep the channel open to vessels of large tonnage. This is the problem which faces the port authorities of Buenos Ayres.

At last the town comes in sight. From out the grey clouds driven by the *pampero* there emerge the massive shapes of the tall elevators—those lofty cubes of masonry so dear to North America. Neither church steeples nor any other prominent monuments. Low, prosaic banks, barely distinguishable from the water, a few clumps of palms here and there, unbroken plains, an utter absence of background to the picture. We are preceded by two pilot boats, their flags flying in honour of the President of the Republic, who is lunching on board a training ship within the harbour.

Very slowly the *Regina Elena* brings up at the quayside. The gangway is put out, and behold a delegation of the Argentine Senate, accompanied by an officer from the President's military household, sent to welcome me. A deputation from the French colony also arrives, having at its head the governor of the French Bank of Rio de la Plata, M. Py. Cordial handshakes: a thousand questions from either side. Friendly greetings are exchanged, some of them taking almost the form of brief harangues in which the mother-country is not forgotten. Journalists swarm round us. As might be expected, the *Prensa*, *Nacion*, and *Diario* have each a word to say. I offer my best thanks to the members of the Senate. Farewell to the excellent Captain with my best wishes. Then I get into the motor-car which ten minutes later drops me at the door of my hotel. I am in the Argentine Republic. Henceforth I must keep my eyes open.

Buenos Ayres first. It is a large European city, giving everywhere an impression of hasty growth, but foreshadowing, too, in its prodigious progress, the capital of a continent. The Avenida de Mayo, as wide as the finest of our boulevards, recalls Oxford Street in the arrangement of its shop-fronts and the ornamental features of its buildings. It starts from a large public square, rather clumsily decorated and closed on the sea side by a tall Italian edifice, known as the *Palais Rose*, in which Ministers and President hold their sittings; it is balanced at the other end of the avenue by another large square with the House of Parliament, a colossal building nearly approaching completion, with a cupola that resembles that of the Capitol of Washington. Every style of architecture is to be seen, from the showy, the more frequent, to the sober, comparatively rare. The finest building is without question that of the wealthy *Prensa*, which we shall visit later.

There is an epidemic of Italian architecture in Buenos Ayres. Everywhere the eye rests on astragals and florets, amid terrible complications of interlaced lines. I except the dainty villas and imposing mansions which call public attention to the dwellings of the aristocracy. I suppose that the business quarters of all cities present the same features. The commercial quarter of Buenos Ayres is the most crowded imaginable. Highways that seemed spacious twenty or thirty years ago for a population of two or three hundred thousand souls have become lamentably inadequate for a capital city with more than a million. The footway, so narrow that two can scarcely walk abreast, is closely shaved by a tramway, which constitutes a danger to life and limb. The traffic is severely regulated by a careful police. But so congested with foot passengers do certain streets become of an afternoon that they have had to be closed to vehicles.

In spite of the wisest of precautions, the problem of shopping in the chief business district is not easily solved. To stroll along, or, still worse, to pause to look in at a shop window, is out of the question. Politeness demands here that the honours of the road be paid to age as to sex; so if by chance, in the confusion, you come upon a friend, you must stand on the outer edge of the pavement so as to check as little as possible the flood of human beings driven inwards by the almost continuous passing of the tramway. It is only just to add that this means of locomotion, which is universally adopted here, is remarkably well organised. Still, there are occasions when one must go on foot, and the municipal government, which has laid out elsewhere broad highways in which cabs, carriages, and motors may take their revenge for the scanty accommodation afforded them in the overcrowded centre, is faced with the urgent necessity of laying out hundreds of millions of francs in a scheme for street improvement that cannot be much longer postponed.

One of the peculiarities of Buenos Ayres is that you can see no end to it. Since on the side of the Pampas there is no obstacle to building operations, small colonial houses, similar to those that attracted my notice at Montevideo, make a fringe on the edge of the city, that extends ever farther and farther into the plain in proportion as building plots in the city area— the object of perpetual speculation—rise in value. Some of brick, some of plaster or cement, these villas make comfortable quarters in a land where no chimney-stacks are needed. The quality of the building, however, goes down naturally as one draws nearer the Pampas. The lowest end of the scale offers the greatest simplification: walls of clay dried in the sun, with a roof of corrugated iron, or the more primitive *rancho,* supported on empty oil-cans, placed at convenient distances, with the spaces filled in with boughs or thatch. One hardly knows whether this outer edge of habitations can fairly be included in the city area or not. The motor-car has been travelling so long that a doubt is permissible. The track is only a more or less level, earth road, which just allows the car to run over its surface but cannot be said to add anything to the pleasure of the drive.

The drawback in this country is the absence of wood, of stone, and of coal. No doubt in the more distant provinces there are still fine forests, which are being ruthlessly devastated either for *québracho* (the tree that is richest in tannin), or for fuel for factory furnaces; but the cost of transport is so great that the more prosperous part of the Republic gets its timber from Norway. Uruguay, on the other hand, supplies a stone that is excellent both for building and for macadam and paving: a heavy expense. As for coal, it is the return cargo of English vessels which carry as inward freight frozen meat and live cattle.

Without comparing in density of shipping with the ports of London, or New York, or Liverpool, a noble line of sea-monsters may be seen here stretching seven miles in length, most of them being rapidly loaded or unloaded in the docks by powerful cranes. The scene has been a hundred times described, and offers here no specially characteristic features.

I should need a volume if I tried to describe the plan and equipment of the docks of Buenos Ayres. Those who take an interest in the subject can easily get all the information they need. The rest will be grateful to me for resisting the temptation to quote long lists of figures copied from technical reports. Here it will suffice for me to state that there are two ports—the *Riachuelo* and the "port of the capital." The former is a natural harbour formed by a stream of the same name. It is used as the auxiliary of the other, which is finely fitted with every appliance of modern science. More than 30,000 craft, sail and steam, come in and out annually, including at least 4000 from overseas.

The big grain elevators have been described over and over again. Those of Buenos Ayres are no whit inferior to the best of the gigantic structures of North America. Each can load 20,000 tons of grain in a day. To one there is attached a mill said to be the largest in the world. Covered by way of precaution with the long white shirt that stamped us at once as real millers, we wandered pleasantly enough amongst the millstones and bolters which transform the small grey wheat of the Pampas into fine white flour. Our Beauce farmers accustomed to heavy ears of golden wheat would not appreciate this species, which, moreover, requires careful washing. We were told that it is the richest in gluten of all known species. Diabetics know, therefore, for what to ask.

The slaughter-houses of the Negra, round which I was taken by M. Carlos Luro (son of a Frenchman) form a model establishment in which no less than 1200 oxen are killed daily, without counting sheep and pigs—a faithful copy of the famous slaughter-houses of North America. The beast, having reached the end of a *cul de sac*, is felled by a blow from a mallet and slips down a slope, at the foot of which the carotid artery is cut. After this operation, the body is hooked up by a small wagon moving along an aerial rail, and is then carried through a series of stages which end in its being handed over in two pieces to the freezing chambers to await speedy shipment for England—the great market for Argentine meat. The whole is performed with a rapidity so disconcerting that the innocent victim of our cannibal habits finds himself in the sack ready for freezing, with all his inside neatly packed into tins, before he has had time to think. "We use everything but his squeals," said a savage butcher of Chicago. Veterinaries are in attendance to inspect each beast, which in the event of its being condemned is immediately burnt.

The first colonists, arriving by sea, naturally built their town close to the port. The capital now, in its prosperity, seeks refinement of every kind, and laments that the approach to the seacoast is disfigured by shipping, elevators, and wharves. The same might be said of any great seaport. Buenos Ayres in reality needs a new harbour, but it looks as if the present one could scarcely be altered.

It is naturally in this part of the town that you find the wretched shanties which are the first refuge of the Italian immigrants whilst waiting for an opportunity to start off again. Here is to be seen all the sordid misery of European towns with the accompaniment of the usual degrading features. I hasten to add that help—both public and private—is not lacking. The ladies of Buenos Ayres have organised different charitable works, and visit needy families; as generosity is one of the leading traits in the Argentine character, much good is done in this way. There are no external signs of the feminine degradation that disfigures our own public streets.

Why is it that this swarm of Italians should stop in crowded Buenos Ayres instead of going straight out to the Pampas, where labour is so urgently needed? I was told that the harvest frequently rots on the fields for want of reapers, and this in spite of wages that rise as high as twenty francs per day. There are a good many reasons for this. In the first place, such wages as this are only for a season of a few months or weeks. Then again, these Italian labourers complain that if they venture far from the city, they have no protection against the overbearing of officials, who are inclined to take advantage of their privileged position. I do not want to dwell on the point. The same complaints—but more detailed—reached me in Brazil. Both the Argentine and Brazilian Governments, to whom I submitted the charges brought against their representatives, protested that whenever any abuse could be proved against an agent he was proceeded against with the utmost rigour of the law. There can be no doubt as to the good faith of the authorities, who have every interest in encouraging the rapid growth of the population in the Pampas. Besides, it must be borne in mind that the elements of immigration are never of the highest quality. Still, I should not be surprised to learn that there was occasion for a stricter control in the direction I have indicated.

So far, I have said nothing of the beauties of the city. It is a pity that amongst the attractions of Buenos Ayres the sea cannot be counted. A level shore does not lend itself to decorative effect. A mediocre vegetation; water of a dirty ochre, neither red nor yellow; nothing to be found to charm the eye. So I saw the sea only twice during my stay at Buenos Ayres—once on arrival, and again when I left. During the summer heat, that section of the population which is not compelled to stay flees to Mar del Plata, the Trouville of Buenos Ayres, a charming conglomeration of beflowered villas on an ocean beach.

A perfectly healthy city. No expense has been spared to satisfy the demands of a good system of municipal sanitation. Avenues planted with trees, gardens and parks laid out to ensure adequate reserves of fresh air, are available to all, and lawns exist for youthful sports. The zoölogical and botanical gardens are models of their kind. A fine racecourse, surrounded by the green belt of foliage of the Argentine Bois de Boulogne, is known as Palermo.

A Frenchman, the genial M. Thays, well known amongst his European colleagues, has entire control of the plantations and parks of Buenos Ayres. M. Thays, who excels in French landscape gardening, takes delight in devoting his whole mind and life to his trees, his plants and flowers. He is ready at any moment to defend his charge against attacks—an attitude that is wholly superfluous, since the public of Buenos Ayres never lets slip an opportunity of testifying its gratitude to him.

Wherever he discovers a propitious site, the master-gardener plants some shoot which will one day be a joy to look upon. He has laid out and planted fine parks. He has large greenhouses at his disposal, and any prominent citizen, or any association popular or aristocratic can, for the asking, have the floral decorations needed for a fête delivered at his door by the municipal carts.

In his search after rare plants for the enrichment of his town, M. Thays has visited equatorial regions—the Argentine, Bolivia, Brazil. As his ambition vaults beyond the boundaries of Buenos Ayres, he has conceived a project, already in process of execution, of founding a great national park, as in the United States, in which all the marvels of tropical vegetation may be collected. The Falls of Iguazzu—greater and loftier than those of Niagara—would be enclosed in this vast estate on the very frontiers of Brazil.

Apart from these plans of conquest, which make him a rival of Alexander, M. Thays is a modest, affable man, who takes a good deal of trouble to look as if he had done nothing out of the common. Were I but competent I would describe the organisation of his botanical garden, which is superior to any to be found in the old continent. More amusing is it, perhaps, to follow him through the various sections in which the characteristic flora of every part of the world is well represented. The Argentine, as may be supposed, has here the larger share. Here are displayed specimens of the principal species of flora to be found in the district lying between the frozen regions of Tierra del Fuego and the Equator: the Antarctic beech, the carob palm, the *québracho* (rendered extraordinarily durable by the quantity of tannin it contains, and in great request for railway sleepers), walnut, and the cedar of Tucuman or of Mendoza—which, by the way, is not a cedar. It is from its wood that cigar boxes are made. It is used in the woodwork of rich houses, for it is easy to handle and highly decorative by reason of its warm colouring. Its fault is that it warps; wherever you find it in house fittings, doors and windows refuse to open or shut as they should.

But you should see M. Thays doing the honours of the *ombu* and the *palo borracho*. The *ombu* is the marvel of the Pampas, the sole tree which the locust refuses to touch. For this reason alone, it has been allowed to grow freely, though not even man has found a way to utilise what the voracious insects of Providence decline. For the *ombu* prides itself on being good for nothing. It does not even lend itself to making good firewood. It is only to look at. But that is sufficient. Imagine an object resembling the backs of antediluvian monsters, mastodons or elephants, lying in the shade of a great mass of sheltering foliage. Heavy folds in the grey rind denote a growing limb, a rounded shoulder, a gigantic head half concealed. These are the tremendous roots of the *ombu*, whose delight it is to issue forth from the soil in the form of astonishing animated objects. When by foot and stick you have ascertained that these living shapes are in reality mummified within a thick bark, you turn your attention to the trunk itself and find it hollow, with a crumbling surface.

Another surprise! The finger sinks into the tree, meeting only the sort of resistance that would be offered by a thin sheet of paper. And now fine powdery scales of a substance which should be wood, but, in fact, is indescribable, fall into your hand. They crumble away into an impalpable dust, which is carried off by the breeze before you have had time to examine it. Now you have the secret of the *ombu*. Its wood evaporates in the open air; at the same time there spring from its strangely beast-like roots young and living shoots of the parent tree. Since it is impossible to burn the non-existent, you cannot, obviously, have recourse to the *ombu* to cook your lunch. Here is an example in the vegetable world of paradox, which has no mission in life but a glorious uselessness. If it were but beautiful I should recommend the *ombu* to poets who profess to prefer the Beautiful to the Useful. But as its appearance does not impress the beholder, the wisest course is to impute its existence to momentary abstraction on the part of the Creator.

The *palo borracho*, on the other hand, is extremely useful, though not without a touch of capriciousness. Its popular name, which signifies "the drunkard," has been given to it on the ground that it seems to stagger; but such a name is a libel. This peaceful denizen of the forest has nothing to do with the alcoholic world. Nor can it be said to attract human society, for its strange trunk, strangled in a collar of roots, and bulging in its middle parts, bristles with innumerable points, short and sharp, which prevent all undue familiarity. These thorns fall with age, at least from the lower part of the tree, but as they exist elsewhere, even on the smallest twig, no animal, from man to monkey, can venture upon its branches.

The trunk, if tapped with a cane, returns a hollow sound. The tree is, in fact, empty, needing only to be cut into lengths to give man all he needs for a trough. The Indian squaw uses it to wash her linen, and the wood, exposed to the double action of air and water, becomes as hard as cement. The unripe fruit, the size of a good apple, furnishes a white cream, which, if not quite the quality demanded for five o'clock tea at Rumpelmayer's, still supplies the natives with a savoury breakfast. Later, when the fruit comes to maturity, it bursts under the sun's rays into a large tuft of silky cotton, dotting the branches with white balls and furnishing admirable material for the birds with which to build their nests. It is for this reason that the species is known as the "false cotton-tree." The exceedingly fine thread produced by this tree is too short to be spun, but the Indians, and even Europeans, turn it to account in many different ways. Soft pillows and cushions are made with it, and I can speak personally of their comfort.

M. Thays was not the man to let us leave without seeing his plantations of *yerba-maté*. Every one knows that *maté*, the Paraguay holly, is a native of Paraguay, whence it spread to Chili, Brazil, and the Argentine. Its leaves, dried and slightly roasted, yield a stimulating infusion that is as much enjoyed by the South American colonists as by the natives. Like kola, tea, and coffee, *maté* contains a large proportion of caffeine, which renders it a good nerve tonic and, at the same time, a digestive.

I have tasted "Paraguay tea," or "Jesuits' tea," on several occasions, but cannot honestly say I like it. The palate, however, ends by getting used to anything. I have a friend who drinks valerian with pleasure. All South America delights in the peculiar aroma of the strengthening but, on first acquaintance, certainly unpleasant *maté*. Existence in the Pampas is strenuous. The days are past when a cow was lassoed to provide a beefsteak for your lunch. The favourite stimulant of the *rancho* is the *yerba-maté* which puts new life into the exhausted horseman. Everywhere in town and country, the first rite in the morning is *maté*-drinking. Men and women carry the little gourd around, into which each in turn dips the tube of the *bombilla*, a perforated disc which travels from mouth to mouth, in the company of devotees.

In the old days, it was the tradition of *maté*-making to give the first infusion —poured off quickly, but invariably slightly bitter—to the servants. Growing familiarity with the herb has practically set aside this practice: in fact, while it is, and probably always will be, the favourite drink of the masses, the aristocracy and *bourgeoisie*, though still appreciating *maté*, drink in preference China tea or Santos coffee, like good Europeans. Yet the consumption of *maté* has increased enormously with the population. It has been calculated that an Argentino spends twice as much in a year on *maté* as a Frenchman on coffee. Until the last few years the Argentine Republic, independently of its home production, imported from Brazil and Paraguay 40 millions of kilogrammes, estimated at 22 millions of francs.

As might be expected, the Argentine Government has shown itself anxious to encourage the cultivation of *maté*. The difficulty lay in the germinating process. In certain provinces of the Argentine, *maté* grew wild, but when sown the crops were a failure. After many trials, M. Thays discovered that the seed only sprouted after long soaking in warm water, and that, strangely enough, the plants thus produced could be propagated without repeating this preliminary process. It appears that in the ordinary course of nature, the fertilising process takes place in the stomach of birds. The Jesuits had made the same discovery, but on their expulsion they carried the secret away with them. M. Thays rediscovered it. More than once an attempt has been made to introduce the habit of *maté*-drinking into Europe. I do not think it will easily come about. It would, nevertheless, be a great boon if *yerba-maté* could with us, as in South America, be substituted for the alcohol which is threatening us with irrevocable destruction.

I cannot leave the Botanical Garden without noting the pleasing effect of the light trellises which are a feature of all large gardens here. In this fine climate, where winter's cold is practically unknown, neither shrubs nor flowers need the protection of glass. An arbour of trellis-work with gay flower-borders forms a winter garden without glass, in which sun and shade, cunningly blended, throw into delicate relief the beauties of the plants. It is not quite the open air, and neither is it the greenhouse. Let us call it a vast cage of decorative vegetation.

CHAPTER III
BUENOS AYRES (*continued*)

Botany and zoölogy are sister sciences. We leave the plants to inspect the beasts in the company of M. Thays, who is always glad to see his neighbour M. Onelli.

The governor of the Zoölogical Garden of Buenos Ayres is a phlegmatic little man, Franco-Italian in speech, and the more amusing in that his gay, caustic wit is clothed in a highly condensed, ironical form. What a pity that his animals, for whom he is father and mother, sister and brother, cannot appreciate his sallies! Not that it is by any means certain that they do not. It seems clear that they can enter into each other's feelings, if not thoughts, since an intimacy of the most touching kind exists between the man and inferior creation, to whose detriment the rights of biological priority have been reversed.

I should like to pause before the llamas, used as beasts of burden to carry a load of twenty-five kilogrammes apiece, or before the vicuñas, whose exquisite feathery fur is utilised for the motor-car, and whose private life would need to be told in Latin by reason of the officious interference of the Indian in matters that concern him not a whit.

M. Onelli has housed the more prominent groups in palaces in the style of architecture peculiar to their native land, and this gives to the gardens a very pleasing aspect.

But first let us enjoy the animals. It is amazing to see the two monstrous hippopotami leap from the water with movements of ridiculous joyfulness in response to the whistle of their governor-friend, and, on a sign from him, open their fearful caverns of pink jaws bristling with formidable teeth to receive with the utmost gratitude three blades of grass which they could easily cull for themselves beneath their feet if these manifestations of joy were called forth by the delicacy and not by friendship. The great beasts became human at sight of their master, if one may thus describe ferocity.

The puma, a sort of yellow panther whose colour has apparently won for him the name of the American lion, came running up to offer his back to the caressing hand of his friend with a hoarse roar that seemed to express rather helpless rage than voluptuousness.

The puma is perhaps the commonest of the wild beasts of the northern provinces of the Argentine, for it retreats from before the approach of man, and is more successful than the jaguar or the panther in escaping the traps or the guns of the hunter.

M. Edmond Hilleret, who has killed several, told me that at Santa Ana, near Tucuman, it was impossible to keep a flock of sheep, as they were always devoured by the pumas in spite of all the efforts he made to protect them. "Yet," he added, "notwithstanding my dogs and my peons the puma can never be seen. He is quite a rarity."

After a short palaver with some delicious penguins newly arrived from the southern ice, with their young, which would die of spleen if they were not fed with a forcing pipe, like an English suffragette, we pause before the grey ostrich of the Pampas, which has been nearly exterminated by the cruel lasso of the *gaucho*.

The grey American ostrich, which should be safe from our barbarous ways since his tail feathers offer no attraction for ladies' hats, is interesting by certain peculiarities in his domestic habits. To the male is left the duty of hatching the eggs, the female preferring to stray. By way of compensation, the paternal instinct is the more keenly developed in the father in proportion as the mother—reprehensible bird!—neglects her duties. Thus before beginning to sit on the eggs, he sets carefully aside two or three of them, according to the number of young to be hatched, and when the little ones leave their shells, he opens them with a sharp blow from the paternal beak, and spreads in the sunshine the contents of the eggs his foresight had reserved; the appetising dish attracts thousands of flies who promptly drown themselves therein to make the first meal of the fledglings. Admirable instance of the contradictory processes of nature designed for the preservation of existing types.

But we have come to the palace of the elephants. There are half a dozen of them beneath a vast dome, and the sight of M. Onelli rouses them all. The heavy grey masses sway from side to side, large ears beat up and down, while the small eyes wink; the trunks are flung inquiringly round, eager for any windfall. One amiable and tame elephant, the youthful Fahda, born on the place, hustles her colossal friends, to clear a way to M. Onelli, who talks to her affectionately, but is unable to respond as he should to her pressing request for cakes. The governor gives us the reason of their friendliness.

"We have no secrets from each other," he remarks gently.

And it was truer than he thought, for the young trunk was softly introduced into his tempting pocket, and brought out a packet of letters which were forthwith swallowed. Thereupon exclamations as late as fruitless from the victim, who thus witnessed the disappearance of his correspondence down the dark passages of an unexpected post-office from which there is no hope of return. [3]

M. Onelli kindly offered us a few minutes' rest in his own *salon*. But what did we find there? The housemaid who opened the door to us carried a young puma in her arms, and I know not what sort of hairy beast on her back. The gnashing of white teeth proceeded from under the chairs and coiled serpents lay in the easy-chairs. Indeed, we were not the least tired! Palermo must be visited.

The celebrated promenade starts nobly at the Recoleta, where the lawns and groves are seen in a setting of harmonious architecture. Carriages of the most correct British style, drawn by superb horses, and noisy motor-cars dash swiftly by. But for the groups of exotic trees one might be in the Bois. Palermo begins well. Unfortunately, we suddenly find before us an avenue of sickly coco-palms, whose bare trunks are covered with dead leaves, giving an unpleasing perspective of broom-handles. This tree, which is so fine in Brazil, is not in its element here. When planted in rows, even in the streets of Rio, it is more surprising than beautiful. It is in groves that it best displays its full decorative qualities. I take the liberty of suggesting that M. Thays should pull up the horticultural invalids and plant eucalyptus or some other species in their place.

But we are not yet at the end of our troubles. Less than two hundred yards down, the railway traverses the avenue on a level crossing. A gate, generally closed, a turnstile for pedestrians, a station, and all the rest of it. After a wait of ten minutes, the train duly passes, and then the motor-car plunges into a roadway, full of ruts, leading to a dark archway which carries another railway across the promenade, making an ugly blot on the landscape. And now we reach a further marshy road, bordered with young plantations, which leads across a leafless wood dividing the railway track from the estuary of La Plata.

A succession of trains on one hand, and a muddy yellow sea on the other: as a view it is not romantic. Gangs of labourers are at work on the roads, which are badly in need of their attentions. No doubt some day this will be a superb promenade. It is only a question of making it, and the first step must be to clear away the railway-lines with their embankments and bridges. This is probably the intention, since I was assured that the level crossing would shortly be swept away. That will be a beginning. M. Bouvard is not likely to overlook the importance of the matter. My only fear is lest the situation should make it impossible for Palermo ever to attain to imposing proportions. But one thing is certain, if M. Thays can get a free hand, the city will not lack a park worthy the capital of the Republic.

Need I say that squares and parks alike are superabundantly decorated with sculpture and monuments both open to criticism? There is nothing more natural to a young people than a desire to acquire great men in every department as early as possible. Yet idealism that is to be materialised must, one would think, have its base set solidly on established facts. In a country whose population offers a mixture of all the Latin races, art could not fail to flourish. It will free itself from its crust as fast as public taste is purified. Works such as those of M. Paul Groussac, or the fine novel by M. Enrique Rodrigues Larreta, [4] the distinguished Minister of the Argentine Republic in Paris, are evidences of the development of literary taste on the banks of the Rio de la Plata. [5]

The sculptor does not appear to have reached quite the same point, but I hasten to add, for the sake of justice, that our own hewers of marble, with a very few prominent exceptions, expose nothing in Buenos Ayres which is calculated to throw into too dark a shade their *confrères* of across the ocean.

France, Italy, and Spain supply some fairly fine statuary for the Latin confraternity. But, as might be readily imagined, a legitimate desire to write history on every square and market-place has given a profusion of monuments to soldiers and politicians. The same mania has been pushed to such extremes in our own land that it would ill become me to make it a subject of reproach to others; nevertheless it behoves us to acknowledge that the Argentine Republic has, both in times of war and of peace, produced some great men. It suffices to mention the names of San Martin (whose statue is being raised at Boulogne-sur-Mer and at Buenos Ayres) and of Sarmiento.

If genius were always at the disposal of Governments, the wish to perpetuate to all eternity the renown a single day had won for them might readily be pardoned. But men of genius are rare, and they are apt to make mistakes like other men. And for the rest, the statues that are put up to their memory serve merely to inspire in our breasts a few philosophic reflections on the danger of a permanent propaganda of mediocrity! Besides, the sculptor has this defect—that he forces himself on the attention of the passer-by. We are not compelled to purchase a poor book or to go into ecstasies over all the Chauchard collection, whereas we are unable to avoid the sight of the statue of Two-shoes by Thingummy. My only consolation is that such monuments will not prevent the advent of other supermen in the future, who, like those of the past, will raise their own monuments in a surer and better manner by their own glorious achievements.

But it is time to leave these men of marble and come to the living, of whom I have so far said not a word. My remark as to the European aspect of Buenos Ayres at first sight must be taken as referring merely to its outdoor life. I do not speak of the business quarter, which is the same in all countries. The man who is glued to the telegraph wire or to the telephone, waiting for the latest quotations in the different parts of the globe in order to build on them his own careful combinations, is, notwithstanding his patriotism, an international type whose world-wide business connection must in time modify his own characteristics and make of him the universal species of merchant.

At the same time, the population of any large European city, while preserving in its general outline the special characteristic evolved by its own history, does yet show a certain trend in the direction of some well-defined types of modern activity whose attributes are the outcome of natural conditions of civilisation the world over. But when transplanted outside Europe, the original characteristics are inevitably modified by the new environment, and the result will be a striking differentiation—North America is an example of this.

In the eyes of our ancient Europe, with its venerable traditions and its base of primeval prejudice, the man who ventures to strike a new root in a colony beyond the sea will have to expiate his new prosperity by some extravagances which will expose him to the fire of the satirical pressman or playwright. This is the reason why South America, having undoubtedly borne in common with every country of Europe some few fantastic types of high and of low ideals, suddenly finds herself represented to the public, for the greater entertainment of the boulevard, as being exclusively peopled with those strange creatures we have christened *rastaquouères*, whose privilege it is to lead a life that is ever at variance with all the laws of common-sense.

If all we ask is a joke at the expense of our neighbours, the Gauls of Paris may give rein to their wit. Still, it may be useful for us all to know that these so-called *rastaquouères*, leaving to petty tyrants the whole field of ancient history, have not only secured to their country by their steady labour its present prosperity, but have also founded in their new domain a European civilisation which is no whit inferior in inspiration to that which we are for ever vaunting. They learn our languages, invade our colleges, absorb our ideas and our methods, and passing from France to Germany and England, draw useful comparisons as to the results obtained.

We are pleased to judge them more or less lightly. Let us not forget that we in our turn are judged by them. And while we waste our time quarrelling about individuals and names, they are directing a steady effort toward taking from each country of Europe what it has of the best, in order to build up over yonder on a solid base a new community which will some day be so much the more formidable that its own economic force will perhaps have as a counterbalance the complications of a European situation that is not tending toward solution.

In spite of everything, France has managed to maintain so far friendly and sympathetic relations with the Republic. Latin idealism keeps these South American nations ever facing toward those great modern peoples that have sprung from the Roman conquest. I cannot say I think we have drawn from this favourable condition of things all the advantage we might have derived from it, both for the youthful Republics and for our Latinity, which is being steadily drained by the huge task of civilisation and by the vigorous onslaught that it is called on to sustain from the systematic activity of the Northern races.

The great Anglo-Saxon Republic of North America, tempered by the same Latin idealism imported in the eighteenth century from France by Jefferson, is making of a continent a modern nation whose influence will count more and more in the affairs of the globe. May it not be that South America, whose evolution is the result of lessons taught to some extent by the Northern races, will give us a new development of Latin civilisation corresponding to that which has so powerfully contributed to the making of Europe as we know it? It is here no question obviously of an organised rivalry of hostile forces between two great American peoples, who must surely be destined both by reason of their geographical situation, as also by mental affinities, to unite their strength to attain to loftier heights. The problem, which ought not to be shirked by France, will be henceforth to maintain in the pacific evolution of these communities the necessary proportion of idealism which she had a large share in planting there.

In following such a train of thought, how can we help pausing for an instant to consider the Pan-American Congress which so fitly closed the splendid exhibition of the Argentine centenary? With the sole exception of Bolivia, every republic of South America sent a representative to the palace of the Congress to discuss their common interests—an imposing assembly, which in the dignity of its debates can bear comparison with any Upper Chamber of the Continent of Europe. For my part, I sought in vain for one of those excitable natures, ever ripe for explosion—the fruit, according to tradition, of equatorial soil. I found only jurisconsults, historians, men of letters or of science, giving their opinions in courteous language, whose example might with advantage be followed by many an orator in the Old Continent. Not, of course, that passions were wholly absent from these debates. In these new countries, where the strength of youth finds a free field for its display, and where revolution and war are the chief traditions of the race, warmth of feeling has too frequently transformed the political arena into a field of battle. But by degrees, as the community takes form and acquires greater weight in every domain of public life, there grows up an imperious need of organised action, and the youthful democrats themselves end by realising that a people can only govern itself when its citizens have proved themselves capable of self-discipline.

Of all the problems which might naturally present themselves in a Pan-American Congress, those that might be expected to call forth implacable opposition were rigorously eliminated. An exchange of views took place, and each delegate was able to report to his principals a number of conclusions calculated to pave the way to future understandings.

When the Congress threw out the proposal to generalise the Monroe Doctrine and apply its principle to the whole of the South American continent, the representative of a large State said to me:

"We shall separate without accomplishing anything."

"It is already much to have avoided all conflict," I replied, "and if you had really accomplished nothing you would still have been useful in that you had met, talked together, understood one another, and parted on good terms."

Perhaps the man whose position was the most delicate of all was Mr. Henry White, the delegate of the great northern Republic, and the distinguished diplomat so popular in Parisian society, who contributed to the utmost of his power towards finding an equitable solution of the Franco-German conflict at the Algeciras Conference. At the Congress of Buenos Ayres, the delegate of Washington had, like the representative of Uruguay, one vote only, and his efforts were directed to making his collaborators forget that he was a "big brother," a very big brother, faintly suspected of tendencies towards an hegemony. It took all the gracious affability of Mr. White to disarm the distrust aroused more especially by the proposal to place Southern America under the banner of the Monroe Doctrine, and thus the Congress could be dissolved without a word of any but good-will and American brotherhood.

The Pan-American Congress was the natural outcome of the great international exhibition by which the Argentine Republic celebrated the centenary of its independence. The great fairs of older times existed with very good reason. There was every advantage to be gained by bringing together at stated times the produce of different districts at a period of the world's history when the deficiency of means of communication placed insurmountable obstacles in the way of producer, merchant, and consumer. To-day, thanks to steampower, every city in the world offers a permanent exhibition adapted to the needs of its public, and the traveller wastes his time when he endeavours to bring back from his journeys some article unknown to his countrymen. For this reason the finest of international exhibitions can reserve no surprises to its visitors. And as for experts, or specialists in any branch of commerce or industry, he is to be pitied who awaits the opening of one of these universal bazaars in order to obtain information on some detail of his business.

There remain evidently the amusements and entertainments which in such gatherings are naturally intended to arouse the pleasure-loving instincts of crowds. But civilisation has pretty well surfeited us with such amusements, which are now better calculated to tempt than to satisfy us. And when the friendly city that summons us to such a show is situated 11,000 kilometres from our shores, it requires a more powerful attraction than this of the "already seen" to induce us to undertake the expedition.

For all these reasons and without seeking any others the Buenos Ayres Exhibition could not be a success either in the way of money or of the concourse of peoples. An unfortunate and ultra-modern strike retarded the arrangements to such a point that on the anniversary day, May 25th, only the section of *ganaderia* (cattle-breeding) was ready. Notwithstanding a multitude of difficulties, pavilions were put up, in which were amassed and docketed in the usual fashion some of those products which the greed for gold brings to all the depots of the world. A few special side-shows were remarkably successful. Of these may be mentioned the English exhibit of the railway industry and the German section of electricity. Some of the buildings were never completed, as that of the Spanish section. France, I regret to say, did not distinguish herself. The omission is inconceivable when one considers what a market might in this way have been found for our manufactures. Apart from some interesting displays by dressmakers, jewellers, and goldsmiths, exhibited in a tasteful pavilion slightly resembling Bagatelle, and called the Palace of Applied Art, we found nothing to send. I admit that for France this was not sufficient. England, however, exhibited a magnificent State railway-carriage—said to be worth two millions—which she presented to the President of the Republic. It is a luxury that the English might very well permit themselves, since almost all the railways of the Argentine are in their hands. And why, if you please? Because the engineer who one day invited tenders for the construction of the first Argentine railway-line found in Paris no support, and from our capital (I have it from his own lips) he turned to London, where the enterprise was carried to colossal proportions.

We could hardly help being represented in the art and sculpture pavilions. I can honestly say that our exhibit, well-organised, was highly creditable to the nation. But, without any tremendous effort, we might have done much better! We reckoned, perhaps, on the Argentine millionaires coming to Paris to look for the works we failed to exhibit in their capital. If only millionaires were concerned, I should say nothing. But it is precisely because the art education of the Argentine people is as yet rudimentary, as might also be said of more than one nation in ancient Europe, that we ought to have attempted to arouse a wider public interest instead of appealing merely to connoisseurs, who are in the habit of getting what they want in the picture-galleries of the Old World. Some excellent examples were shown, no doubt; that was the least we could do. Our home artists would not risk the experiment of creating a kind of exhibition-museum, which might have been a revelation of French art and have had the effect of arousing the need of the Beautiful which is latent in every nation, and at the same time inviting that intelligent criticism which is a powerful factor in the development of taste in connoisseurs.

There is no art museum worthy the name in the Argentine Republic. You must exist before you can add adornment. If, however, I may judge by what I saw in a few private galleries, the time is at hand when the need for large art collections will be fully acknowledged in the south as it is now in the north; there, forty years ago, I know by personal observation that the ground was less fully prepared than it is to-day in the Argentine, while now we see the treasures of Europe being eagerly bought up in order that the New World may soon vie with the Old on this point.

I must not omit to say a word on the retrospective exhibit of "colonial days." A centenary celebration implies a history and a past, and this history is remarkably well illustrated by the instruments of civilisation now in the hands of the founders. What a contrast there is between the more than sumptuous railway-carriage of which I spoke just now and the archaic coaches, fat-bellied barouches, and Merovingian chariots which used to pick a painful way across the pathless Pampas, transporting from plantation to plantation families that had but little prospect of ever amassing more than they needed for a bare daily life. Utensils of the simplest, bespeaking a time when wood was scarce. Weapons of the clumsiest, undressed skins as a protection from the occasional blasts of the *pampero*. In a period when the horse was the universal means of locomotion—he still is as a matter of fact, to a very great extent, since in the country the little children must mount their ponies to go to school—the equipment of the horseman was a pompous bedizenment in Spanish guise, from his heavy brass ornaments to the rowels of monstrous spurs. All this belongs to the ancient times of scarcely fifty years ago, and when you meet a *gaucho* on his thick-set horse, his feet in weighty wooden stirrups hanging vertically like wheels, you realise that the modern miracle of iron roads has not been able to entirely wipe out the primitive machinery of a world of colonists.

The section of Argentine produce—cattle, timber, plants, fruits, cereals, etc.—is specially interesting to foreigners. To describe it would be to write the economic history of the land. I heard on all sides that the cattle exhibits were exceptionally fine. I am not astonished, now that I have seen in the shows and on the *estancias* (farms) the finest of stock for breeding purposes. We know that out on the Pampas the rearing of horses and horned cattle as well as of sheep has developed enormously. I shall have occasion presently to return to the subject when I speak of the famous freezing-machines which supply the English markets with meat slaughtered in Buenos Ayres—to say nothing of the live cattle exported. The only detail that I shall give here is that the event of the day has been the purchase by a meat-freezing company of five oxen for beef at the price of 25,000 francs apiece (£1000). This looks like madness, and perhaps it is. We are beginning to learn in Europe to what point the craze for advertisement is carried by Americans. I only quote this fact because it throws more light on certain traits of character than any number of traveller's tales could do.

Grain-growing—wheat and maize—like that of flax (of which they burn the stalks for want of knowing how to utilise them) has recently grown enormously. I shall return to this subject also later on, when I speak of the Pampas, with their immense stretch of arable land between the Andes and the sea, yielding every kind of harvest without manure and almost without labour. Wherever the locomotive makes its appearance there blossoms forth a fertile strip of country on either side of the line, which on the plan of the administrators symbolises an instant rise in value of the property whose produce has henceforth a quick means of transport to its market. Had I not firmly resolved to abstain from quoting figures and facts cut out of books of statistics, I could easily dazzle the reader by showing him the fantastic increase in the crops of maize alone, standing in gigantic ricks round the *estancias*, pending the moment when they will be handed over to the gigantic elevators to be flung on board the English and German cargo-boats.

Strolling through the galleries in which are accumulated the exhibits of Argentine agricultural produce, you are forced to admire the variety of species yielded by a soil that produces clover two and a half yards in height! I say nothing of the fruits and vegetables, because at that season of the year I could not try them. Neither seemed to me to compete with European varieties. As for the tropical fruits, with the exception of the oranges and pines, they are astonishing, I confess, but I cannot give them any other praise.

In the section of Argentine timber is to be seen in the front rank the "false cedar" and the marvellous *québracho,* of which I have already spoken. No other wood can be compared with this in respect of the quantity of tannin it contains. For this reason the immense forests of the northern provinces are being devastated to supply the manufacturers. Railway-sleepers and stakes for the wire-fencing that marks out the immense stretches of Pampas are the principal employment for *québracho*, irrespective of the extraction of tannin. As the demand increases, and the idea of replanting does not seem to have occurred to the Argentinos, it is reasonable to foresee the moment when the Government of the Republic, having neglected to husband its resources, will have only vain lamentations to offer to its customers. The day may be far distant; I do not dispute it. Such an improvident policy is, none the less, reprehensible. How many years, moreover, must elapse between the planting of the young *québracho* and its maturity? Indeed, the same remarks might be made of all the other species of timber.

When you have seen tree-trunks that were many centuries in growth falling bit by bit into the maw of a factory furnace, without any attempt being made to replace them, when you have been saddened by the spectacle of the marvellous Brazilian forests blazing in every direction to make room for coffee plantations that will presently spring up amongst the charred trunks, you realise keenly that there is no more urgent need in these great countries than a complete organisation of forestry. If in some parts of Brazil the soil will no longer yield freely without the help of manure, the water system, at all events, remains unchanged. In the Argentine Pampas the case is very different, for the reason that the watercourses disappear into the ground before reaching the sea. When the immense forests of the highlands have disappeared to make way for plateaux open to wind and sun, can we doubt but that the already terrible scourge of drought will be still further aggravated, and its disastrous effects on cattle and harvests be even more redoubtable than they are at present?

I must resist the temptation of dwelling on the interesting exhibits of the South American Republics. I should never finish. Neither must I wander any farther from the Argentine capital to set down reflections that will more fitly suggest themselves later. Nevertheless I cannot leave the exhibition without mentioning the extraordinary establishment in which the Rural Society holds its annual cattle-shows—vast stables and stalls, constructed according to the latest pattern on English model farms. There is accommodation perhaps for more than 500 horned cattle, or horses, and for 700 or 800 probably in the paddocks, while 4000 sheep can be penned under a single roof, the whole completed by an enclosure for trials with seating accommodation for 2000 persons.

These shows take place every year in October. They are closed by a sale at which the beasts are put up at auction. No better system of gauging the progress of the breeding industry could be devised. As many as 4000 animals have been brought together for these shows, collected from all parts of the country, including stallions of the best breeds, Durham and Herefordshire cows, to say nothing of pigs, llamas, and poultry. Agricultural machinery and dairy implements also find a place here, of course.

It is in this colossal cattle-rearing city that the greatest effort of production ever made has been concentrated. I saw at Rosario a magnificent cattle show. But the great Fair of Buenos Ayres outdoes anything to be offered elsewhere of the kind. I shall have to return to the subject when I come to the *estancias* and the vast herds that belong to them. Here it suffices to note that the Argentine breeders do not shrink from any expense in order to obtain the most perfect stallions. England is, of course, the chief market for the frozen meat, which is carried as return cargo by the coaling-boats. Naturally the farmers of the Pampas endeavour to suit the tastes of their customers. This is why the finest specimens of British cattle-farms find their way every year to Buenos Ayres. It is not surprising that the horse-breeders have adopted the same course, though full justice is done to the qualities of French breeds. Still, the English breeder best understands how to make an outlet for his wares, whilst the French prefers to sit in the sun on the plains of Caen to wait until the foreigner comes to ask him as a favour for his animals.

FOOTNOTES:

[3] One word about M. Onelli's interesting work, *À Travers les Andes*, an accurate account of his journey in Patagonia. When describing to me the customs of the natives, he was good enough to promise me a few arrowheads collected in the course of his expedition. They reached me the following day with this letter:

"MY DEAR SIR,—After rummaging amongst my drawers, I finally found the arrowheads you wanted. The book which accompanies them, a humble homage to yourself, describes the places in which I found them. If you are good enough to glance at it you will find several photographs of the descendants of the makers of these arrows. The Tchuleches Indians, who to the number of rather more than 2000 live in the southern half of Patagonia, say, when shown one of these arrowheads, which are to be found all over the arid plateau they inhabit, that they were the usual weapon of the Indians of olden times who travelled on foot. We know that they did not know the horse until a hundred and fifty years ago, at most, and, in fact, one may say that the Stone Age represented by these arrowheads only ended in Patagonia a half-century ago. The arrows to be found in Patagonia demonstrate in a contrary manner the influence of civilised industries, since the heads the most clumsily made are the most modern. The Indians lost little by little the art of making them when they learnt to make the shafts of fragments of knife-blades, or of iron obtained from the Christians, and since then they have completely abandoned the work to adopt firearms. In the preparation of guanaco skins, the Indian women, naturally more conservative than the men, still use the old system of scraping the under side of the leather with scrapers made of stone, in every way similar to the tool used by prehistoric man in European lands. Nowadays, having no means of making them, they search in their leisure moments in the ancient dwellings of their forefathers in order to find a flint scraper, which they carefully use and preserve.

"The arrow age still subsists in the north of the Republic among the Indians of the Chaco forests. Their arrows are made of hard wood. On alluvial soils no flint can be found, just as none can be had in the province of Santa Fé, and nearly throughout the whole of the province of Buenos Ayres (a region larger than all France), without a single pebble!—a fact which renders it extremely difficult to keep up good roads across a flat country of crumbling soil without lime. The highway is turned into soft mud by traffic and rain; yet observe the enormous increase of railway lines.

"As for the art of making arrowheads, the Stone Age still reigns among the Onas and Lakaluf, natives of Terra del Fuego; but alas! the art has degenerated. The natives of the seacoast, always on the lookout for a whale, dead or wounded, and for fragments of wrecks of sailing vessels rounding Cape Horn, have discovered that bottle glass is the easiest material to work upon for their arrows, and their poor language is thus enriched with a new word; to express 'glass' they say 'botel,' by the natural *quid pro quo* of a tongue which in adopting a new word confuses the name of the object with that of the material of which it is made.

"The opaque black arrowhead is of basalt, the most abundant kind of rock in Patagonia, but also the most difficult to use in the manufacture of such small objects. Obsidian—the little black point of flint—is more generally used.

"The twisted forms are moulds of flint of the inside of a tertiary fossil mollusc, the 'turritella,' very common in the strata of the Rio Santa Cruz cliffs, and which Indian women often wear as ornaments. In the hope you will excuse my bad French, since I have had the presumption to write direct to you instead of being translated into good French,

"I am, my dear sir, yours, etc.,

"CLEMENT ONELLI."

[4] *La Gloire de Don Ramire.*

[5] I quote these two names because they are best known among us in France. But Argentine literature cannot be dismissed in a word. The struggle for independence could not fail to inspire songs to be caught up from ear to ear and sung everywhere, and in the same way the spread of education has naturally turned many minds to literary composition. The struggle with the metropolis and the flame of civil war irresistibly impelled the individual into the arena to take public action, and from the vortex there issued a new nationality. It is from such a period of strife that the first history of a people takes its origin, and the record of deeds wrought under the influence of such excitement is the material from which a nation's archives are derived, fixing for ever the memory of actions that will be revered by the generations to come. In this way, the noble harangues of Moriano Moreno to the Provisional Government, the eloquent proclamations made by General Belgrano after the battles of Salta and Tucuman, the noble letters of San Martin are impressive lessons for all humanity; time can have no effect on the exalted nobility of thought and artistic mode of expression that are here held up before us. Under the savage dictatorship of Rosas, all voices were silenced. Still, Sarmiento from his exile in Chili launched from the heights of the Andes his virulent pamphlets against the odious tyrant. When liberty was regained, Press and rostrum sent forth a legion of writers and orators, at whose head we must place Bartolome Mitré and Nicolas Avellaneda. To come down to our own time, the list of distinguished writers meriting each a special notice would be long indeed.

CHAPTER IV
FOREIGN COLONISTS IN ARGENTINA

It is now time to return to the city to get a little better acquainted with its inhabitants. As a matter of fact, the features upon which I have touched—the town, port, promenades, palaces, settlers' houses, agricultural products, manufactures, or commerce—do more or less reveal the native, and although I have said nothing of his person beyond that he looks very like a European, my reader has certainly gathered some light as to his way of living.

To the Argentine *extra muros*, the citizen of Buenos Ayres is the *porteño*—that is, the man of the port, the townsman kept, by the sea, in constant contact with Europe, and more readily undertaking a trip to London or Paris than to Tucuman or Mendoza. On his side, while professing great esteem for the provincials (for in the Argentine patriotism amounts to mania), the *porteño* is inclined to pity those who pass their lives far from the capital; while the countryman mocks good-humouredly at his strange compatriot who knows naught of the *Campo*, whence are brought to his door the corn and cattle which are the outcome of the highest and mightiest efforts of their common national energy, and which by his means are to be exchanged for European produce in an ever-widening and developing trade.

This is, however, but a superficial judgment that we may permit ourselves to make; but if we look more closely into the national character, we shall perceive that if the *porteño* is the nearer to Europe and hastens thither on the smallest pretext; if he is more thoroughly steeped in European culture; if he takes more interest in the doings of the Old World, attaching the greatest importance to its opinion of his own country; if it is his dearest ambition that the youthful Argentine Republic shall comport herself nobly among the old peoples of a weary civilisation; if it is his constant care to obtain from beyond sea the advantages gained by experience, to be turned to account by his own nation—we should be greatly mistaken in assuming that European contact or descent could lead either citizen or farmer, *porteño* or *estanciero*, to prefer to his own land that Old Continent which his forefathers deserted, in the hope, already realised, of finding on this virgin soil, fertilised by his own labour, a better chance of success than the Old World could offer him.

While the physiognomy of the streets of Buenos Ayres is wholly European in symmetry, style, and even in the expression of the faces to be seen thereon, yet this people is Argentine to the very marrow of the bones—exclusively and entirely Argentine. New York is nearer to Europe, and New York is North American in essence as completely as Buenos Ayres is Argentine. The difference is that in New York, and even in Boston or Chicago, North Americanism is patent to all eyes in type, in carriage, and in voice, as much as in feeling and manner of thinking; whereas the piquancy of Buenos Ayres lies in the fact that it offers the spectacle of rabid Argentinism under a European veil. And, strangely enough, this inherent jingoism, which in some nations that shall be nameless assumes so easily an offensive guise, is here displayed with an amiable candour that is most disarming, and instinctively you seek to justify it to yourself. Not satisfied with being Argentine from top to toe, these people will, if you let them, Argentinise you in a trice.

To tell the truth, there are some (I have met a few) who speak ill of the country—and these critics are people who have not even had the excuse of having been unsuccessful in their business affairs here. There are systematic grumblers everywhere, who endeavour to give themselves importance by finding fault with their surroundings. Those who are not pleased with their stay in a foreign country should remind themselves that nobody prevents them from returning to their own.

I have already mentioned that many Italians cross the sea for the harvesting in the Argentine, and then, taking advantage of the difference in the seasons, return home to cut their home corn. This backward and forward movement has grown enormously. But in the long run the attraction of a land that overflows with energy defeats atavistic proclivities and weakens roots that are centuries old. And as soon as the settler has become the owner of a few roods of the new soil, he is irrevocably lost to Europe.

I have not sought to conceal the fact that the largest number of immigrants make the mistake of stopping at Buenos Ayres, whose population is thus increased out of all proportion with the development of Argentine territory. This mass of working people, who necessarily remain easily accessible to

European influences, offers apparently an excellent field for revolutionary propaganda. Anarchists and socialists spare no pains to make proselytes here, in order to strengthen their hands. A violence of speech and action has in this way given to certain strikes a truly European aspect. Still, in a country in which there is a constant supply of work, it is hardly possible that disturbances arising rather from doctrine than from existing social evils can take any hold on or materially affect any considerable extent of territory.

If I am to believe what I heard in all parts, the Russian anarchists have a specially redoubtable organisation. To mention only the most recent of events, it is known that the Chief of Police, who had directed in person some ruthless repressive measures, was killed in the street by a bomb thrown by a Russian, who was protected from the full severity of the law by his tender age. [6]

Last June, a few days before I left Europe, a bomb was thrown by some unknown person in the Colon Theatre, falling in the middle of the orchestra and wounding more or less seriously a large number of persons. The Colon Theatre, in which opera is given, is the largest and perhaps the handsomest theatre in the world. [7] The open boxes of the pit tier, like those of the first two tiers and orchestra, present, when filled with young women in evening dress, the most brilliant spectacle that I have ever seen in any theatre. In such a setting, imagine the catastrophe that could be caused by a bomb! [8] The injured were carried out somehow or other, the house was emptied amid loud and furious outcries, and, the damage having been repaired in the course of the following day, not a woman in society was absent from her place at the performance of the evening. This is a very fine trait of character which does the highest honour to the women of Argentine society. I am not sure that in Paris, under similar circumstances, there would have been a full house on the night following such a disaster.

It is easy to understand, however, that the fury of the public found expression in an Act of Parliament of terrible severity, directed immediately against any suspicious groups. The criminal in the present case has not yet been discovered, though during my stay in Buenos Ayres there occurred a sensational arrest which led the authorities to believe they had laid hands on the guilty man. A state of siege was in some sense declared, lasting all the time I was in Buenos Ayres; and the Government obtained extraordinary powers, to be used only against organisations believed to be anarchical. The penalty generally imposed was transportation to Terra del Fuego, under conditions that no one would or, perhaps, could describe to me. I am without the necessary returns for establishing the results obtained. Some complaints reached me from the more populous quarters affirming that the innocent had been punished; all I could do was to hand them over to the authorities. I can testify that in my presence, in any of the circles of Buenos Ayres society that I was able to observe, no anarchist outrages were on any single occasion the subject of conversation. More than once I led up to it. The reply invariably was that the question was one for public authority, that the Government was armed and would take action, and if further powers should prove necessary they would be granted. Then the topic was changed.

There is no doubt that the Argentine Government, like that of Great Britain, is resolved to finish, once for all, with crimes which arouse only horror in all the civilised world. In the course of a hasty visit I had occasion to pay to the Police Department, in the company of the City Superintendent, Señor Guiraldès (at the very moment of the arrest of the man who was believed to have thrown the bomb in the Colon Theatre), I could see that not only is the force a very powerful one, but that it has at its head men of energy and decision who are determined to repress deeds of violence, of which all or nearly all are committed by persons not of Argentine nationality. [9]

While on the subject, one may note that the Argentine police have adopted and perfected the system of identification of criminals by the marks of the thumb. First the imprint of all ten fingers is taken, so as to make mistake impossible and arrive at absolute certainty; then, acting on the principle that it may be as useful to identify an honest man as a bandit, identification certificates are issued to the public, for a small fee, containing an enlargement of the thumb imprint.

A crowd of people waiting at the door of the office that makes and furnishes these documents showed that the public fully appreciated their usefulness. Young men and old were submitting in silence to have their ten fingers smeared with a sort of wax not easily removed by soap and water. Each in turn departed well pleased that the stigma of "Unknown" would never be attached to his grave. It appears that it has become the fashion to register one's thumb at the police-station before starting on any journey. Señor

Guiraldès told us that his own son, now in Europe, had taken this precaution before exposing his person to the risks of the elements and the unceremonious manners of Parisian *apaches*.

In the days of the stage-coach Parisians used to be laughed at for making their wills and taking out passports before starting on a journey to Étampes. Now behold! By other routes we have returned to the good old days. And funny as it may appear to those of us who like to believe that civilisation in South America is more or less rudimentary, it is precisely this country which thus, in scientific fashion, guards against the barbarous ways of the capitals and even the country districts of Europe.

There was recently a story of an Argentine who was drowned on our coast and whose body was subsequently washed up on shore, with the head frightfully mutilated. As, however, the telltale thumb had been preserved he was quickly identified. If this story had been told me in time I should certainly have allowed as much of my person as was necessary to be dipped in wax instead of venturing to start on my homeward journey without the simple proofs of identity which would suffice to place beyond doubt the status of any Jonah in the depths of a whale. As it is, in spite of my imprudence, I reached home with my head still on my shoulders. Pure luck! Never again will I trust myself at sea without this elementary precaution, which would so radically have changed the fortunes of Ulysses in rocky Ithaca.

After this digression, which is only excused by the importance of the subject, I want to finish what I began to say about the rabid Argentinism of our friends. I had a great surprise one day when speaking respectfully of the fine qualities of the Spaniards. Some highly cultured men present interrupted me, and criticised severely the race from which they had sprung in terms one might have expected from an Anglo-Saxon, but not from a Latin. Therefore I must ask my readers not to imagine that the Argentinos are merely Spaniards transplanted to American soil. No! The real Argentino, though he would never confess it, seems to me convinced that there is a magic elixir of youth that springs from his soil and makes of him a new man, descendant of none but ancestor of endless generations to come.

That there is indeed a regenerating influence in this youthful land is proved by the power it wields over newcomers of whatever origin. The Italian in particular is Argentinised before he is *argenté*. In the provinces, as in Buenos Ayres, I had a hundred thousand examples of this before my eyes. You ask a child, the son of an immigrant, whether he speaks Italian or Spanish. He answers haughtily, "At home we all talk Argentine." Another, unable to deny that he was born in Genoa, although he claimed Argentine nationality, murmured by way of excuse, "I was so little." I may add that in the primary schools where these replies were made to me the teaching was the epitome of Argentine patriotic spirit, as might be guessed from the pictures and inscriptions on the walls. [10] But Alsace-Lorraine and Poland are witness to the fact that unless the heart be wholly won authority may labour in vain.

As I want to be wholly sincere here, I must admit that the French take this Argentine contagion with remarkable facility. I should grievously wrong our own excellent colony, however, if I did less than justice to its ardent patriotism. It is only when tried that love grows and grows purer. In absence the fatherland seems the dearer in proportion as it is connected with the recollection of sufferings that left us stripped of all but honour.

The public work of the French colony speaks loudly for it. Its most important achievement is the French Hospital, founded long ago, but, thanks to its Governor, M. Basset, and its chief physician, Dr. G. Lauré, it is invaluable. As I was leaving the building after a visit I shall not soon forget, the Chairman of the Board of Directors showed me a bust of Pasteur standing among the trees, and asked what I thought of a suggestion to place near it a figure of Lorraine. Although the symbolism in the two statues would be entirely different, I warmly concurred in the plan. There is, after all, a delicate connection between these two manifestations of the soul of France—the desire for knowledge and the courage to hold.

These men, who have presented to the city of Buenos Ayres a monument worthy of France in commemoration of the friendship of the sister republics, and who, on the occasion of the floods in Paris of last year, sent a cheque for 400,000 francs to assuage the worst of the distress, never miss an opportunity of showing their loyalty to the mother-country. Yet how many sons of France one meets at every step who have gone over to the Argentine, head and heart, beyond all possibility of return!

One large manufacturer of the port of Buenos Ayres is a nephew of a member of our National Assembly of 1871. I noticed, when inspecting his very remarkable establishment, that he speaks French less fluently than Spanish, while his two brothers, who pay frequent visits to Paris, have become thorough Argentinos.

Again, I might take the case of one of our most eminent compatriots who left France in his twentieth year, but who has remained French to the very marrow of his bones. His son is an official of high position in the Argentine. Doubtless his marriage with a woman of the country laid the foundation for this South American family. The atmosphere of the home is naturally altered, and his material interests, indissolubly riveted to the soil that feeds him and his family, attune the settler insensibly to new ways, and gradually transform his whole habit of mind to the new pattern.

Can anybody explain why this is not the case with the French who try their fortune in North America, and why in Canada the two races live side by side in all harmony but never mix? It must be that "blood is thicker than water," as says the English proverb, and that the Latin element blends more readily with a Latin agglomeration than with an Anglo-Saxon community. Here I have seen, over and over again, that after two or three generations nothing remains of the original stock but the name.

I know of but one instance where the Latin organism has been completely assimilated by a northern race, and that is the French emigration to Germany in consequence of the revocation of the Edict of Nantes. But in that case a community of religious fervour, strengthened by an odious persecution, was the active agent in the blending of the Latin mind and character with that of Germany. We all remember that the first German Governor of Alsace-Lorraine was the descendant of a French emigrant. Some of us may recall the furious address of the learned Dubois-Reymond to the youth of Prussia in 1870, urging them over the frontier of the land from which their ancestors were driven by the sabres of the dragoons of Louis XIV.

To return once more to our Franco-Argentinos, I ought to say that the severe application of French military law but too often embitters them against the mother-country. In its haste to increase its population, the Argentine awards nationalisation to the children of foreigners born on Argentine soil, and nationalisation carries in its train military service. It is the same system adopted by ourselves in Algiers toward Spanish colonists. The consequence is that the son of French parents duly registered at the French Consulate, in order to preserve for him his father's nationality, finds himself later called simultaneously to serve under two flags on opposite sides of the ocean.

What is he to do? In the Argentine, where military service is very short, are all his future prospects, while in France no place has been kept open for him. If France were in danger and called to him for help he would not hesitate, but, failing that, his actual surroundings make it hard for him to decide. The majority respond to the call to the Argentine flag, and by so doing fall into the class of *insoumis* on French soil, except in cases where the father, with a forethought that cannot be approved, has omitted to register the birth at the Consulate.

If I remember rightly, ten only out of forty youths called up leave Buenos Ayres annually to answer to their names at the French roll-call. One wonders whether the result be sufficient to justify steps that might easily trouble our relations with the French colony in this country. For the young *insoumis* can never set foot on French soil without finding the *gendarmerie* after him. Yet his business will call him inevitably to Europe. Where will he take his orders when France has shut her doors to him? England, Belgium, Switzerland, and Germany are open to him. I heard recently a story about a Frenchman of Buenos Ayres who ventured to Lille, and had only just time, at a warning from a friend, to escape over the border.

I need not dwell on the matter, but it is easy to see how detrimental the present state of the law is to French families living in the Argentine, Brazil, and other American countries, as well as to France herself. We manage in this way to drive from the national fold a number of young men who would in time of danger respond heartily to a call from the motherland.

Wherever I went I heard the same cry. The Consuls and the French Minister could only reply, "It is the law." But the Frenchman who follows the Flag in some foreign land demands an alteration in a law which ought not to be applied with the same rigour to youths living in Basle, Brussels, Geneva, and to those who have found a field for their activities across the sea.

To me it seems only justice to establish a distinction in our legislation between these two categories of French subjects. For example, I heard of the case of an eminent politician—M. Pellegrini, the son of an inhabitant of Nice, and therefore French—who, in his youth, got into difficulties in the way described with the French recruiting service, and who later, having risen to the position of President of the Argentine Republic, received the Grand Cordon of the Legion of Honour. The red ribbon or the Council of War—which seems the more appropriate reward to citizens of this kind? Of course, we must all regret that valuable citizens should thus be taken from France at the moment when she needs every one of her children. At the same time we must consider that a Frenchman who has become Argentine is by no means lost to France, as might be the case in the United States, for instance, where the Latin is rapidly submerged by the irresistible flood of Anglo-Saxonism.

In the Argentine, on the contrary, the Northern races prove merely a useful element of methodical intelligence and tenacity, which is in time engulfed by the great Latin wave. There are important German colonies in Brazil, and even in the Argentine. Both English and North Americans have prosperous manufactories there. Yet in a race that has preserved integrally its Latinity, all this is of but secondary interest, and the tendency remains to travel steadily in the track of peoples of Latin stock, among whom it may without presumption be said that the French exert the most powerful influence.

For this reason any Frenchman of average intellectual and moral value who becomes incorporated in the Argentine nation must almost infallibly at the same time—for I doubt if any Frenchman is ever really un-Frenched—materially aid in permanently strengthening French prestige.

What are we to think of men like M. Paul Groussac, who holds an eminent place in Buenos Ayres, but who would equally in his own land have reached the very front rank? M. Groussac, having gone through our naval training school, set out to see the world. One day, his pockets empty, he arrived at Buenos Ayres, where courageously he hired himself as *gaucho*—that is, keeper of the immense flocks of the Pampas, whose members run into their thousands—and he undertook to drive a train of mules to Peru. He accomplished the journey successfully, covering the same route four times in all, each journey taking four months. Later we find him acting as schoolmaster. In Tucuman he carried on the work of the French outlaw, Jacques, who, having escaped to the Argentine after the *coup d'état* of

December 2d, devoted himself entirely to public education on lines taken up later and developed by President Sarmiento. We had the pleasure of seeing in the place of honour at the Training College of Tucuman the portraits of the two French founders, Jacques and Paul Groussac. From time to time the latter brother has published various literary works, notably some short stories in which Argentine life and character are brilliantly set forth, and the name of their author has achieved a wide celebrity. Then M. Hilleret, the great French sugar manufacturer of Santa Ana, placed a large capital at the disposal of Paul Groussac with which to start a daily paper destined to reveal, in the person of its editor-in-chief, a writer of remarkable force.

To-day you may hear that Paul Groussac is the leading Spanish writer of our times, which by no means prevents him from contributing some brilliant articles to our own *Journal des Débats*, amply proving his mastery of his mother-tongue, not to mention a curious study by him of that literary enigma the *Don Quichotte* of Avellaneda.

In 1810 a Public Library was founded by decree of the first Revolutionary Junto, on the initiative of Secretary Moreno. It was opened March 16, 1812, its nucleus being drawn from the convent libraries. In 1880, after the proclamation of Buenos Ayres as capital of the Federation, the Public Library became the National Library, and in 1885 Paul Groussac was appointed Governor. In an interview with President Roca, who cannot be accused of any partiality for him, Groussac obtained a grant of the building intended, alas! for public lotteries, in which the library might be installed. He set to work immediately. The National Library of the Argentine, under the control of M. Groussac, is now without a rival in South America, and can bear comparison with many similar institutions on the Old Continent.
[11]

One of the pet hobbies of M. Groussac is now to open a French *lycée* in Buenos Ayres, with the support of both Governments. His eldest son, an Argentino, has just been appointed to the post of Under-Secretary of State in the Office of Public Instruction by M. Saënz Peña.

Strangely enough all the fine qualities of this illustrious compatriot of ours have been lost sight of for the reason that through some defect—I had almost said vice—in his character he has won the reputation of being the surliest of bears. Having myself also, to some extent, a reputation for being less than amiable I wondered whether the two of us might not come to blows if we met. Considering in some sort my bald head a protection, I ventured into the bear's den, and found only the most affable and genial of men, whose claws were of velvet and his tusks of sugar. Thus we made friends at once, and I found that the much-dreaded beast had nothing terrible about him, unless it was a strong accent of the Gers.

Since that day I have done my best to dispel so injurious a prejudice against the man. I can only explain its prevalence by the words of Tacitus, who remarked of his father-in-law, Agricola, "He chose rather to offend than to hate." It is a rare enough trait among men this, which leads them, like Alceste, to declare their real opinion rather than stoop to the indignity of falsehood. It may very easily happen that in this way such men may offend the talker who asks only cheap flattery, though actuated themselves by the kindliest feelings towards their fellow-men.

If we consider for a moment the sentiment aroused in us by the general practice of using words to conceal our thoughts, we must recognise that we are the first to suffer by this universal weakness—not to say cowardice—in that we only expect from others what we ourselves give, namely, hypocritical phrases, leading to crooked actions, and causing that silent but lasting dislike which forms the principal obsession in the life of many among us. If it is a less offence to inspire than to harbour dislike, let us absolve the men who fail to win universal regard, but who are nevertheless wholly incapable of harming a creature.

Unless I am misinformed, we shall soon have the pleasure of seeing Paul Groussac in Paris. A Chair of History of the Argentine Republic has been founded at the Sorbonne, and there is talk of offering it to him. Certainly no one could better perform its duties. Yet it would surprise me if he could in this way break off his multitudinous engagements in the Argentine. They say he will in person open the course of lectures. I can promise an intellectual treat to his hearers.

I did not hear of any Germans or Englishmen who had, to the same extent as the Italians and the French, undergone transformation into Argentinos. The German, whose fundamental roughness—to call it by no stronger name—is frequently masked by good humour, works his way into all classes of society, but without losing any of his original traits. M. Mihanowitch, who is at the head of a colossal business of river and sea transportation, must, notwithstanding his Austrian origin, be considered as an Argentino, though he is surely of Slav blood.

The English invariably retain their individuality. I am told that in Patagonia, where they are carrying on sheep breeding on a scale that leaves Australia in the rear, they have built up cosy dwellings, where every night they change into their smoking-jackets for the family repast, and never miss taking a holiday of two or three months in their native land. They never become Argentinos. This, however, does not prevent their being at the head of the business world of La Plata, where they exert a powerful influence on the industrial and commercial life of the people.

It would have greatly interested me to study the foreign colonies more closely, but time was lacking. Of the Spanish, the only man I was able to see anything of was M. Coelho, the distinguished Governor of the Spanish Bank of La Plata, whose untiring energy reaches out daily in new directions; he gave me many proofs of kindness, for which I am sincerely grateful.

It is certain that the recent visit of Field-Marshal von der Goltz to the Argentine must prove useful to German influence. As we know, it is the Germans who are responsible for the present organisation of the Argentine Army. Their Government, wiser than some others, did not hesitate to send to La Plata some of their most skilled officers, who were naturally received by Argentine society with the deference that was their due.

The eminent legal scholar, Professor Enrico Ferri, lately re-elected Deputy of the group that we should call "Independent Socialists," is and has long been the official mouthpiece of the Italian colony. Gifted with a perfect urbanity, an impartial mind, lofty ideals, and generous eloquence, he quickly attracted the notice of the public, and soon vanquished the suspicions of the Extreme Right, who feared his Socialist views, and the opposition of the Extreme Left, who bore him malice for having broken away from them. M. Saënz Peña's Cabinet has been well advised in calling on M. Enrico Ferri to take over the management of the penitentiary system.

I have mentioned the principal features of the French colony, and shall hope to be forgiven if lack of space has prevented me from doing full justice to its members. I have spoken of M. Py, the distinguished Governor of the Banque Française de la Plata, who is admirably assisted in his work by the manager, M. Puisoye. It would be unpardonable to omit the name of Mme. Moreno (of the Comédie Française), who has so thoroughly mastered the Spanish tongue that she has opened and carried to success a *conservatoire*, in which she trains pupils for the stage. It would be the less excusable to forget this lady in that she is frequently to be met at receptions, where her elocution, both in prose and in poetry, delights her Parisian-Argentine public. Whilst waiting for the Académies to confer on women the right to be learned, let us venture to proclaim their cleverness even when it is but an adjunct to feminine charm.

CHAPTER V
ARGENTINE EDUCATION, HOSPITALS, AND ASYLUMS

If the different foreign elements contributed by the Latin peoples fuse so readily into an Argentine race, it is none the less true that Spanish metal bulks the heaviest in the ore. Language, literature, history, give a bias from which none can escape. The ancient branch transplanted to this youthful soil sends up its shoots towards another heaven, but the original sap circulates unendingly in the living tree. The Argentine is not, and firmly refuses to be, a Spanish colony. It has successfully freed itself from the historic shackles—those of theocracy, first of all—which have so disastrously tied and bound the noble and lofty impulses of a people eminently fitted to perform exalted tasks. And hence, notwithstanding a large alluvion from Italy, symbolised by the monument to Garibaldi, notwithstanding the growing influence of French culture, the atavism of blood preserves an indelible imprint which will characterise the Argentine nation down to its most distant posterity.

The visit of the Infanta Isabella on the occasion of the Centenary Fêtes in honour of the independence was a happy thought on the part of the Spanish Government. The Princess, escorted by M. Perez Caballero, the present Spanish Ambassador in Paris, was everywhere received with rapturous enthusiasm. It was easy to see that the struggles of the past, now relegated to the annals of the dead, had left no bitterness in the people's heart. There was universal pleasure at the graceful action of the now reconciled parent in thus stretching a hand to the son who, with impetuous ardour, had thrown off the yoke of dependence, and the public found a subtle pleasure in showing that the chivalrous courtesy which is part of the tradition of the race had lost none of its flower in this American land. After the severe measures taken to repress anarchical violence, a rumour spread that the life of the President of the Republic was in danger. Perhaps there was nothing in it. Unfortunately, it was one of those things that can only be verified by experience. At all events, the Infanta Isabella chose to ignore the danger.

With the utmost simplicity, but also with the utmost courage, she showed herself everywhere by the side of the Chief of the State, and to the lasting credit of the Argentine reputation, everywhere she was greeted with hearty applause.

Here, then, is a base, immutably Spanish through all the changes that one can foresee, together with a fusion and perfect assimilation of the Latin elements in the immense influx of European civilisation: such is the first condition of Argentine evolution to be seen and studied in the city of Buenos Ayres. To make the picture complete, we must notice an important contribution of Indian blood that is very marked everywhere. I shall return to this later. As for the national character, since I am only jotting down a traveller's impressions, and not attempting to present to my readers a didactic study, it is, I think, better to allow its features to spring naturally from the subject under consideration as we go along, rather than first to make statements that I must next attempt to prove.

I have already mentioned the extreme kindness of Señor Guiraldès, the City Lieutenant, who is for the Argentine capital what M. de Selves is for Paris. Like our own Prefect, he is appointed by the President of the Republic, and I may say that although there are inevitably from time to time differences with the Municipal Council, the system has given good results as applied to a place in which there are so many conflicting elements. Señor and Señora Guiraldès, like all the upper class of Argentine society, possess the most perfect European culture, and they do the honours of their city with a charming grace that delights the foreign visitor. Now that I am at a distance from them, I consider that I may with propriety pay sincere homage to their courtesy. Whenever I found I had a little time to spare I used to telephone to Señor Guiraldès, who had once for all placed himself at my disposal. He invariably replied by hastening to my door, and together we consulted as to tours of inspection; it was agreed that I should choose the institutions to be visited so that there might be no suspicion of collusion. In this way I was enabled to visit all the State or municipal establishments that interested me. When by chance we found some evidence of official oversight, Señor Guiraldès's satisfaction was boundless.

"At least," he cried, "you will not tell me that your call had been announced beforehand."

Then, to check any inordinate vanity, I told him the tale of an adventure that happened once to a certain Minister of the Interior who visited the prison of Saint Lazare.

A ring at the bell.

"I want to see the Governor."

"He has gone up to town."

"Then I will see the chief clerk."

"He is away on leave."

"The chief warder?"

"He is laid up."

"Can I speak to the Sister Superior?"

"She has just gone out."

"Well, are any of the prisoners at home?"

The gaoler, smiling amiably: "I believe so."

Argentine officials, like their French brethren, are both fallible and zealous, and while it was impossible that in so many visits there should be no ground for criticism, yet I am anxious to declare publicly how admirably kept were the schools, of whatever degree, the hospitals, asylums, refuges, and prisons; they were not only adapted to all the requirements of therapeutics, hygiene, and the canons of modern European science, but they showed a genuine effort to do better than the best. I should have been glad to have there some of those who make a practice of disdaining these countries that started very long after us, but that can already give us some salutary lessons through institutions such as those I have named, which are here brought to a pitch of perfection that is in many cases unknown with us.

My readers will not expect me to take them with me round all the establishments that I visited with Señor Guiraldès. They would fill a book, and I should need to dip into the innumerable volumes of reports and notices which Argentine benevolence added to my personal luggage. This, however, does not come within my subject.

None will be surprised that the schools attracted my attention first. The School Question is too vast to be handled here in detail. But I saw professional schools (*Écoles industrielles de la Nation*), and primary schools that would be models in any land. All the arrangements irreproachable, and the children scrupulously clean. Demonstration lessons in abundance. Lessons on the land and its mineral, vegetable, and animal productions, specimens of each being passed from hand to hand, accompanied by explanations summarised in synoptic tables. A lesson on the anatomy and physiology of the lungs was illustrated by the breathing organs of an ox and a sheep (higher primary class for young girls), which appeared to awaken great interest among the scholars. Specimens in pasteboard coloured like life, showing the different parts of the organism, allow these rudimentary demonstrations to be carried fairly far.

The primary schools, under the management of the National Educational Council, are free, and include the school material obligatory in theory for children of from six to twelve years of age. But the population of Buenos Ayres grows more rapidly than its schools. Hence the inconvenient expedient has been adopted of dividing the pupils into two categories, one attending school of a morning and the other of an afternoon, with the result that one half the children are always wandering about the streets while the others are drinking at the fountain of knowledge. This is a system that has nothing to recommend it. It is difficult to understand why the Argentine capital postpones making a pecuniary sacrifice which is certainly not beyond its means, and which is imperatively necessary. The criticism is the more justifiable in that untold sums have been spent on certain buildings which are veritable palaces, as, for example, the President Roca School. About a hundred private, lay, or denominational schools, kept for the most part by foreigners, take in the children who are crowded out of the public schools. At Buenos Ayres, as in other parts of the country, the number of pupils in this category is far too large. There are provinces where the deficit of schools is such as to constitute a real scandal in a civilised nation. [12]

I shall never forget the heart-broken tones of a child of ten whom I met in the Pampas of the Buenos Ayres province and whom I questioned as to his occupations.

"I want to go to school. Papa does not want me to."

The father was a Mexican. The eyes of the child thus condemned by paternal stupidity to mental darkness were full of intelligence. How much trouble we take to make the best of our land! How apathetic we are when it is a question of developing the greatest force in the world, that which sets in motion all the rest—human intelligence! Is it not inconceivable that in France, after nearly half a century of labour, we still find every year a large number of wholly illiterate men among the conscripts called up to serve with the Flag? This state of affairs, which is sad enough at home, would be reckoned a great success in the *Campo*, where distances are such that the children have to go to the primary schools on horseback, as I have elsewhere mentioned. But when a school is within reach, the folly of parents must not be permitted to debar their children from its advantages.

The municipal and State schools are entirely undenominational. This rule obtains throughout the Argentine, where it is accepted without a murmur. The numerous religious Orders have their own private schools in virtue of the recognised principle of liberty of teaching. It might surprise a European to see that the Catholic clergy of the Argentine do not attempt to fight the undenominational character of the public schools which elsewhere has aroused such violent hostility. To my mind this cannot be explained by a want of religious fervour amongst priests and monks in the Argentine. But circumstances which it would take too long to explain have taught the Argentine clergy to make an *outward* practice of toleration. If questioned on the subject, the Argentino will reply: "Our clergy hold themselves aloof from politics."

And this seems to be the case. The religious world appears to be no party to political differences. The social influence of the Roman hierarchy is none the less powerful on what remains of the old colonial aristocracy and (with few exceptions) on the women of the class known as superior. Practically, the official relations of Church and State in the Argentine approach very close to separation.

I shall say nothing of the secondary schools and colleges, of which I saw but little. They are placed under the immediate control of the Minister of Public Instruction. There are no resident students. This, in the opinion of all, is the weakest spot in their educational scheme. Amédée Jacques, one of the exiles of our December *coup d'état*, introduced our classical curriculum into the Argentine, but it met with no success. Since that time, here, as at home, there has been strife between the partisans of the classic and those of modern, or even technical, education. Great battles have been fought, and the only result is that the cause of education has suffered from both parties. The opening of a French *lycée*, which I have reason to believe will shortly take place, may help to restore the classics to the position which in my opinion they ought to hold in every civilised country.

In certain branches higher education has made great strides. Law and Medicine in particular have a staff of eminent men in their colleges. Any man who has made his mark in Europe is sure of a choice audience there, drawn from both professors and students. I had the pleasure of being present at the first of Enrico Ferri's lectures at the Law schools. His subject was Social Justice. The powerful and glowing eloquence of the orator was never displayed before a public better prepared to profit by his lofty teaching on humanitarian equity.

It is not in vain that so many young Argentines have made their way to the universities of France, Italy, and Germany. As soon as I set foot in the hospitals here I had an impression that I was in the full stream of European science, and that the Argentinos were determined to be second to none in the perfection of their organisation.

I noticed an excellent bacteriological institute managed by a compatriot of ours, M. Lignères, and some agricultural schools that are turning out a competent body of men for the development of the Pampas.

The hospitals impressed us very favourably. The New Hospital for Contagious Diseases, situated some kilometres from the centre of the town, comprises a series of model buildings, all strictly isolated, of which each is devoted to a special disease. At the Rivadavia Hospital, for women only, the *Cobo* wards (for pulmonary tuberculosis and surgical operations) are particularly admirable. Everywhere the latest improvements as regards the appliances for the patients, the sterilising halls, and operating theatres, and also as regards surgical appliances. Nothing has been overlooked that can increase the efficaciousness of the hospital schools: amphitheatres for classes, diagrams, specimens, etc. The laboratories are so luxurious that they would make our own hospital students envious. It was here that Dr. Pozzi, our eminent compatriot, performed in May, 1910, a series of operations, every one of which proved successful; while his German fellow-practitioner, whose scientific acquirements are unquestionable, met with very different results. The same may be said of Dr. Doléris, who held a course of demonstration lessons in Buenos Ayres, and whose operations were also crowned with entire success. The Rivadavia Hospital has a fine *annexe* of supplementary work: consultations for outpatients, electro- and radio-therapy, dispensary, etc. I must also mention the sumptuous recreation-rooms for the use of convalescents, and the gardens, exquisitely kept.

In the maternity wards (at Alvear as at Rivadavia) we find the same care for ultra-modern comfort, combined with the strictest cleanliness. I must not forget a very curious obstetrical museum with diagrams, anatomical specimens, and a series of admirable preparations exemplifying the different stages of gestation. A small cradle should be noticed (a German invention, I believe), ingeniously attached to the mother's bed and taken down with a single movement of the hand. Very happy instance of simplification. Everywhere—in the design of the buildings, in the fittings, laboratories, sterilising- and operating-rooms—the influence and products of Germany were patent. On the other hand, the French culture of doctors and surgeons, masters and pupils, was easily discernible, and all were greatly indebted to the classics of our Paris and Lyons Faculties. I could not see the evidences of this in the hospital libraries without remembering regretfully the churlish reception that is given in some of our hospital schools to modest foreign *savants*.

At the same time, I will not conceal the fact that Protection of the most extreme sort flourishes among the Argentine physicians, who are very anxious to defend themselves against European competition. I was told that there are no less than thirty-two examinations imposed on a doctor from the Paris Faculty before he is permitted to write out the simplest prescription for a *gaucho* of the Pampas. We may be allowed to find these measures highly exaggerated.

There is a splendid Asylum for Aged Men kept by French Sisters of Charity in a condition of the daintiest cleanliness, and managed by ladies of the city. The Argentinos claim that their women are very zealous in all charitable works. Doubt was thrown recently in the Chamber on this statement. I am not competent to judge.

One original institution—the Widows' Asylum—is a sort of settlement composed of small apartments of one or two rooms, on a single floor. In the courtyard opposite the gate is a small shed, in which is placed a stove for open-air cooking, possible in this fortunate climate all the year round. The rents are very low for widows having more than four children.

The lunatic colony of Lujan, to which its founder and manager, Dr. Cabred, has given the significant name of The Open Door, deserves a more detailed description. It consists of an estate of six hundred hectares on the Pacific Line seventy kilometres from Buenos Ayres, and here twelve hundred patients are accommodated in twenty villas—graceful *chalets*, surrounded by gardens and containing each sixty patients. These villas are fitted up with everything necessary for clinotherapy and balneotherapy, with fine recreation-rooms. The colony is enclosed by a line of wire; not a wall, not a wooden fence—everywhere unrestricted freedom and a wide, open horizon.

We have erected a monument in Paris to the memory of Pinel, in which he is represented as breaking the chains which mediæval ignorance heaped on the mad inmates of Bicêtre as late as 1793. But if you visit our asylum of Sainte-Anne, you are tempted to ask in what this "modern" establishment differs from an ordinary prison. I hasten to add that in the other asylums of the Department of the Seine we are beginning to develop the open-air treatment. Long ago the system of placing certain patients out in the country amongst peasant families was planned and adopted. The Open Door treats all mental patients, of whatever degree of madness, on the plan known out here as "work performed in liberty." In the confusion of cerebral phenomena the widest freedom is given to the reflex action of unconscious or quasi-unconscious life. If a patient has learnt a trade, he finds at once in The Open Door an outlet for his energies, for it is with the labour of the lunatics that the carpentering, masonry, scaffolding, etc., of these villas was executed. Those who have no trade are given a technical education, and often acquire great skill. The difficulty is to persuade the newcomer to begin to work. If he refuses, he is left alone. "He is left to feel dull." Then he is invited to take a walk, and once on the spot where work is proceeding, he is offered a tool that he may do as the others are doing.

"I have met with only one refusal," said Dr. Cabred. "One patient tried calmly to prove to me that life was not worth the labour necessary to preserve it. I must confess that he nearly convinced me, and I often try to find the flaw in his reasoning, though never, as yet, with success. It is a little hard when the apostle of lunatic labour is brought to ask himself if the lunatic who refuses to work is not acting on a better reasoned conviction than his more submissive companions. At any rate, he is the only man in the colony who does nothing. He spends his time reading the paper or dreaming, without saying a word. When I go to see him he mocks at me, declaring that it is I who am the fool, and, indeed, to support his laziness is not, perhaps, the action of a sane man."

There is not a strait-waistcoat or a single appliance for restraint in the whole colony. Excitement or attacks of violence all yield to the bath, which is sometimes prolonged to twenty-four or thirty hours if necessary.

Separate *chalets* for the manager and his staff, for the water reservoir, the machinery, laundry, dairy, kitchens, workshops, theatre, chapel. Outside, agricultural labour in every form, from ploughing to cattle rearing. Only the superintendents who direct the work are sane, or supposed to be. In spite of this assurance it is not without alarm that one watches madmen handling red-hot irons or tools as dangerous for others as themselves. As may be supposed, they are not put to this kind of work until they have been subjected to long trials.

Our visit to The Open Door lasted a whole day, and still we had not seen everything. From first to last we were followed by a mad photographer, who took his pictures at his own convenience and reprimanded us severely for rising from lunch without first posing for him. Four days later a series of photographs, representing the various incidents of our day at The Open Door, was sent to me, bound in an album—by a madman, of course, and sent by another madman to a person mad enough to believe himself endowed with reason.

Need I add that we had been received to the strains of the *Marseillaise* and the National Argentine Hymn, performed by a mad band, which, all through lunch, played the music of its repertoire! Ever since, I have wondered why a certificate of madness is not demanded from every candidate for admission to the Opera orchestra.

As for journalism, do you suppose that no room was found for it in The Open Door? The excellent Dr. Cabred is not a man to make such omissions. We were duly presented with a copy of the *Ecos de las Mercedes*, a monthly paper, written and published by the madmen of The Open Door, with the intention, perhaps, of making us believe that other journals are the work of individuals in full possession of their common-sense—prose and poetry; articles in Spanish, Italian, and French; occasionally a slight carelessness in grammar and in sequence of thought, but, on the whole, not wandering farther from their subject than others.

Finally, to wind up the day's proceedings, we were treated to a horserace ridden by lunatics. Sane beasts mounted by mad horsemen, galloping wildly, by mutual consent, in a useless effort to reach a perfectly vain end. Is not this the common spectacle offered by humanity?

Meantime, one honest madman of mystic tendencies, decorated with about a hundred medals, pursued us with religious works, from which he read us extracts, accompanied by his blessing. I wondered whether this form of exercise was included in Dr. Cabred's programme, since he claims to make his lunatics perform all the acts of a sane community. A similar scruple occurred to me at noon, when I was invited to take a seat at a well-spread table.

"Is your cooking done by madmen?" I inquired, not without anxiety.

"We have made an exception in your favour," was the contrite reply.

And now another question arose to my lips.

"Since you have clearly proved that the mad are capable of performing any kind of task, will you tell me why you give yourself the lie by placing at the head of The Open Door a man who appears to me in possession of all his faculties?"

"Yes; that is a weakness," replied the Doctor, laughing. "But, after all, what proof have you that I am not literally fulfilling all my own conditions? Did I not tell you that one of my patients, who may quite possibly be the most enlightened of us all, pronounced me a raving lunatic when I invited him to work? If he is right, then all is as it should be at The Open Door."

I did not wish to vex the kindly doctor, who is the architect of so admirable a monument, but there was still a doubt in my mind: Was it possible to give the illusion of freedom to these madmen by merely suppressing the walls? They offer no resistance when called to co-operate in all kinds of open-air labour, and find, if not a cure, at least relief from their malady in this simple treatment; but did they really believe themselves free? I did not ask the question, for the answer was given by an old French gardener, one of the inmates of The Open Door, who, over-excited by our presence there, suddenly began to rave.

"For twenty-five years," he shrieked, "you have kept me prisoner here!"

Here, then, was a man whose life was spent out of doors at the work with which he had been familiar all his life, and, although no sign of restraint was visible, he was conscious of imprisonment. It is true that modern determinism has reduced what we call our "liberty" to the rigorous fatality of an organism which leaves to us merely the illusion of free will, [13] while imposing on us the impulse of some superior energy that we are forced to obey. Oh, Madness! Oh, Wisdom! Oh, vacillating sisters! is it indeed true that you wander hand in hand through the world?

To whatever philosophic solution our own madness or reason may lead us, let us hasten to conclude the subject by stating that The Open Door is a model establishment, which, thanks to Dr. Cabred, enables the Argentine to give the lead to older peoples. I will only add that it is the rarest thing for a patient to escape (if I may use so unsuitable a word), since the natural conditions of the surrounding Pampas would render life therein impossible; and the lunatics on the way to recovery who are given leave of absence to stay a few days with their friends before being finally set at liberty invariably return punctually to the colony. Who can tell if some lunatic, restored to reason, might not secretly refuse to believe himself cured, and elect to pass the rest of his days happily at work under the glorious sky amongst these peaceful creatures, where the troubles and worries of the world, with the eternal competition and conflict which are the scourge of our "sane" existence, are unfelt and unknown? Such a case might lead Dr. Cabred to put up a similar establishment for the wise.

From the lunatic asylum to the prison is not such a leap as some of us may think. The asylum lifts out of the relative orderliness that we have managed to establish in the conditions of civilised life all those who, by lack of mental balance, might introduce unbearable disorder. And might not this elemental definition be equally applied to the one or the other class of unfortunates? I beg my reader not to be alarmed at the fearful gravity of the problem. If it be true that no philosopher has ever been able to find a solid foundation for the right that man has assumed to "punish" his fellows for transgressing his laws, at least all will readily admit that, notwithstanding some obvious imperfections, society has attained to manifest superiority over the state of barbarism in which brute force alone rules, and that it is therefore inadmissible that those who would transgress the general laws on which society has been based should be allowed to destroy the fabric so laboriously built up.

In moving out of its path those who would live within its pale in defiance of its laws, society but exercises its natural right. [14] The real question open to dispute is rather the treatment to be meted out to these rebels. In the primitive code of the *talion* nothing was more simple—an eye for an eye, a tooth for a tooth—thou hast killed; I kill thee. Thou hast inflicted injuries; I in my turn shall injure thee, and I expect to deter thee from future crimes by fear of the pain in store for thee. Such "justice" has the double advantage of being speedy and readily comprehended of a rudimentary intelligence as long as the temptation has been resisted. But when evil instincts, that none asks of Nature, have caused the fall of delinquents, the morbid moral sense, more or less distorted, which urged them on to violent deeds, makes them conscious solely of the violence of which they are now the object, and drives them to take sinister revenge. Thus they are prevented from exercising their calmer judgment, from which, by the mere force of reaction, there might spring a desire and hope for a new life within the pale of the established order of things.

And seeing it had been left for 1793—the epoch of a universal outburst of fraternity, manifested first by the permanent institution of the guillotine—to give us in Pinel a man of enough simple common-sense to break the chains that bound the mad, is it unreasonable to think that without freeing criminals (since not even at The Open Door are the lunatics let loose upon the public) one might yet seek some system of improvement and reformation to be applied in the establishments in which we keep our prisoners? There will always be some incurables—that is certain; but because incurables exist in every hospital and asylum, ought we to argue therefrom that it is useless to fight against an evil that is beyond human powers?

The reader may suppose that I should not have ventured to set down these considerations of social philosophy without a good reason. The principles I have thus summarised, at the risk of wearying those who look only for amusement, are now held by every criminalist worthy the name. But since this new conception makes its way very slowly with even the best-intentioned of Governments, which are the more strongly imbued with the prejudices of the masses in proportion as they are the more impregnated with the democracy, and since the transformation of our existing prisons would be very costly, we have as yet not got farther than the inclusion of the words "reform" and "amendment" on programmes that are very far from being put in execution.

Shall I give an example? It is evident that the time-sentence must inevitably restore a prisoner sooner or later to society. Is not, therefore, the public interest bound up in his returning with a good chance of leading a regular life, and not falling back into the disorder that was the cause of his temporary removal? And is not the very first condition of this fresh start the possession of a trade with sufficient skill therein to ensure some chance of success? If, then, we can give technical instruction in our prisons, and at the same time improve the intellectual and moral standard of the prisoner; and if, on his discharge, we can place the man whom society has thus—temporarily only—removed from its midst, in a position immediately to earn an honest living, instead of throwing him on his own resources, to be again confronted with the same temptations—would not society in this way infinitely multiply the sum total of the probabilities that its money and trouble would have the desired effect? I think, in theory, this argument will be readily admitted. Unfortunately, the difficulty is that it is much more economical to draw an immediate profit from prison labour than to reverse the problem and spend more in order to place an instrument of reform in the hands of the delinquent, with always, of course, a risk of failure.

In the United States great progress has been made in this direction, and if I appear to have gone a long way round to introduce my readers to the Central (men's) Prison of Buenos Ayres, my excuse is that to my mind the Argentine Republic has far surpassed all that has been attempted hitherto in this department of work. And to say truth, I feared that in bluntly and without comment giving a description of what I have been permitted to see, I might jar the spirit of routine that has taken hold of certain communities, notwithstanding their revolutionary changes of appellation.

I shall say nothing of the material side of the place, which very much resembles our own prisons. The prisoners are locked into their cells at night, but by day they are told off into the different workshops which are intended to perfect them in their own trades or give them a new one. The wages question is placed on much the same basis as with us, except that, the food being more abundant, the men are able to put aside the greater part of what they earn. (The diet consists principally of *perchero*—boiled beef— the staple article of food amongst the masses.) Conversation is allowed, but only in a low voice, and as long as work is not hindered thereby. Rations are distributed in the cells by the prisoners themselves, who take their meals with the door open, and frequently add a cigarette to the menu. There are books in every cell, with the essentials of school stationery. There are fourteen classes and fourteen masters. All the inmates attend the adult classes, which include such subjects—in addition to the theory of their own special technical work—as history, hygiene, morality, and in each an examination is held at the end of the year.

Both Governor and masters testify to the general application of the pupils. The land surveying class grows with special rapidity, in view of the constant demand for surveyors in the Pampas. A vast lecture-hall, which makes a theatre when required, is decorated with drawings, casts, and charts by the hand of the pupils. Lectures are given both by masters and prisoners when the latter are sufficiently advanced, or when their former studies have qualified them for the task. On one occasion M. Ferrero, who has, I believe, published an account of his visit to the Central Prison of Buenos Ayres, was present when a prisoner gave a lecture on prehistoric America.

"And the old offenders?" I asked as I went out.

"There are some," replied the Governor, "but not many. Our system of re-education is powerfully backed up by the permanent offer of work from all parts of the Pampas. Moreover, the greater number of our crimes are what are called 'crimes of passion.' The Italian and Spaniard are equally prompt with the knife. A large number of these men have killed their man in a fit of furious excitement, but they will be thought none the less of for their 'irritability' when they return home. Our point of view is this: Every time a man commits an offence or a crime, it becomes the duty of the community to begin, immediately, the work of re-education. Probably in no country shall we ever do all we might for the individual offender. But when one member of the social corporation falls he must be made over again. This is what we are trying to do, and I admit it is the greatest joy to us to see the success of our efforts. I have seen most of the prisons of Europe. Did you notice amongst our inmates that expression of the tracked beast which you find on all your prisoners? No. Our inmates have one idea only—to begin life again and to prepare, this time, for success. This is the secret of that tranquil, confiding air of good children at their task which you must have observed on so many faces; and this, perhaps, takes the place of repentance, which is not given to all."

"And you are not afraid your comfortable building will prove an attraction to people who are at a loss to know what to do with themselves?"

"That has not happened so far. Such a fear—though I cannot believe you are speaking seriously—shows you do not take into account the superior attraction for every human creature of liberty."

With that I left, having learnt a very interesting lesson from the Argentinos, whom so many Europeans are generously ready to teach.

FOOTNOTES:

[12] The census of 1909 showed that public instruction had since 1895, the date of the last census, made great progress. In these ten years the Argentine has opened 2000 new schools. In 1895, 30 per cent. of the population were in the schools; in 1909, 59 per cent.

The Lainez Act enjoined on the National Educational Council the duty of opening elementary schools, giving the minimum of instruction, wherever they were needed.

In the census of 1909 every child from five to fourteen years was made the subject of a separate card of psychophysical details on the initiative of Dr. Horacio G. Pinero. This card contained twenty-one questions: age, nationality, parentage, height, weight, thoracic measurements, size of the head, weight of the body, anomalies, deformities, stigmata, anterior diseases, sight, hearing, objective perception, attention, memory, language and pronunciation, affectionateness, excitability, temper.

[13] "If the idea of liberty be in itself a force, as Fouillée maintains, that force would be scarcely less if some wise man should one day demonstrate that it rested on illusion alone. This illusion is too tenacious to be dispelled by reasoning. The most convinced of determinists will still continue to use the words 'I will' and even 'I ought' in his daily speech, and moreover will continue to think them with what is the most powerful part of his mind—the unconscious and non-reasoning part. It is just as impossible not to act like a free man when one acts as it is not to reason like the determinist when one is working at science" ("La Morale et la Science," by Henri Poincaré, *La Revue*, June 1, 1910).

[14] "If some day morality were forced to accept determinism, would it not perish in the effort to adapt itself thereto? So profound a metaphysical revolution would doubtless have less influence on our manners than might be thought. Penal repression is not of course in question; what we now call

crime and punishment would be known as disease and prevention, but society would preserve intact its right which is not to punish but simply to defend itself" (Henri Poincaré, *loc. cit.*).

CHAPTER VI
ARGENTINE TYPES, MANNERS, AND MORALS

I had very good ground for stating that a salient characteristic of the Argentinos was a desire, not only to learn from Europe but to carry to the farthest possible pitch of perfection every institution begun, whether public or private, and to surpass their model. The obvious danger in all rapidly-developed colonial settlements is the acceptance of the "half-done," an almost obligatory condition in the early stages of development, and one whose facility of attainment is apt to militate against the persistency of effort after that precision of completion which alone can give good results. This defect, in fact, constitutes the principal reproach brought by the systematic Northerners against the impulsive Latin races, whose temperamental traits lead them to content themselves with a brilliant start, leaving thereafter to imagination the task of filling in the blanks left in the reality by this unsatisfactory method of operation.

I confess that in setting out for South America I was prepared to find that I should need the greatest indulgence if I would escape the danger of offending by discourteous but candid criticism. This was due to the fact that I was insensibly influenced partly by a few sociologists who discuss these matters carelessly, and partly by the folly that leads us to overlook the claims of consanguinity and urges us ever along those paths that England and Germany have opened. But not at all. If the prodigious expansion of the great North American republic may have inclined me to fear for the South American republics anything approaching to comparison, it is my belief that any impartial observer will rejoice to recognise the robust and generous development of some of the most promising forces of the future, in young communities that are clearly destined to attain to the highest grades of human superiority.

In 1865 Buckle, who was a man of no ordinary mental calibre, did not fear to write in his *History of Civilisation* that the compelling action of land and climate in Brazil was such that a highly civilised community must shortly find a home there. The event has amply justified the bold prophecy. In the South American republics, as in the United States and elsewhere, there are different degrees of fulfilment, of course. At the outset, while waiting for land to acquire value, all peoples have had to be satisfied with an approximate achievement. But in the Argentine, Uruguay, and Brazil, to speak only of countries I have visited, it is plain that nothing will be left half done, and the capacity to carry all work methodically forward to its end, in no matter what field of labour, promises well for the future of a race.

You do not require to stay long at Buenos Ayres to find that this quality exists in a very high degree in the Argentino.

I have mentioned the European aspect of Buenos Ayres—the least colonial-looking, probably, of any place in South America. But I noticed at the same time that the Argentino refuses to be simply a Spaniard transplanted, although *society*, in Buenos Ayres, traces its descent, with more or less authenticity, from the *conquistadores*, and did originally issue from the Iberian Peninsula. If we go farther and inquire what other influence, beside that of soil and climate, has been exercised over the European stock in the basin of the Rio de la Plata, we are bound to be struck with the thought that the admixture of Indian blood must count for something. The negro element, never numerically strong, appears to have been completely absorbed. There is very little trace of African blood. On the other hand, without leaving Buenos Ayres, you cannot fail to be struck by some handsome half-castes to be seen in the police force and fire brigade, for example, and the regularity of their delicate features is very noticeable to even the observer who is least prepared for it. The Indian of South America, though closely akin to the redskin of the North, is infinitely his superior. He had, indeed, created a form of civilisation, to which the *conquistadores* put brutally an end. There still subsist in the northern provinces of the Argentine some fairly large native settlements which receive but scant consideration from the Government. I heard too much on the subject to doubt the truth of this. Not but what many savage deeds can be laid to the charge of the Indians, as, for example, the abominable trap they laid for the peaceful Crevaux Mission in Bolivia which led to the massacre of all its members. Still, in equity we must remember that those who have recourse to the final argument of brute force are helping to confirm the savages in the habit of using it. In the interest of the higher sentimentality we must all deplore this. But our implacable civilisation has passed sentence on all races that are unable to adapt themselves to our form of social evolution, and from that verdict there is no appeal.

Not that the native of the South is incapable, like his brother of the North, of performing a daily task. I saw many natives amongst the hands employed by M. Hilleret in his factories in Tucuman. Neither can it be said that there is any lack of intelligence in the Indian. But the fact remains that he finds a difficulty in bending the faculties which have grown rigid in the circle of a primitive state of existence to the better forms of our own daily work, and this renders it impossible for him to carve out a place for himself in the sunlight under the new social organism imported from Europe by the white men. With greater power of resistance than the redskins of the other continent, he, like them, is doomed to disappear. Yet in one respect he has been more fortunate than his kinsmen of the North, and will never entirely die out, for he has already inoculated with his blood the flesh of the victors.

I am not going to pretend to settle in a word the problem of the fusion of races. I will only observe that the inrush of Indian blood in the masses—and also to a very considerable extent in the upper classes [15]—cannot fail to leave a permanent trace in the Argentine type, notwithstanding the steady current of immigration. And if I were asked to say what were the elemental qualities contributed to the coming race by the native strain, I should be inclined to think that the Indian's simplicity, dignity, nobility, and decision of character might modify in the happiest way the turbulent European blood of future generations.

After all, the Argentino who declines to be Spanish has, perhaps, very good reasons for his action. Here, he has succeeded, better than in the Iberian Peninsula, in ridding himself of the Moorish strain, which, though it gave him his lofty chivalry, has yet enchained him to the Oriental conception of a rigid theocracy. Why should not native blood have taken effect already upon the European mixture, and, with the aid of those unknown forces which we may class under the collective term of "climate," have prepared and formed a new people to be known henceforth by the obviously suitable name of "Argentinos"? All I can say is that there are Argentine characteristics now plainly visible in this conglomeration of the Latin races. The objection may be made that the "Yankee" shows equally strongly marked characteristics, which distinguish him from the Anglo-Saxon stock, while we know that he is unaffected by other than European strains. This is undeniable, and in his case soil, climate, and the unceasing admixture of European types suffice to explain modifications which are apparently converging towards the creation of a new type or sub-type.

It is remarkable that the character of the Americanised Englishman, having passed through a phase of Puritan rigidity in the North and aristocratic haughtiness in the South, has, for some inexplicable reason, burst out into a temperament of highly vitalised energy that may be summed up in the characteristic formula of a universal "go-aheadedness." The South American, on the contrary, having started with every kind of extravagance in both public and private life calculated to destroy the confidence of Europe, is obviously now undergoing a settling-down process with a marked tendency to adopt those principles of action of which the North is so proud, while at the same time retaining his affection for Latin culture.

It is easier to generalise about the Argentine character than to penetrate beneath its surface. It is naturally in "society," where refinement is the highest, that traits which best lend themselves to generalisation are to be seen in strongest relief. The American of the North is, above all, highly hospitable. If you have a letter of introduction, his house is open to you at once. He establishes you under his roof and then leaves you to your own devices, while keeping himself free to continue his daily occupation. The Argentino receives you as kindly, though with more reserve. Although I know but little of the business world, I saw enough of it to gather that money enjoys as much favour there as in any other country; but the pursuit of wealth is there tempered by an indulgent kindliness that greatly softens all personal relations, and the asperities of the struggle for life are smoothed by a universal gentleness charming to encounter.

In their family relations the differences between the social ideals of the North and South American are plainly visible. The family tie appears to be stronger in the Argentine than, perhaps, any other land. The rich, unlike those of other countries, take pleasure in having large families. One lady boasted in my presence of having thirty-four descendants—children and grandchildren—gathered round her table. Everywhere family anniversaries are carefully observed, and all take pleasure in celebrating them. The greatest affection prevails and the greatest devotion to the parent roof-tree. Not that the Argentine woman would appear to be a particularly admirable mother according to our standard; for, on the contrary, it is said that her children are turned out into the world with very bad manners. How, then, are we to explain the contradictory fact that such children become the most courteous of men? Perhaps a certain wildness in youth should be regarded as the noisy, but salutary, apprenticeship to liberty.

All that can be seen of the public morals is most favourable. The women—generally extremely handsome in a super-Spanish way, and often fascinating [16]—enjoy a reputation, that seems well justified, of being extremely virtuous. I heard too much good about them to think any evil. They were, from what I could see, too carefully removed from the danger of conventional sins for me to be able to add the personal testimony that I have no doubt they merit. As to their feelings, or passions, if I may venture to use the word, I know nothing and therefore can say nothing. Are they capable of the self-abandonment of love, of experiencing all its joy and all its pain —inseparable as these but too often are? They did not tell me, so I shall never know. The most I can say is that they did not give me the impression of being made for the violent reactions of life as we know it in our daily European existence. I hope no one will see in this statement a shadow of criticism. It is, indeed, a compliment if you will admit that in an Argentine family love's dream is realised in the natural, orderly course of events. But if it were otherwise, it would still be to the highest credit of the women that in their *rôle* of faithful guardians of the hearth they have been able to silence calumny and inspire universal respect by the purity and dignity of their life.

Above all, do not imagine that these charming women are devoid of conversational talent. Some ill-natured critics have given them a bad reputation in this respect. Their principal occupation is evidently paying visits, and they gossip as best they can under the circumstances, considering that neither their friends nor their foes give any ground for tittle-tattle. This deficit might cause conversation to languish. Dress and news from the Rue de la Paix are a never-failing topic. [17] May not this be true in other lands? It has also been said that the beauties of Buenos Ayres are as prone to speculate in land as their menkind. It is quite possible. None will be surprised to learn that they gave me no information on this head either. They are credited, too, with being very superstitious, and are supposed to attach great importance to knowing exactly what must not be done on any given day of the week, or to what saint they should address their petitions. Here, again, I can give no authentic information. Naturally, had I been present at any of their meetings, the first condition of an exclusively feminine company would have been unfulfilled. It seems to me more reasonable to believe that the many works of public charity in which the ladies of Buenos Ayres take a share would account for much time and also for much talk.

Further, I may in all sincerity remark that if female education be not one of the points in which the Argentine Republic has left us behind, it is none the less a fact that I was happy enough to meet many charming women who were perfectly capable of sustaining a thoroughly Parisian kind of conversation supported by a fund of general information. And, moreover, they added a charm of geniality and real simplicity that are not too common on the banks of the Seine.

I have not spoken of shopping, which is the main occupation of the fair sex in North America, for the reason that at Buenos Ayres I saw none. I mentioned that the footwalks of the business quarter—including Florida, the handsomest and busiest of the streets—were blocked to such an extent that it was impossible to walk there two abreast. You do not expect to hear that there are any elegant toilettes in the crowd. And, in fact, in the central streets no women go afoot for pleasure. Some go about their business with hasty step, and that is all; the others receive the tradesmen at home, or take their chance of calling in the motor-car, which, after five o'clock, will probably not be allowed in the street to which they want to go. What is left, then, for the daily stroll? Only the wide avenues of the suburbs, where there is no particular attraction, and Palermo—the unique and inevitable Palermo, or rather, a part of Palermo, with the Recoleta, which makes a fine beginning for a public promenade.

In these circumstances it is evident that the aspect of the pavements of Buenos Ayres suffers by the absence of the fair sex. It might be thought that at Palermo, where the walks lead amongst flowers, lawns, and groves, our Argentinos would recover the use of their limbs and guard against their dangerous tendency to an over-abundance of flesh. Not at all. Social conventions do not allow of this. Our classics, men of mature mind, were fond of saying, with the Apollo of Delphi, that excess in all things is bad. Buenos Ayres has not yet reached to this degree of wisdom, and its female society, not satisfied to follow closely after virtue, seeks to add to their fame the spice of a reputation that leaves absolutely nothing to be said. For this reason they guard against even a chance encounter that might appear compromising. And so the fair sex only consent to walk on the Palermo under the protection of a rigorous rule of etiquette which enacts that to stop and talk on a public road with a lady whom one may meet later in the day in some *salon* is a sign of unpardonable ill-breeding. Decidedly we are far from Europe.

To complete the exotic air of the place, know that all husbands are jealous, or, at least, so they say, and it must be supposed there is some foundation for the statement. As far as I was able to judge, they are as amiable as their wives, and appear by no means to harbour tragic intentions towards any man likely to arouse their resentment. No. But if by chance, after dinner, you remain chatting quietly with one or two ladies, and in the inevitable ebb and flow of a *salon* you find yourself for a moment left alone with one, be sure that her husband, more genial than ever, will promptly appear on the scene to claim his share in the talk. At home this would appear strange, since we do not impose the spectacle of our private intimacies upon the public. Yet may not this very air of detachment upon which we insist lead, both in public and in private, to some of the tragedies of life? Is it wrong for a married couple to love each other? And when two hearts are united in this way how can a feeling so powerful fail at times to betray itself by some outward manifestation? Let us take heed lest, in laughing at others, we denounce ourselves. A man in a very high position, who is the father of a lad of twenty, volunteered to me the information that in the whole course of his married life he had nothing to reproach himself with, and that if by some misfortune he had transgressed the marriage law, he should have considered himself wholly unworthy of the woman who had given her whole life to him. No doubt the woman in question, who happened to be standing near us as we talked, fully merited his homage. Yet I wondered, as I listened to his noble and simple speech, whether one could find many Frenchmen to make in all candour such a confidence to a perfect stranger, or, supposing one found such a one, could he say as much without an embarrassed blush? Whatever may be the secret opinion of my reader, I hope he will agree with me in thinking that the advantage in this delicate matter is decidedly on the side of the Argentino, whose sane morality is the best of auguries for the community he is trying to found.

I should like to say something about the Argentine girl. The difficulty is that I never saw her. Every one knows that in North America the young girl is the principal social institution. She has got herself so much talked about that neither Europe nor Asia can help knowing her. In Argentine society, as in France and in Latin countries generally, the young girl is a cipher. She may be seen, no doubt, in the home, at concerts, where she figures in large numbers for the satisfaction of our eyes, at Palermo, at the Tigre, [18] and the Ice Palace—very respectable—where she skates under her mother's eyes, and, finally, at balls, whose joys and special rites are the same the world over. But all this does not make of the South American girl an element of conversation and social doings as in the United States. She remains on the edge of society until the day of her marriage. At the same time, the Argentine girl must not be supposed to resemble very closely her sister in Latin Europe. Less educated, perhaps, but more vivacious and less timidly reserved, she shows greater independence, they tell me, at Mar del Plata, which is the sole common meeting-ground for wealthier families, since the Pampas offer no resource outside the *estancia*. [19] At the Colon Theatre and at the Opera she is seated well in view in front of the box, making the whole ground floor an immense basket of beribboned flowers, and there, under the eye of her parents, the young men who are friends of her family are permitted to pay their respects to her. Must it be confessed? It is said that she makes use of borrowed charms, applied with puff and pencil, following in this the example of her who should rather prevent than abet? This must, however, be libel, for whenever I ventured a query on the point, I was met with a shrug of the shoulders and a burst of laughter. In such a case, the man who can laugh sees always more than smoke.

The father is not a negligible quantity, whatever may be said of him. I saw very plainly that it is entirely untrue that he takes no interest in his children's upbringing. I may have come across a few specimens of idle youth engaged in flinging their *piastres* into the gutter, but as regards heads of families, there is no comparison between the number who here are seeking distractions, illicit or otherwise, for a useless existence and those of the same type to be seen in any capital of Europe.

But while I have here said nothing that is not strictly true, I am not trying to represent the Argentine husband as the phœnix of the universe. Money is so plentiful that it may well be responsible for some sins, and, on occasions, I suspect that the city can supply opportunities of committing them. Even so, it is wise to maintain the strictest reserve on the subject, for Buenos Ayres smacks strong of the small country town, and there is abundance of pointed arrows for culprits who allow themselves to be caught. Still, as long as society has not decreed the total suppression of the bachelor....

None can deny that gambling occupies too large a place in the life of a certain number of the newly rich. But are we indeed justified in pretending to be more scandalised at what takes place amongst our neighbours than at home? What might I not write about the development of our *casinos*? To satisfy this vice in the masses the Argentinos have established lotteries, which now add to the temptations, powerful enough already, provided by race meetings. The evil is universal; I can but note it.

The form of gambling which is special to Buenos Ayres is unbridled speculation in land. In Europe it is constantly stated that all the work of Buenos Ayres, as of the Pampas, is done by foreigners, whilst the Argentino himself sits waiting for the value of his land to treble, quadruple, decuple his fortune without effort on his part. This might easily be true, since the value of property has risen with giddy rapidity of late years. Sooner or later, of course, there must be a reaction; this is obvious. But until that day dawns it must be admitted that, in a country where every self-respecting mortal owns a bit of land, large fortunes have been realised before the fortunate proprietor has raised as much as a finger. Our fellow-countryman M. Basset told me that on his own estate the rise in value of his waste ground allowed him to recoup himself for all he lost on his arable land. Under these circumstances, it is really not surprising if prices form a general subject of conversation. It was, in fact, on a larger scale, but with less excitement, a repetition of the Fair of Mississippi stock, in the Rue Quicampoix, with this difference, that there is here some foundation for it, though it is by no means inexhaustible.

But while there is no denying that land speculation occupies a special place in Argentine life to-day, it is also incontestable that all ranks of society are here, as elsewhere, devoting their energy to some great agricultural, commercial, or cattle-rearing enterprise. The *estancia* needs a head. Herds of ten thousand cows must be well looked after if they are to be productive in their three departments—dairy, meat, or breeding. The magnificent exhibits that we see at shows are not raised by the sole grace of God, and the "big Argentinos" with whom I had the privilege of chatting not only spoke of their *estancias* with a wealth of detail that showed a close interest, ever on the watch for improvements, but also frequently I was given to understand that they had other business which claimed part of their time. And many of them surprised me by their readiness to discuss topics of general interest that happened to be engrossing the attention of Europe at the time.

The growing interest taken in all kinds of labour on the soil and the need of perfecting strains of cattle both for breeding and for meat have led the larger owners to group themselves into a club, which they call the Jockey Club. The name suffices to denote the aristocratic pretensions of an institution that has, nevertheless, rendered important services to the cause, as well for horned cattle as for horses. The sumptuous fittings lack that rich simplicity in which the English delight. The decorations are borrowed from Europe, but the working of the club is wholly American. The greatest comfort reigns in all departments of the palace, whose luxury is not allowed to dissemble itself. The cuisine is thoroughly Parisian. Fine drawing-rooms, in which the light is pleasantly diffused. A large rotunda in Empire style is the show-place of the club, but, like Napoleon himself, it lacks moderation. A severe-looking library, reading-rooms, banqueting-rooms, etc.

To explain the amount of money either amassed or flung away here, it must be remembered that all the receipts taken at the race-courses—less a small tax to the Government—come back to the Jockey Club, which is at liberty to dispose of them at will. Hence the large fortune of the establishment, which has just purchased a piece of land in the best part of Buenos Ayres, for which it gave seven millions; and here it is proposed to erect a palace still more grandiose. I saw in the papers that the Jockey Club intends to offer to the Government the building they now occupy in the Rue Florida, and it is believed that the Foreign Office will be moved there. You see, the Argentine cattle breeders have found very comfortable quarters and enjoy themselves there.

M. Benito Villanueva, the Chairman of the Jockey Club, is a senator, extremely prominent in the business world, who joins the most superlative form of North American "go-aheadism" with the graceful urbanity of European *bongarçonnisme.* He is in close touch with all classes in the capital, and if he cannot be said to have a hand in everybody's business, it is certain he could if he would. People who have never set eyes on him speak of him by his Christian name, and as there are not two "Benitos" of that calibre this is accepted as a matter of course. Very unceremonious, very quick of perception, and with a dash of the modern aristocrat in his bearing, he is a manager of men who would make any sacrifice to gain his end. His small black eyes are as bright as steel, and gave me an impression that it would not be agreeable to have him for an enemy. Like any man who combines politics with large business interests, he has his adversaries, but he appears entirely oblivious of them. His *estancia*, the "Eldorado," with its racing stables and prize cattle, the Senate, which he attends with great regularity, and the innumerable commercial enterprises in which he is engaged (to say nothing of the admirable Jockey Club), make him one of the busiest men in Buenos Ayres. Nevertheless, he always found time to waste in my company, and showed me much both in and out of Buenos Ayres. I found every one in the capital obliging to a degree, and it would be rank injustice to place M. Benito Villanueva in a category by himself under this heading. I will only say, therefore, that if many equalled him, none surpassed him.

Who better fitted to do the honours of the Palermo racecourse than M. Villanueva? Modern arrangements, elegant fittings; no convenience missing. The Jockey Club Stand has a first-class restaurant on its upper story, where its members who are just sufficiently interested in the racing to make their bets can enjoy at the same time the pleasures of the table and a view of the winning-post. Betting is fabulously high. But the racecourse is open to the same objection as Palermo. What is to be said of the hideous embankment of yellow clay that bars the landscape? Surely the setting of a racecourse is not without its importance. As far as the convenience of the situation goes, this one leaves nothing to be desired. But really, seeing the small part played in an afternoon's racing by the events themselves, how is it that the artists who laid out this hippodrome neglected to provide a lovely view for the joy and repose of the visitors' eyes? They talk of masking the slope by plantations, but the trains that traverse the course from one end to the other will still remain visible. I have nothing against this form of amusement, though I think it almost a pity not to reserve it for the delectation of the *ranchos* out on the Pampas, since there is no part of the plain where it might not be enjoyed. Then the displaced railway would allow of a cutting which would let in a great flood of light as far down as Rio.

The racing public, from horses to humans, being everywhere the same, there would be nothing to say of either professionals or spectators, had I not noticed that the fair sex of Buenos Ayres, as seen in the stands, were wearing with confident grace the latest creations of Parisian fashions, and more than made up in quality for their possible inferiority in quantity as compared with a Longchamp gathering. I will not say that there were not a few errors in technical details here and there. But it was pleasant to see that some of our audacious Parisian freaks, contrary to what one might imagine, find only the faintest of echoes in these brilliant meetings. The reason is that the cunning display of eccentricities by beauties who have nothing to lose cannot here, as at home, react on the toilettes of society women by consequence of a universal search after novelties whose sole object is to attract attention. The reason is simple. In Buenos Ayres there is no *demi-monde*, for the few belles who cross the ocean to come here are birds of passage merely, and cannot be said to form a class. When present they avoid the grandstands of the racecourse and take refuge in the paddock, where their loneliness makes them rather an object of public pity.

Still in Señor Villanueva's company, I had the pleasure of visiting the Tigre, the finest recreation ground open to the inhabitants of Buenos Ayres. But do not be misled by the name to fancy that it is a menagerie. There were, it appears, in distant ages, some few great cats that ventured as far as the mouth of the Parana in order to steal a breakfast at the expense of the citizens of the capital. Times have greatly changed. It is now the honest Argentino who comes here to get a meal after having taken proper steps to ensure the absence of the tiger. The delta of the Parana is formed by an inextricable network of channels, dotted with innumerable islets, whose luxuriant vegetation has won for them the pretty name of a "Venice of Gardens." In all this floating land imagine trees of every kind leaning over the water as though attracted by the moving reflection of their foliage; call up a picture of orchards in the glory of their spring or autumn dress; fling amongst the groves an orgy of wild and cultivated flowers; people the shade of the branches with large and small boats filled with merry young people, whose song and laughter blend with the music of the oars, and you will have an idea of the pastimes that the Tigre can offer. *Quintas, chalets*, built on piles, hotels, restaurants, wine-shops, resorts of all kinds, suited to all classes of society, provide a peaceful asylum for fête days and holidays, far from the turmoil and bustle of Buenos Ayres. Following the stream upwards, past miles of wood and water, there are still more picturesque sites to be visited, where man has not yet set his hand, and the boat glides in and out of these beflowered waterways as far as Parana, whence come the big boats from Paraguay laden with oranges, their decks shining in the sunlight like some quaint palace of ruddy gold.

The Tigre is reached by railway in twenty minutes, and a skiff bespoken in advance awaits you at the station. But Señor Villanueva, whom nothing can daunt, wanted to try a new road, said to be just finished, in his motor-car. Now, carriage roads are not a strong point in this country, where no stones are to be found. However, after a journey that recalled at times the passage over the rollers at Auteuil Lock, we duly and miraculously reached the Tigre without quite wrecking the car, but not without some damage to our more sensitive and intimate organs. Wherefore we were assailed by a longing for the *chaises-longues* and easy-chairs of our hotel, which drew us forthwith to the booking-office of the railway-station, whence modestly and quickly we made our way back.

Since the subject of hotel furnishings thus comes under my pen, why not say at once that in the Argentine, as in Brazil, the internal arrangements of the houses show that the greater part of the time is spent out of doors? Italy, with its open-air life, was naturally the land to which the Argentino turned for architects to supply florid furniture, meant rather to look at than to use; and when to this is added cheap German goods with their clumsy designs, one may be pardoned for finding a lack of grace as of comfort, to a French way of thinking. [20] In aristocratic *salons* the best Parisian upholsterers have at least left their mark—with a little overcrowding in effect, if the truth must be told. In a few, where "antiques" were discernible, there were evidences of an appreciation of just proportions and simplicity. But my criticisms must be taken in the most general way possible.

It is in the hotels that one feels the farthest from Europe, and this in spite of a manifest attempt to do things well. A continual change of servants and a bad division of labour ensure infinite discomfort for the traveller. There is, it is true, central heating, but it works badly. Is the *pampero* blowing? The pipes of the radiators shake the window-panes with their tempestuous snorting and bubbling, waking you out of your sleep with the suddenness of their noise; but they diffuse only cold air. [21] An electric heating apparatus, hastily put in, must be used to supplement the other. Do you want to lock up some papers? You may, perhaps, after a long search, find a key in your room, but it will assuredly fit none of the locks. As I was tiresome enough to insist, the manager, anxious to oblige me, ordered his own safe to be placed in my apartment, with all his accounts therein. When I found the drawer that was placed at my disposal, I found money in it! Oh, marvellous hospitality!

To the new houses in the town chimneys are being added. The European who comes to the Argentine for the winter months—June, July, August—can be delighted with the change. But, meantime, he suffers keenly from the cold, for if the sun shines perseveringly in a cloudless sky, an icy south wind will prove very trying to Europeans who are not accustomed to such sharp contrasts. [22] As for the summer season, which I have not tried, every one talked of its charms, the greatest being, apparently, to go and wipe one's brow at the Tigre, at Mar del Plata, or on the *estancia*, in default of the mountain resorts within reach of the Brazilians.

It is difficult to speak of Argentine cookery—which is rather international than local—always excepting those households that boast a French *chef*. The influence of Italy, with her macaroni and her cheese, predominates. The vegetables are mediocre; the fruit too tropical, or, if European, spoilt by the effect of the tropics. Lobsters and European fish, imported frozen, are not to be recommended; table water is excellent. The national dishes, *puchero*, or boiled beef, good when the animal has not been slaughtered the same morning; *asado*, lamb, roasted whole—savoury souvenir of my excursions in Greece, where it is to be met under the name of *lamb à la palikare*. I might add a long list whose sole interest would be the strange-sounding names given to familiar dishes. Still, as the main conditions of man and communities are necessarily unvarying, is it not in appearances and forms of expression that we find variety?

FOOTNOTES:

[15] I might instance a statesman who has all the externals and probably also the prudent wisdom of a pure *cacique* of olden times.

[16] I shall not take the liberty of attempting a description of Argentine beauty. Let me only mention their large black eyes, heavily shaded, the delicately golden skin, beneath which there pulses a generous blood, and the sweet and ever youthful smile.

[17] "Six dresses are sufficient for me for one season in Paris; in Buenos Ayres I want quite a dozen," says an Argentine belle who was until recently a member of the Parisian diplomatic world. The more limited circles of Argentine society and the proportionately keener rivalry of personal luxury may explain the difference.

[18] This is the name applied to the group of islands forming the Delta of the Parana.

[19] An estate devoted to agriculture and cattle rearing.

[20] The dearness of living in Buenos Ayres and especially of rents is a common theme among travellers.

[21] I understand there is a scheme for adding a system of central cooling for summer use in hotels and private houses in hot climates. Nothing would be easier or more useful. Even in our own land there are many days in the season when we should be glad of cool radiators.

[22] It is often said that Buenos Ayres has a "Nice winter." This is strictly true. The sun is rarely wanting, and the *rôle* of the Mistral is played by the pampero with great success.

CHAPTER VII
ARGENTINE POLITICS

Writing about a country, with no dogmatic intention, but drawing at haphazard from memory impressions received, has this advantage, that instead of setting down general theories that are always open to argument, certain living traits may be seized upon which, by the very fact that they are open to more than one interpretation, demand the constant collaboration of writer and reader. The method—if one may apply so big a word to so small a result—gives me an opportunity of making a few observations about the organisation and working of the Argentine Government.

It seemed quite natural to the intellectuals of a democratic Republic that a democrat should come out to talk to them about democracy, to discuss the serious problems it presents and the solutions that time is more or less rapidly working out for them. Nevertheless, it is not without some legitimate trepidation that one faces a public completely unknown, proud probably of its achievements, ardently hopeful certainly for the future, and inclined, no doubt, thanks to the very sincerity of its labours, to be carried away by an excess of jealous susceptibility. I was quickly reassured. The consciousness of a great work accomplished, a keen appreciation of the finely organised effort whose astounding results are revealed anew each day, give to the Argentine people too just a confidence in the value of their activity for them to see more in any courteous criticism than a good opportunity of improving on their past—on condition, naturally, that the criticism appear to be well founded. The critic is thus disarmed, and lets fall his weapons for fear lest a shaft intended only to graze the skin should penetrate deeper and inspire a weakening doubt in the mind of men who are engaged, body and soul, in a tremendous struggle after social progress.

In matters of government the Argentinos are neither better nor worse off than any people of Europe where freedom of speech has begun its work. But, notwithstanding the astonishing rapidity of assimilation that distinguishes this land, there is as yet too little homogeneity in the masses for the possibility of any influence from below, on the problems of the day, apart, of course, from matters that make appeal to patriotism, which inevitably provoke unanimity. There are many other countries of which, in spite of appearances to the contrary, the same might be said.

Here, as elsewhere, politicians, who are the more or less official mouthpieces of that vague concourse of general opinions which we call the mind of the public, may very easily mistake the ephemeral demands of a party for the permanent interest of the country.

A point to be noticed is that faction fights, which have for so long brought bloodshed into the cities and villages of South America, are now disappearing. It is scarcely possible, none the less, for all traces of violence to depart, leaving no reminder of movements which have made of political changes one long series of hysterics. Autocracy and sudden upheavals are inseparable. This is the lesson that the races of the Iberian Peninsula have best learnt from their governors. In Brazil, where an admirable economic movement goes hand in hand with a remarkable development of orderly progress and civic peace, recent events have shown what fires are smouldering beneath the molten streams of a dying volcano. It is to be hoped that our friends will not be found lacking either in the patience or the courage necessary to impose on the public a salutary respect for law! In Uruguay, a land of Latin amiability, the rage of revolution has frequently broken out; and if, to all appearances, there is calm to-day, Whites and Reds still exhibit mutual hostility without troubling to find reasons that might explain, if not justify, recourse to arms. The Argentinos appear farther removed from the danger of revolutionary shocks. "Wealth has quieted us," said a politician. This is no new thing. All activities profit by undisturbed work and lose by deeds of violence. Lucrative labour and the fear of losing what has been acquired go to make up a fund of prudence.

But while, happily, in the Argentine there is no present menace of revolution, I cannot deny that in the provinces I often heard rumours of it. Insurrection seemed imminent. Precautions were taken to protect arsenals. And when I inquired the reason for such a movement, I was invariably told that no one knew, but that no doubt there were malcontents. One need not go as far as the Argentine to seek for them. As all these alarms ended in nothing, I must put them down as a verbal echo of a vanished epoch. I can but admire the profound peace that has succeeded to the fury of the past, for the Argentino who, in revolution, exposed his person so light-heartedly did not fear to take the life of his enemy.

But can it be affirmed that in no department of the Administration there has survived some trace of the cavalier methods of former days? Is it true that some officials do as they like with the people committed to their charge, and inflict treatment that is passively borne for the moment, but may lead to terrible reprisals later? It was often stated in my hearing, but I could never obtain any proof. I shall not make myself the echo of slanders and calumny, which, in all lands, are the weapons used by public men against each other. I will only take the liberty of reminding my Argentine friends that one never need fear excess on the side of a watchful control over Government offices.

M. Thiébaud, the Minister of France, presented me to M. Figueroa Alcorta, the President of the Republic. [23] He gave me the most cordially courteous of receptions, prompted, of course, by the respect and friendship that Argentine statesmen have for France. The President's first words were an inquiry as to whether I was as comfortable at the Palace Hotel as at the *Hôtel du Mouton*, in Chantonnay (Vendée). This showed me that the President of the Argentine Republic was a reader of the *Illustration*, for a photograph of that more than modest establishment was recently published in the columns of the review on the occasion of an expedition I made to my native country, when I put up at the little inn. I assured him that the resources of Buenos Ayres were infinitely superior, and from this we wandered off into a very interesting talk about our two countries.

M. Figueroa Alcorta was Vice-President of the Republic when the death of President Quintana called him to the supreme *magistratere*. I fancied that a good many people found it hard to forgive him this unlooked-for good fortune. Some journalists thought it funny to create for him the reputation of a "Jettatore," an inexhaustible subject for spiteful tales in the Opposition sheets. They say the story has not been without influence on the feminine world, specially prone to superstition. M. Figueroa Alcorta appears to bear the misfortune with calm courage. He talks of the Argentine with a modesty that does not exclude a just pride, and for France he had only sympathetic admiration. Let me say also that President Saënz Peña, whom I twice saw in Buenos Ayres, is a devoted friend to France and French culture. It is my duty to add that M. Saënz Peña's attention has been called to certain lapses in the administration, and he is firmly resolved to put an end to them.

The Minister of Foreign Affairs, M. de la Plaza, has, since my journey, become Vice-President of the Republic. He is rather heavy and cold in appearance—with the silent gravity of the *cacique*, it is said—but he is a man of profound culture and keen mind, and it is not impossible that his taciturnity and slowness of speech are merely diplomatic. He enjoys the reputation of being a thorough Anglomaniac, but this, fortunately, does not preclude him from being also a Francophil. [24]

I must mention the Minister of Public Works, M. Ramos Mexia, who was continued in his important office by President Saënz Peña when the Cabinet was new-formed. In a country where great public works are constantly being undertaken, an upright mind and an iron will, united to a spotless reputation, are all needed to resist the overtures of the large European firms that are clamouring for contracts. A vast field for quarrels, more or less veiled personal attacks, and unending recriminations. I do not want to recriminate myself, or, indeed, to touch on any delicate questions; yet I must regret the preference that has been shown for Krupp cannon, when innumerable experiments have demonstrated the infinite superiority of French guns.

I have already pointed out that England, by our wilful negligence, managed to obtain the right of building practically the whole of the railway system. She has done the work to the satisfaction of the public, and the same may be said of the way Germany has installed the electric systems. France triumphs in the ports of Rosario, Montevideo, Pernambuco, Bahia-Blanca, and Rio Grande do Sul. That is all I can say, for at the moment there exists the keenest European competition in the harbour works of Mar del Plata and Buenos Ayres. Some complain that Ramos Mexia has been too favourable to England. He is, however, first and foremost an Argentino, and he uses his right to take the best from each country.

If there has been in the past some little friction, I fancy it is now over; it hardly could be otherwise, for M. Ramos Mexia is a warm admirer of French culture, and as well acquainted with our classics as our contemporaries, beside being a regular attendant at the lectures at the Sorbonne and Collège de France whenever he is able to take a little recreation in Paris. Need I add that Mme. Ramos Mexia is the most French of all the Argentinos whom I met—French in the graciousness of her welcome and French in charm of conversation.

We know that in the Argentine (and perhaps in all South American republics, with the exception of Chili) Ministers are not responsible to Parliament. In Chili, Parliamentary coalitions amuse themselves by knocking over Ministers like ninepins. In the Argentine it is the rule—to which there are exceptions—for Ministers to follow the President, whose agents they are, having the sole function of obtaining from the Chambers the funds required to carry on the administration. Before I weigh up the advantages and disadvantages of this system, which was imported ready-made by South America from the north, let me record the surprise I felt when I discovered that, notwithstanding the absurd stories told of the lack of measure in "hot countries," a South American assembly could give a lesson in dignity to more than one European Parliament. In England, as we know, measures have been taken to prevent personal questions from being introduced into debates, where the interests of the public alone occupy members' attention. Here the chivalrous temperament of Castile suffices as a guarantee against excesses of language or abuses at the hands of the majority. For instance, in some cases a speaker is granted only ten minutes in which to give the merest sketch of his Bill. If the orator be a member of the minority, however, Speaker and Chamber make it a point of honour to let him take as long as he likes. If he goes too far the rule is applied; but this, I was assured, never happens. Finally, "it is our constant rule," said a member well qualified to make the statement, "not to let slip allusions in the course of a debate that might hurt the feelings of a colleague. This requires no effort. It is just a habit one can acquire." May the "habit" be shortly acquired in all lands!

Now that the tide of free civilisation is setting towards a dissolution of all autocratic Powers, from Russia to Persia, and even to China, instituting the parliamentary system which we have come to regard as the best instrument for controlling and liberating the democracy, it is a remarkable fact that, in practice, Parliament is much criticised, more particularly in countries where it was only obtained after long and painful struggles. The reason, to my mind, must be sought in the unpardonable waste of time in debates, where free rein is given to a puerile love of theatrical display. In the absence of any salutary check on the humours of orators, too little attention is given to bringing the discussions to a practical conclusion. A good reformer should be able first to reform himself.

It is less the Parliament than the executive that attracts the European observer of American institutions. This is because Parliament is dominated by the executive, instead of being itself the dominating power. The South American republics hastened to copy the Constitution of the United States of the North, which is the original creation of the revolution of 1776, and adapted, in a marvellous degree, to the needs, idea, and sentiment of the country. Adopting its text, if not its spirit, the South Americans fell into the same error as Europe has done in copying the English Constitution in the letter, but not in the spirit and sense given to it by the people whom it justly claims to express.

Without entering on a discussion that would lead me too far, I could not refrain from remarking that in actual working the North American institutions have become distorted in South America, a change rendered inevitable by the different level of public education and the geographical distribution of the population. It was in the nature of things that the earliest civilisation should partake of the constitution of states or provinces destined later to form a federation, but as long as the Motherland imported the sovereign authority from outside, the struggles between a budding liberty and an unchecked autocracy were unceasing. Once self-government had been proclaimed, it became obligatory to constitute such elements of public life as should make its exercise possible. Now, for this, it is not enough to draw up a code of principles. We cannot, then, be surprised if the South American races, fondly attached to their own institutions, which maintain the principle of an autonomy of federated States and provide for their idealism a verbal satisfaction, inestimable, as they think, are yet (just like other nations now undergoing democratic evolution) far enough from an adequate realisation of their idea. We can scarcely expect any concerted political action from men (often of foreign birth) who are scattered all across the Pampas and separated by enormous distances. And, as regards the cities, great or small, a political *élite* will more easily organise itself—especially where an absence of public opinion facilitates the abuse of power—than will the "sovereign people" be brought to exercise their sovereignty (and this we see even in Europe).

Hence the evils often made public, which are but striking examples of what we see elsewhere; notably, the indifference of the electoral body, evidenced by the contemptibly small number of voters who answer the summons to the ballot—and of these few some have been brought thither by who knows what means! To this public apathy must be added the abstention of the middle classes, always difficult to incite to a common political action, who thus leave a wider field than is desirable to the machinations of the professional politician, with his methods, direct or indirect, of bringing pressure upon the elector.

I have no hesitation in speaking of the evil. But at the same time I must point out that if the mind of the public—such as the intellectual *élite* of the nation have made it—experiences some difficulty in getting used to the slow methods of organised political action, the independent spirit and personal dignity of the citizens are so strong [25] that a force of public opinion is gradually evolving which, in spite of some backsliding, will soon be powerful enough to impose its decisions on the world of political intrigue. For instance, it is frequently said that the President of the Republic does, in effect, nominate his successor by reason of his authority with the State Legislature, and there is a grain of truth in the assertion. Yet if it were strictly true, the same party would remain in perpetuity in power, and this we know is not the case. Thus public opinion, when it pronounces itself with sufficient decision, can, with the help of a wholesome fear of revolt, vanquish all resistance and bring in its candidate. In this way any eventual abuse of personal influence is, in effect, prevented, and this is precisely what happened in the case of the election of M. Saënz Peña. I fear that nowhere are institutions worked according to rule. Before throwing stones at the Argentine, let us look at our own deficiencies.

The weak place in South American constitutions, as organised on the theory of Jefferson, appears to us Europeans to lie in the fact that too much power is vested in the individual. In our continent this would open the door to the danger of a reconstitution of the forces of the past, whose only hope now lies in the possibility of a surprise. In America a federation of divided Powers offers so many different centres of resistance (providing always that each State Government enjoys a real autonomy) to any attempt at usurpation. The American of the South is no less attached than his brother of the North to the principle of autonomy of States. It only remains for him to make it a reality.

As a matter of fact, moreover, the theoretic independence of Ministers and Parliament does not hold together, in view of the omnipotence of the representative assemblies in matters of finance. This system has the advantage of making a series of crises impossible, but a Minister must, and always does, disappear when a succession of votes proves that he no longer possesses the confidence of Parliament.

In America, as in Europe, the Press is the highest power after the Government. I say "after," because we must believe the Constitution. It is, however, only too true that the moral paralysis that distinguishes certain "popular leaders," whose chief anxiety is to trim their course to every wind that blows, leaves to any one who claims to speak in the name of public opinion a degree of authority before which the individuality of the pretended governing body, in spite of its pomp of speeches, is apt to disappear.

But although the Press plays unquestionably a very important *rôle* in the Argentine, it did not appear to me that the evil went as far as this. Not but what, perhaps, the man who owns a newspaper is as much inclined here as anywhere to make the most use he can of its influence. But in a land that calls out the best in any man, even the Latin, usually so easy a prey to the designs of the political revolutionary, manages to preserve enough independence of character to offer an effective resistance to projects that are too flagrantly opposed to his own calmer views.

Argentine statesmen, worthy the name, are not content to hold opinions of their own; they are perfectly capable of the tenacity necessary to put a scheme into execution and carry it through. Clearly the advantages that go to make up the success of the Argentine Republic would count for nothing were there no strong minds to grasp the higher principles of public interest and no strong hearts to enforce their practice. The Argentine is a battlefield where every kind of moral force, including politics and sociology, is now in the full heat of action, and exposed to all the chances and changes common to weak humanity.

Public activity is here, as in all countries, manifested chiefly by means of parties, a necessity, practically, which has at least as many advantages as disadvantages. Casuists have argued much about the relative qualities of "human" parties and those of any given intellectual symbol. The Argentine Government is not based upon a traditional or historic fact, but on a theory of right in which originates an organisation of justice and liberty that can only pass from principle to practice when the citizens are capable of clothing its bare bones with the living sinews of action; but this fact in no sense changes the problem, since man without the intellectual symbol or idea can be only a disturbing force, and the idea in politics has no value apart from the man who can give it life.

The old-fashioned Press of ideas has made prodigious strides since the days of Armand Carrel, and the modern reader is more especially greedy for facts. With these before him he forms his own opinions, and the most the writer can do is to prepare the way towards a given deduction, without being able to discount its acceptance with any certainty. In reality, the Argentine Press is no better and no worse than that of any free countries; and, whether as regards news or party politics, the newspapers are extremely well conducted. [26] Not but that you may find occasional violence of language, as happens everywhere, but there are extremes which the public will not tolerate. There are no pornographic Press and no pictures of a kind to defile the eyes of every passer-by. On this we may congratulate a race whose healthy energies find too continuous employment in the sunshine for them to develop any tendency towards the excesses of "civilised" corruption.

The *Prensa* is, as we all know, the leading newspaper of the South American continent. Under the skilful control of its founder, M. Paz, the *Prensa* has reached a state of prosperity which, within the limits of its field of action, makes it the equal of any advertising agency in the world. It is a paper that has to be reckoned with by every party, for although not officially attached to any group of politicians, it obviously seeks—while maintaining the principles of democratic evolution—to hold the balance between all parties, ready if necessary to intervene at the critical moment. Just now its general editor is M. Ezequiel Paz, who seems in every way capable of carrying on his father's work. M. Zeballos is credited with being the fount of inspiration of the paper. The ex-Minister of Foreign Affairs is at the same time a literary man, a legal expert, and a historian. His writings on questions of law are highly esteemed in Europe. An untimely dispute with

Brazil drove him out of office, and gave him the leisure he is turning to account now. M. Paz is enjoying a well-earned rest in Europe, but he retains supreme control of the sheet; and a gorgeous palace that he is building in the best part of Buenos Ayres would appear to point to an intention of returning to the country before long. If he does I cannot help pitying him, for he will require nothing less than the Court of Louis XIV., or perhaps of Xerxes, to fill this showy dwelling. The business quarters of the *Prensa* are in the Avenue of May, and if smaller in dimensions, they are no less magnificent. The building is one of the sights of the city. How shall I describe it? It would fill a volume. Every department of the paper is lodged in a way that unites the most perfect of means to the end in view. Simplicity of background, a scrupulous cleanliness, comfort for every worker therein, with a highly specialised method that gathers together all the varied workers on the staff to direct them towards their final end and aim, namely, promptness and accuracy of news. With all this there are outside services, such as a dispensary, so complete it would need a specialist to catalogue it, and suites of apartments that are placed at the disposal of persons whom the *Prensa* considers worthy the honour. I confess that I thought less luxury in this part of the building would have been more to the taste of the poor distinguished men who are lodged there, since a comparison with their own modest homes would be wholly to the disadvantage of the latter.

The *Nacion* is a party organ in the best sense of the word, following the exalted traditions of Bartolome Mitre. It has been compared with our *Temps*. My friend Antonio Piñero exercises considerable influence here over the descendants of the great statesman. But for the quiet and invaluable help given by the *Nacion*, all of whose interests lay in the opposite direction, [27] we should never have succeeded in getting the law establishing literary proprietorship through Parliament. It is my duty as well as my pleasure to take this opportunity of offering my grateful thanks in the quarter where they are due.

The *Diario*, in its turn, deserves special mention on account of its editor, M. Manuel Lainez, senator, who has a rare command of the most refined of Parisian critical talent, the sting of which does not exclude mirth. M. Lainez is one of those journalists who excel in detecting the weak spot in men and things and take a delight in driving home the shaft of a caustic phrase. He dissects with ease, and disguises the depth of his own knowledge under a thin veil of irony. I know of no more charming talker. Whether or no his wit has injured his political prospects is a point I am not able to decide.

Then I must mention the *Argentina*, which seemed to me an honest news organ; and finally, I must not neglect the photographic papers, the *P. B. T.* and the *Caras y Carietas*, in which the spoken word gives place to the picture, according to the formula lately invented amongst us. Both have a large circulation.

We all remember the words that Ibsen has placed in the mouth of his "Enemy of the People" about papers being edited by their readers. No doubt the gazette, nowadays, seeks less to establish an idea than to conform to the supposed feelings of the masses in whose hands is the key of success. Its educational influence has, of course, been in consequence greatly reduced; still, a remnant exists. The culture, slow but inevitable, of the masses must in time have a good influence on the Press that caters for them. Photography, when genuine, and the cinematograph, which vitalises it, have a real educational value. The trouble is that nothing is sacred to the Argentine photographer. He is omnipresent and enjoys the execrable privilege of being at home in all homes. You give a dinner-party to friends or relations. With the dessert there appear some pale persons, draped in black, who disturb servants and guests to set up their complicated lenses on the spot that strikes their fancy. Then comes the blinding flash and a poisonous puff of smoke, and the master of the house hastens to thank the intruders for the outrage. The *diable boiteux*, who lifted the roofs of houses, has been surpassed. When an unfortunate Argentino wants to offer his heart (always accompanied by his hand) to the lady of his choice, let him begin by doubly locking all the doors and hermetically closing the shutters, if he wishes to be safe from intrusion!

I alluded just now to the voting of the Law of Literary Property. [28] As may be supposed, such an excellent Act was not carried through without long preparation. I could give a list of men who, on both sides of the ocean, worked in favour of this act of justice and literary honesty. From the moment that Argentine statesmen realised that purely intellectual labour had proprietary rights in the same way as every other kind, and that to defraud its owners of the proceeds was to place themselves outside the pale of civilisation, they made it a point of honour to yield to the representations made to them from all parts of the world. Is it not extraordinary that a law which was diametrically opposed to the interests of persons particularly well placed to defend them should have been voted unanimously without a single protest? All honour to the Argentine Republic, not only for the act itself, but for the nobility with which it was performed.

It would be an affectation on my part to pass over in silence the public which did me the honour to come to listen to my lectures on democratic evolution as it manifests itself in history and in contemporary events. The subject is not wildly amusing. It is, however, one of those that are of surpassing importance to-day, and none can ignore it. Unfortunately, the general public cannot acquire any trustworthy knowledge of it by scrappy reading indulged in between the hours of the day's work; and if in the tumult of party passion the public are to be of any real service to their Government in solving it, the problem calls for more than a hasty and summary judgment founded on insufficient data. And yet was it not too much to expect of people who are engrossed all day by their own affairs to come to listen to the statements of a public man, against whom there must necessarily be some prejudices on a question of pure doctrine? The majority of workers are not free of an afternoon, and the "upper classes," even the most cultured—in Europe, at least,—are too distrustful of democratic movements in general to waste an hour on a subject that worries them. Happily, the history of American peoples has never been embittered by race hatred engendered by centuries of oppression, and revolts of which it is to be hoped that we have now seen the end. In the North, as in the South, a formula frightens nobody. Society has been built up on a new idea embodied in language that was once the terror and scandal of the Old World. When put in practice, however, these ideas and their verbal expression have stood the test of a century of trial; and the "practical" men of the new continent, while no less alive to social needs than any others, are, perhaps, more ready than the rest of us to make an experiment that can be recommended by right and by reason. There is here neither middle class nor aristocracy in the sense that we attach to those terms in the Old World. All are workers who, having reached the top rung of the ladder, are ready to hold it steady for other feet to climb, rather than to overturn it and retard the advance of those behind.

Thus, beside the small aristocracy formed of the last vestiges of the original Spanish colony, I had the pleasure and honour of finding a large public of

European culture and wide intelligence, eager to hear what any European might have to say about an idea whose course he was honestly seeking to trace, whether bearing on the political and social experiences of Europe or on the more or less rational experiments of which their own land is the theatre. Their unbiassed criticism and independent opinions are all one could hope to find in an audience one is trying to influence. The very best public possible, prepared to surrender or resist according to the intrinsic value of the arguments presented. The element of resistance came, perhaps, from the feminine section, slightly actuated by snobbishness, and either holding itself aloof by way of protest against the possible utterance of ideas too bold to be acceptable, or attending the lectures in order to get some understanding of the subject so as to discuss it afterwards.

As regards language, there was no difficulty. Every one here understands French, reading and speaking it like the speaker himself, and showing by their gestures that no shade of meaning was lost on them. What better could one wish? By the grace of winged words the mind of France has flown across the ocean, and we may rejoice in the fact and found great hopes for the future on it. It is therefore with the greatest pleasure that I offer my heartfelt gratitude to this admirable audience for their constant kindliness and for the encouragement that I found in their remarkable idealism and determination.

FOOTNOTES:

[23] I take this opportunity of thanking M. and Mme. Thiébaud for the friendly welcome I found at the French Legation.

[24] If to Argentine diplomacy the rigidity of our famous chapel on the Quai d'Orsay be unknown, they have none the less given us first-class men—such, for instance as the present Minister for Foreign Affairs, M. Ernesto Bosch, who is much esteemed in the French political world, and his worthy successor in Paris, M. Enrique Rodriguez Larreta.

[25] It pleases me to note the triumph of pride over vanity shown in the fact that the Argentinos have deliberately renounced the childish folly of orders.

[26] Thanks to the difference in the clocks, the Buenos Ayres newspapers are able to publish in their morning editions news appearing at the same time in London and Paris.

[27] The *Nacion* publishes a Library of translations of the best works in French (fifty per cent. of the whole), English, Russian, German, Italian, to say nothing of Spanish and Argentine works in the original.

CHAPTER VIII
PAMPAS LIFE

Every capital is a world in itself—a world in which national and foreign elements blend; but to understand the life of a nation one must go out into the country. A vast territory, ten times the size of France, extending from Patagonia to Paraguay and Bolivia, will naturally offer the greatest diversity of soil and climate, representing differing conditions of labour as well as of customs and sometimes of morals. Our ancient Europe can in the same way show ethnical groups with sufficiently marked features (such as in our French provinces) which a long history has not been able to destroy or even to modify.

It is quite another matter when, on a continent with no history at all, you get men of every origin spread over it, brought thither by a community of interest and in the hope of cultivating the soil by their labour. I have already said what racial characteristics subsist. The colonist will, of course, at first do all he can to remain what the land of his birth has made him; the first evidence of this is his tendency to fall into groups and form national colonies. But the land of his adoption will in time surely force upon him the inevitable conditions of a new mode of life, the very necessity of adapting himself to changed conditions making of him a new creature, to be later definitely moulded by success.

The Pampas are not the Argentine. They form, however, so predominant a part that they have shaped the man and the race by imposing on them their organisation of agricultural labour and the development of their natural resources. Whilst manufactures are still in a rudimentary state and are likely to remain so for a long time to come owing to the lack of coal, the Pampas from the Andes to the ocean offer an immense plain of the same alluvial soil from end to end, ready to respond in the same degree to the same effort of stock-raising or agriculture. An identical stretch of unbroken ground, with identical surface, identical pools of subterranean water, no special features to call for other than the unchanging life of the *Campo*.

Naturally, the first experiments were made in the most rudimentary fashion on the half-wild herds of cattle that could not be improved unless the European market were thrown open. As soon as this outlet was assured the whole effort of skill and money was directed towards the improvement of stock, and the progress made in a few years of work far exceeded the brightest hopes of those early days. And as at the same time a powerful impetus was given to wheat-growing, the Pampas from one end to the other of their vast extent immediately took on a dual aspect: cattle farms (herds grazing on natural or artificial pastures), and acres of grain (wheat, oats, maize, and flax)—this is the only picture that the Pampas offer or ever can offer to the traveller. The system of cattle-breeding, primitive in the extreme at a distance from railroads, improves in proportion as the line draws nearer; wherever the iron road passes there is an immediate development of land under cultivation.

All this goes to make up a man of the *Campo*—the *estanciero*, colonist, peon, *gaucho*, or whatever other name he may be called. Certain conditions of living and working are forced upon him from which there is no escape. Whether landed proprietor, farmer, servant, or agricultural labourer, the vastness of the plain which opens in front of him, the distance between inhabited dwellings, the roughness of the roads, leave him no other means of communication but the horse, which abounds everywhere and can be unceremoniously borrowed on occasion. The man of the *Campo* is a horseman. He is certainly not an elegant horseman, whose riding would be appreciated at the Saumur Cavalry School. No curb; only a plain bit is used, whose first effect is to bring down the animal's head and throw him out of balance, whilst his rider, to remedy this defect, raises his hands as high as his head. To the unsightliness of this picture is added an unstable seat. As very often happens in similar circumstances, instinct and determination more or less making up for all mistakes, the rider manages approximately to keep on his beast's back, thanks partly to the fact that the horse is rarely required to go at more than a moderate pace over level ground. The hoof never by any chance can strike on a stone, though it may be caught in a hole; the active little *creole* horse excels in avoiding this danger. One can ask no more of him. (I shall have something to say later of the way wild horses are broken in.)

On his enormous saddle of sheepskin, the peon or *gaucho*, his hat pulled well down over his eyes, his shoulders draped in the folds of the *poncho*,—a blanket with a hole in it for the head to pass through,—is encumbered with a whip whose handle serves on occasion as a mallet, and a lasso, with or without metal balls, coiled behind his saddle. He makes a picturesque enough figure in the monotonous expanse of earth and sky, where *rancho* or tree, beast or man, stand out in high relief against a background of glaring light. Without sign or syllable, his eyes fixed on the empty horizon, the man passes through the silence of infinite solitude, rising like a ghost from the nothingness of the horizon at one point to sink again into nothingness at another. When riding in a troop, they talk together in low tones. There are none of those outbursts of fun that you might expect in a land of sunshine. It is the gravity natural to men brought face to face with Nature in the pitiless light of sky and earth where no fold or break in the surface arrests the glance or fixes the attention.

Still, there are those gigantic herds of horned cattle or horses which fill an appreciable portion of the melancholy plain—"green in winter, yellow in summer." I say nothing of the great flocks of sheep because there were none in the districts which I visited. When you talk of a herd of ten thousand cows, you make some impression on even a big farmer of the Charolais. Well, I can assure you that out in the Pampas ten thousand head of cattle is a small affair. You see a dark shadow that rises on the horizon that might be either a village or a group of haycocks, until the vague shifting of the mass suggests to your mind the idea of some form of life. The lines show clearer, groups break off and stand out, pointed horns appear, and at last you find you are watching the tranquil passage of a monstrous herd, whose outlines are stencilled in black upon the whiteness of the sky-line like the Chinese shadow pictures I saw on one occasion at the *Chat Noir* (in Montmartre) when the flocks of the patriarchs were flung upon the sheet. So distinct are the shapes here that you lose the sense of distance and are astonished at the harmony of nonchalant impulse, as irresistible as slow, which can thus set in movement this huge living mass and make it pass before us like a vision of Fate. The dream fantasy is the more striking because it changes so rapidly. Withdraw your eyes a moment from the picture, and it is entirely altered. The heavy mass of migrating cattle seems now to have taken root at the opposite extremity of the horizon, whilst in the depths of the luminous distance shadowy patches of haze more or less distinct betoken further living bodies, some stationary, some in motion. These are mirages of the Pampas of which none takes any heed; but upon me they made a powerful impression, for I saw in them the whole tragedy of this land, from the tuft of grass on which the eyes of the beast first saw the light down to the last step of that fateful journey which ends at the slide of the slaughter-house.

The rapid travelling of the motor-car multiplies one's point of view. The vast estates on the Pampas, which run from two to a hundred square miles in extent, are further divided into large sections bounded by wire fencing to limit the wandering of the herds. The roads are marked out by a double row of wire. What dust and what mud may be found thereon, according to weather conditions, may be imagined, since there is not the smallest pebble to be found there. Yet vehicles do, it appears venture along these paths, and even arrive at their destination. You may also meet flocks of sheep and oxen on them, and families of pigs engaged in breakfasting on a sheep that has been relieved of its skin. In less than an hour its bones, picked clean, are scattered along the way, where in process of time they will contribute precious phosphates to the soil. Naturally, on such a "road," the automobile does not yearn to travel; rather does it prefer the green smoothness of the immense prairie. Here there are no police regulations to annoy the motorist. No other law but your own fancy and a certain thought for the savoury lunch that is awaiting you at the next *estancia*. When you reach it you will discover that the monstrous herds on the horizon were merely these gentle creatures, placid in their happy ignorance of the fell designs that are the hidden causes of man's kindness to them. Do we astonish them? Or are they wholly indifferent? Their eyes are fixed on our panting machines as ours are on the grazing beasts, and not a spark is struck by the meeting of the two intelligences, the one so calmly definite and the other too soon checked in its effort to understand. Obedient to the *rebenque* (whip) of the peon, the herd, which in motion looks so threatening, allows itself to be stopped or led by the cries and rapid movements of the horsemen going at a hand-gallop. The sight of any object that waves in the wind (whether coat or *poncho*) is equally effectual.

If one expects the cows, which are penned for milking (three quarts a day as an average), the only apparent relations between man and beast consist in the easy use of this instrument of terror. Nothing is done for the flock except to provide the mill which automatically feeds the water-troughs, and to see to the safe arrival of the bulls intended to improve the breed, and to select those from the herd destined for the freezing machines; for all their other needs Providence is expected to provide—quite a different *régime* from that prevailing in our French stock-farms. Of shelter against wind or sun there is none. The grass is there when the drought has not burnt it up, also an ugly thistle which no one troubles to pull up and which sometimes overruns the pasture. Of Nature's scourges, the drought is the most to be feared, for it falls with fearful suddenness on great stretches of the *Campo*. In the absence of rain, neither turf nor forage nor harvest can be looked for; for the cattle, death is certain. Winter in any case is a hard season for them. Their coats lose their gloss, their flanks fall in, and their pointed bones witness to their sufferings, which the icy breath of the *pampero* does nothing to assuage. With the spring comes the hope of rain. But if this hope is betrayed, nothing can save innumerable herds from starvation and death. Forage is always stored for the more precious of the stock, but to feed the herd is out of the question. The Pampas then become one vast cemetery where hundreds of thousands of dead cattle are lying in heaps beyond all possibility of burial. It is the custom to leave the body of the beast that dies by the way to the tender mercies of the wind and the sun, the rain and the earth, into whose wide-open pores the remains are little by little absorbed. The birds of prey and dogs are valuable assistants but wholly insufficient. One of my friends told me that it was by no means uncommon for the dogs to return to the farm from the *Campo* bearing a horrible smell about them. For my part, if I was often revolted by the spectacle of putrefying carcasses lying about the Pampas and seen either on my walks or from the railway-train—some even lying festering in pools close to dwelling-houses—I cannot say that my olfactory nerves were ever troubled. I occasionally spoke of the danger of poisonous fly-bites, but I got only vague replies.

In my personal experience, whenever I met something disagreeable on my walks about the Pampas, the carcass was invariably completely mummified, the skin being so thoroughly tanned that the object might have been carefully prepared for a museum of comparative anatomy. But when death was recent, and the summer season had set in, with its attendant flies, I should certainly avoid the neighbourhood.

It will surprise no one to hear that I took the liberty of calling the attention of two or three statesmen to the dangers of this unfortunate custom and the detestable impression it is bound to make on travellers. The reply invariably was that the Argentine was suffering, and would, no doubt, continue to suffer for some time to come, from a lack of hands and that the thousands of animals which under normal conditions perished in the Pampas could never find grave-diggers. When, therefore, a dry season killed off as many as ten thousand sheep on a single ranch, there was no alternative but to bow to the inevitable.

We see that cattle-rearing in the Argentine has its ups and downs. At every turn Nature intervenes with its elements of success or disaster. Man's *rôle* is to furnish a minimum of labour, and by the force of circumstances, he is compelled to reckon on quantity for his modicum of success; but the fact does not prevent his successful efforts to improve the quality. As I have already said, he will give any prize to secure a fine strain. It is naturally from England that he gets his stock for breeding, since the customers for his meat are chiefly English. On all hands I was told that the results were most satisfactory. As regards their breed of horses, the result is manifest. But as for the cattle, I take the liberty of disagreeing with those who declare that the Argentine can send to our slaughter-houses at La Villette meat as fine as our own at half its price. If, however, I am firmly convinced that our palate would not readily be satisfied with the frozen meat that seems to please the English, I am quite aware that there is a distinction to be drawn between the choice beasts, generally magnificent, that make such a show at exhibitions and the common run of the average flock, amongst which truth compels me to admit there are some very indifferent animals. It will require a long time and a change of system on the cattle-rearing farms for the Argentine ever to equal the fine products of our French breeders. It cannot be otherwise as long as the young animal, bred somewhat at haphazard and born on the open camp between the corpses of some of its relations, is left to grow up as best it can, exposed to every change of temperature. Everywhere I came upon young calves abandoned by their mothers as soon as born, and only sought out when the time for feeding came round; it cannot be said that the stock would bear comparison with the average produce of a Norman or Charolais byre. Not all the quality of its mother's milk will suffice to make up for the ground lost by neglect.

As I have said, the troops of horses seem to have lost the least. I speak less of their appearance than of their action, which often seemed to me remarkable. You cannot imagine the pleasure it is to glide swiftly across the Pampas in a motor-car with a troop of young horses on either side of you, neighing and galloping to keep up with the machine. But do not, pray, call them "wild horses."

Tradition to the contrary notwithstanding, I believe there are no wild horses in the Argentine. There are horses, and there are horsemen who treat them brutally under the pretext of breaking them in. This is a survival of ancient times which not even the universality of the horse in civilised countries can destroy. Any English squire will get more out of a young horse by quiet skill and kindness than can ever be obtained by the useless and cruel lasso, to which I shall return later.

I have shown you the Pampas alive with the swarms of their new civilisation. We are far enough from the romantic descriptions so dear to story-tellers. We all know now that the redskin of North America bears no resemblance to the portraits painted of him by Chateaubriand or Fenimore Cooper. The Pampas, in full process of evolution, are getting more human and losing their distinctive features. They were once as bare, to quote the joke of a poet, now a member of the Académie Française, "as the speech of an academician"; man has undertaken to raise up orchards, groves, and even forests. Once they were the refuge of more or less innocent beasts. The son of Adam, by the mere fact of his presence, treads out all life that cannot be made of use to himself.

I said that the *ombu* was the only tree that flourished in the Pampas, for the simple reason that the locusts devour every other vegetable product, including clover, crops, and trees of all sorts. The damage caused by these insects, which descend in clouds and destroy in a moment the harvest, is only too well known by our Algerian colonists. Wherever the cloud descends vegetation vanishes. In a few hours every leaf is gone from the tree, and only the kernel, clean and dry, is left on the branch as a mute witness of the irreparable disaster. I did not see the locusts, but I was shown the result of their work, most conscientiously carried out. Men who have put long months of toil into their land see, with impotent rage, all the fruit of their toil swept off in the twinkling of an eye. The Government lays out some millions yearly to assuage in some sort the mischief done. But the only remedy applied up to the present consists in making such a din on the approach of the baneful host as to induce them to go on farther and land at a neighbour's. As altruism, this course is not above reproach. Another way is to dig ditches in which to bury them alive, but this is mere child's play. If you inquire the origin of the scourge you will get the sulky reply that the pest comes from Chaco, and that some men have travelled thither to verify the statement, but the country proving impenetrable, the project has for the moment been abandoned. I hasten to place these insufficient data before the European public.

Alone victorious over the locusts by the repugnance it inspires, and over man by its glorious uselessness, the *ombu* here and there spreads its triumphant arms near some ranch; occasionally, on the pasturage of the *Campo*, it may be seen extending its shelter to some quadruped that shuns the rays of the sun. Around his *estancia* the farmer plants his orchard and his ornamental thicket, which will flourish or not at the will of the insects. After the passage of the destructive horde it requires at least two years for the country to recover. The eucalyptus, owing to its rapid growth, gives very good results, but the favourite tree in the Pampas is the *paraiso*—the Tree of Paradise—which is admirable rather for its flower than its form, and withstands to some extent the locust, through sheer force of resistance. Occasionally one comes upon a small wood, in which the *ornevo*—the cardinal—sings and the dove coos.

For the *Campo* has a whole population of running or flying creatures, whose principal virtue is that of being satisfied with little in the shape of a shelter. The gardens and parks of the *estancias* provide a natural asylum for a world of winged songsters, in whom man, softened by isolation, has not yet inspired terror.

But the Pampas in their nudity are not without signs of life. There is the guanaco, smaller than the llama, larger than the stork, which has already retreated far from Buenos Ayres. The grey ostrich, formerly abundant, has been decimated by the lasso of the *gaucho*, who, at the risk of getting a kick that may rip him open, attacks the beast that struggles wildly in the bonds of the cruel rope, drags out his handsomest feathers, and then lets him go. The really "wild" ostrich has disappeared from the Pampas. Numbers may be seen from the window of the train, but they are all confined in fenced parks, and are really in captivity.

I cannot be expected to give a list of all the creatures that swarm on or under the soil of the *Campo*. There is nothing to be said about the prairie-dog, which has been systematically destroyed on account of the damage it does. I must mention the *tatou*, a small creature with a pointed muzzle, something between a lizard and a tortoise, and with the shell of the latter. It burrows into the ground, as certain of our European species do. The *gaucho* considers its flesh excellent, declaring that it tastes like pork. Perhaps the surest way of getting the taste of pork is to address oneself to the pig himself, here popularly known as the "creole pig," a lovable little black beast that plays with the children in tiny muddy pools in the neighbourhood of the ranches.

Passing by the hare (imported from Europe), the small partridge, and the martinette (*tinamou*), to which I shall return presently, I may mention the plover (abundant) and the birds of carrion, which settle all disputes for the possession of the ground according to the dictates of a boundless appetite, and the small owl, so tame that it rises every few yards with a cheerful cry to come down again a few yards farther on, following all your movements with a questioning eye. At the mouth of its burrow, or on the stake that marks the boundary of the ranch, its pretty form is a feature in the landscape. Finally, I must not forget the *ornevo*, to be found near the *estancias* and in the woods, a charming, tame little bird, that chatters all the time like a good many people, and builds a mud nest in the branches, in the shape of an oven divided into two apartments, whose tiny door opens always to the north, whence comes the warmth. If you lose yourself in the forest you need no compass but this. The *gauchos* hold the bird in pious respect. Legend has it that he never works on Sundays at his nest. Here is one who wants no legislation for a *repos hebdomadaire* any more than he does for the regulation of the liquor sale. Oh, the superiority of our "inferior brethren"!

I heard a good deal about the great lakes in which thousands of black-necked swans and rose-pink flamingoes may be seen at play. I was never able to visit these fascinating birds. To make up for this M. Onelli presented me with two handsome black-throated swans, which, however, were not able to stand the climate of Normandy.

Having thus sketched the principal features, it remains to fill in the picture of the ranch and *estancia*. I have shown you the primitive cabin of the

Robinson Crusoe of the *Campo*. I have drawn a picture of the colonist and the *gaucho*; it is not necessary to go back to him again. I have shown the diverse elements of his existence. The railway has not changed anything in it except by abolishing the interminable rides of earlier days and the tiresome monotony of convoying freight waggons to the town markets. The railway, moreover, brings within reach of the ranch the conveniences of modern furniture.

In the huts of the half-castes, near Tucuman, the only piece of furniture I saw was a pair of trestles, on which was laid the mat which served as seat, bed, or table—the kitchen being always outside. In the Pampas, dwellings that look modest, and even less than modest, generally boast an easy-chair, a chest of drawers, with a clock, a sewing-machine, and gramophone, which, when fortune comes, is completed by a piano. The gramophone is the theatre of the Pampas. It brings with it orchestra, song, words, and the whole equipment of "art" suited to the æsthetic sense of its hearers. Thus on all sides dreadful nasal sounds twang out, to the great joy of the youth of the colony.

The morals of the *Campo* are what the conditions of life there have made them. Men who are crowded together in large cities are exposed to many temptations. When too far removed from the restraint of public opinion, the danger is no less great. In all circumstances a witness acts as a curb. In the Pampas as it used to be, the witness, nine times out of ten, became an accomplice. Between the menace of a distant and vague police force and the ever-present fear of the Indian, the *gaucho* became a soldier of fortune, prepared for any bold stroke. With his dagger in his belt, his gun on his shoulder, and the lasso on his saddle-bow, he rode over the eternal prairie in search of adventures, and ready at any moment for the drama that might be awaiting him. To his other qualities must be added a generous hospitality, that dispensed to all comers his more or less well-gotten goods; he had in him the material for an admirable leader in revolutionary times. I saw no revolutions, and I hope the Argentine has finished with them for ever; but the periodic explosions that have taken place there are not so ancient but that an echo of them reached my ear. I shall leave out of the question, of course, all more remote circumstances that might serve at hazard to put a body of adventurers in motion. You were on the side of General X or General Z, according to the hopes of the party; but, in reality, that had little to do with it. When the signal was once given a military force had to be organised, and the means adopted were admirably simple. Any weapon that could be of use in battle was picked up, and a band would present themselves at the door of an *estancia*.

"We are for General X. All the peons here must follow us. To arms! To horse!"

And the order would be obeyed; otherwise, the *estancia* and its herds would suffer. With such a system of recruiting, troops were quickly collected, and a few such visits would suffice to bring together a very respectable force of men. My friend Biessy, the artist, with whom I had the pleasure of making the journey, witnessed just such a scene one day at an *estancia* which he was visiting. He was chatting with the overseer when the man, hearing a suspicious sound, flung himself down and put his ear to the ground. A moment later he rose, looking anxious.

"There are horsemen galloping this way. What can have happened?" And sure enough, a minute later, there appeared a band of men so oddly equipped that at first they were taken for masqueraders. It was carnival time. The leader, however, came forward and called on the overseer to place all his peons at the service of the revolutionaries. Biessy himself only escaped by claiming the rights of a French citizen. And do not imagine that all this was a comedy. The dominant sentiment in their camp was by no means a respect for human life. On both sides these brave peons fought furiously, asking no questions about the party in whose cause they happened to be enrolled. The overseer of a neighbouring *estancia*, who was talking with M. Biessy when called to parley with the revolutionaries, was shot dead a few hours later for having offered resistance to them.

If men are thus unceremoniously enrolled—I use the present tense because one never knows what may happen—it may be imagined the horses are borrowed still more freely. A curious thing is that when the war is over, and these creatures are again at liberty, they find their way back quite easily to their own pastures.

The overseer of one *estancia* told me that the last revolution had cost him 600 horses, of which 400, that had been taken to a distance of from 200 to 300 kilometres, returned of their own accord. How they contrive to steer their course over the Pampas, with their inextricable tangle of wire fencing,

I do not undertake to explain. When I inquired of the overseer whether it were not possible to steal one of his horses without being discovered, he replied, "Oh, it is like picking an apple in Normandy! It often happens that a traveller on a tired horse lassoes another to continue his journey. But on reaching his destination he sets the animal at liberty, and he invariably makes his way back to the herd."

I have already spoken of the time when the *gaucho* would fell an ox to obtain a steak for lunch. In some of the more remote districts it is possible that the custom still subsists. But it is none the less true that a growing civilisation and the railway, which is its most effectual and rapid instrument, are changing the *gaucho*, together with his surroundings and his sphere of action. The *gaucho* on foot is very like any other man. His flowing necktie of brilliant colour, once the party signal, has been toned down. His *poncho*, admirably adapted to the climatic conditions of camp life in the *Campo*, is now used by the townsmen, who throw it over their arm or shoulder according to the variations in the temperature. The sombrero, like the slashed breeches or high boots, is no longer distinctive. There remains only the heavy stirrup of romantic design, more or less artistically ornamented, but now often replaced by a simple ring of rope or iron. The days of roystering glamour are passed. The heavy roller of civilisation levels all the elements of modern existence to make way for the utilitarian but inæsthetic triumph of uniformity. Yet a little longer and the life of the *Campo* will be nothing but a memory, for with his picturesque dress the type itself is disappearing.

The modern *gaucho* has preserved from his ancestors the slowness in speech, the reserved manner, and scrutinising eye of the man who lives on the defensive. But to-day he is thoroughly civilised, and can stroll down Florida Street, in Buenos Ayres, without attracting any attention. It is in vain that the theatre seeks to reproduce the life of the *Campo*, as I saw it attempted at the Apollo. What can it show us beyond the eternal comedy of love, or the absurdities of the wife of the *gaucho* who has too suddenly acquired a fortune? Both subjects belong to all times and all countries, in the same way as every dance and every song are common to any assembly of young humanity. Long before the gramophone was invented the guitar was the joy of Spanish ears to the farthest confines of the Pampas. Between two outbreaks of civil war, when men were rushing madly to meet death, joyous songs and plaintive refrains alternated beneath the branches of the *ombu*, where the youth of the district met, and the sudden dramas of the ranch made them the more eager to drink deep of the pleasure they knew to be fleeting. They danced the *Pericou* and the *Tango*, as they still do to-day; but the audacious gestures in which amorous Spain gave expression to the ardour of its feelings have now passed into the domain of history. The "Creole balls," where may be seen graceful young girls in soft white draperies, dancing in a chain that resembles our *Pastourelle,* have been reproduced on postcards and are familiar to all. There are, there will ever be in the Pampas—at least, I fondly hope so—graceful young girls dressed in white and destined to rouse the love instinct which never seems to sleep in an Italian or Spanish breast. But the trouble we take to reconstruct on the stage, for the edification of travellers from Europe, the real *Tango*, in all the antique effrontery of its ingeniousness, proves that the heroic age, made up of the *naïf* and the barbarous, is fast losing its last vestiges of character in the wilderness of civilised monotony. The *Tango* is disappearing rapidly. On the other hand, at Rio de Janeiro, in the flower of my seventieth year, I actually figured in the official quadrille of the President of the Republic, to the shame of French choregraphy. Alas! alas!

CHAPTER IX
FARMING AND SPORT

Roman civilisation ended in those *latifundia* which, amongst other causes, are usually considered to have brought about the ruin of Italy. The immense estates of the Argentine *Campo* were not built up, however, by the expropriation of small farmers, as was the case in decadent Rome. They are simply the result of wholesale seizure of land at the expense of the savages who were incapable of utilising it. Without discussing the origin of all landed property, or to what extent our legal principles and our practice agree, I simply note the fact that the *conquistadores* and their descendants set down as *res nullius* whatever it suited them to appropriate.

The principle once established (this is the commencement of every civilisation), there remained only to fix the approximate extent of land likely to satisfy the appetite of the European newcomer. Do you remember a fine story, by Tolstoy, of a man who was given, by I know not what tribe of the steppe, as much land as he could walk round in a day? Once started, the sole idea of the poor wretch was continually to enlarge the circumference. It was only at the price of a tremendous effort that he completed the circle, falling dead at the moment of accomplishing his journey. The first settlers, who followed the Genoese, took probably less trouble, though their greed was as great. But as the land depends for its value on labour, the result for Tolstoy's hero and for the *conquistadores* was not so very different. Thus, when the first ploughshare turned the first sod, the estate, whatever its proportions, had to bear some relation to human capacity. The large domains of to-day—measuring from two to a hundred square miles—have proceeded from still larger ones, and gradually, as the much-needed labour comes forward to undertake the task, we shall see the further cutting up of preposterous holdings.

This is inevitable in the near future, and this alone will render possible scientific farming, which is highly necessary for the development of agriculture. A farmer who knows nothing of manure of any sort, who is making his first experiments in irrigation, and who burns his flax straw for want of knowing how to utilise it, will, for a long time to come, continue to swamp the markets of Europe with his grain and his meat, but only on condition that he is satisfied with small profits and gives quantity in place of quality. These are the conditions of life on the *Campo*, such as I have tried to sketch them.

It remains for me to introduce the chief agent in this huge movement of cattle-rearing and agriculture, who, in his own person and that of his overseers, administers the Pampas; he is the owner of the *estancia*, the *estanciero*.

The word *estancia*—since it represents something non-existent with us—is not easy to translate. Let us put it down as the most sumptuous form of primitive ownership. I might call it the seat of an agricultural feudalism if the peon were a man to accept serfdom—something resembling a democratic principality, if the two words can be coupled together.

When we meet him on the boulevard, the *estanciero*, who talks of his immeasurable estate and his innumerable herds, seems to us a fabulous creature. It is quite another matter to see him on horseback amidst his peons in the Pampas, which, in default of the customary features of private property, appears in its nakedness to be nobody's land—that is to say, everybody's land.

The contrast between the *estanciero's* personal refinement and the English comfort of his family abode, and the primitive rusticity of the surrounding country, suggests the inconsistencies of barbarism undergoing the civilising process.

As I have already observed, the results obtained are due to a progression of efforts in which the chief, even if assisted by an overseer, necessarily plays a large part. For although it is easy to dazzle the European with fantastic figures, without sacrificing the truth, it is wise to remember that success is not automatic, and that from the elements alone (to say nothing of locusts) serious difficulties are to be expected. M. Basset, whose competence is beyond question, told me that, having lost money in conducting experiments on a large estate, he decided to sell the place. In the meantime land had gone up in value, and he was able to recover himself on the sale of the unworked plots. "I should have made a lot of money," he concluded, "if I had not farmed any of my land." This shows that in the Argentine, as elsewhere, there are risks to be run. The *estanciero* takes these risks, but if he were content to wait on chance to enhance the value of his land, he would not contribute as largely as he does to the wealth of the Rue de la Paix.

We are always being told that the word dearest to Creole indolence is *mañana* ("to-morrow"), but the exigencies of economic success tend to modify customs. The Argentino, like the Yankee, is more and more inclined to do over-night the work that might be put off to the morrow. At all events, absenteeism is unknown on the *estancia*, for this would spell ruin at short notice. It is true the *estanciero* has the reputation of mortgaging freely his estates, and, when a good harvest makes it possible, of hastening to purchase more land so as to increase his output. What can I say, unless that every economic error must be paid for sooner or later, and that in spite of whatever may remain of "Creole indolence," all are forced in the end to seek their profits in an improvement of the system of cultivation?

Grand seigneur I called him—a *grand seigneur* on colonial soil, where his dwelling is a rustic palace that is something between a farmhouse and a mansion. Simple in structure, wood being the principal element, it is built on the ground-floor, colonial fashion. The comforts of English life are reflected in the large rooms, and both furniture and the domestic arrangements are admirable. Large and rich pieces of furniture belong to the days when difficulties of travelling made a provision of the sort indispensable. Large bookcases, filled with heavy volumes, denote a time before the coming of the railway to scatter on the winds leaves from the Tree of Knowledge. Here is every inducement for reflection—paintings, or, rather, pictures; massive plate, goldsmiths' work won as prizes in cattle shows, whose medals fill large frames, to say nothing of photographs of prize beasts. And, better than all the rest, was the hospitality of other times. Now that every one travels without ceasing, the ancient hospitality has lost its savour. There still linger vestiges of it in those countries where civilisation is not advanced enough to protect the traveller from unpleasant contingencies. Let me hasten to add that amongst these one need not count the risk of starvation in an *estancia*. No doubt the abundance of cattle counts for something. In any case, the *estanciero* is admirable in this respect. I wish I could give unstinted praise to the *upchero*, the *asado*, of which I have already spoken. But I shall not be able to do that until the

Argentino has got out of the habit of handing the meat to the cook while it is still warm, for this requires a power of mastication which European debility denies to our jaws.

All kitchen-gardens are alike, and you cannot expect to find the pleasure-gardens of an *estancia* laid out by a Lenôtre. Even if that miracle had been worked, what good would it be when the locusts had passed over it? In one *estancia*, near Buenos Ayres, considered the handsomest in the Argentine, which the kindness of its owner throws open to any foreign visitor, I beheld a park of a thousand hectares, where, amid the groves of tall trees, animals wander, giving the illusion of wildness. The grey ostriches that are there imagine, perhaps, that they are free. We admire some handsome bulls which are stalled here. The eucalyptus, planted sometimes singly and sometimes in broad avenues, towered above us at a height no other tree could rival. In this favoured spot the rich vegetation has nothing to fear from the locusts. Every species grows freely, as it will. For this reason, the overseer, anxious we should miss none of the rare species on which he prides himself, led us, with an air of mystery, to the edge of a low hill, where, with an authoritative gesture, he stopped us before an ordinary-looking tree, destitute of leaves, which had to me a familiar air.

"Yes, it is an oak you are looking at. An old European oak in the Argentine. What say you to that?"

I admit with prejudice that it is an oak, though at the same time confessing that I have seen others more favourable. And at the risk of being misunderstood, I acknowledge that it is not European flora that most interests me in the Argentine Republic.

The special feature of this fine park is the quarter reserved for the bulls. The specimens I saw, which were led past us, are magnificent beasts, bearing witness to methodical and prolonged selection. The best English breeds are gloriously represented, not only in the beasts imported from Europe, but also in Argentine-bred animals, which would do honour to any country.

The management and staff of the stables are entirely English. Stallions of world-wide fame are paraded by English stud-grooms that we may admire beauty of line united to beauty of action.

Now we were to see the trainers at work, not upon "wild" horses, since they belong to bygone days, but simply upon young animals that have not yet been ridden. As a matter of fact, the problem here is exactly the same as with us, but I venture to think that our system is vastly superior. The colts are collected in an enclosure called the corral. Pray do not conjure up a picture of Mazeppa's steed, with fiery eye and bristling mane, as depicted in the favourite chromo. There is nothing here but ardour of youth and grace of movement. The object is to accustom the horse to man and his needs. This our Norman boys quickly achieve by a mixture of skill and kindness which does not preclude firmness of hand. The system of the Argentine peon is very different. First he catches the neck of the animal in a noose and leads him out of the enclosure to a piece of rough ground. There, with a few movements of the lasso, the limbs are so tied that the simplest movement must make the unfortunate victim lose his balance and bring him heavily to earth at the risk of breaking his bones. The creature is terrified, naturally. Meantime, five or six men run in upon him—each an expert in his own way; and when he is so bound he can no longer move, the bit is adjusted and a sheepskin saddle adroitly buckled. All that now remains is to set the animal on his feet so that the horseman may mount. The rope is then relaxed as swiftly as it was tightened, and the colt, on his four feet, firmly held by the head, his eyes blindfolded, might perhaps get over his fright if his two forefeet were not still tied together by a last knot to prevent him running away. The peon gives the signal, and as the last loop is removed he leaps into the saddle and urges his mount straight ahead with the air of riding a savage brute and with a lavish use of his riding crop. Two horsemen, called "sponsors," accompany him, rending the air with their cries and beating the creature with pitiless crops. By the time he has travelled two hundred yards in this way the horse is mad with terror, and asks nothing better than to be allowed to stop. Perhaps there are exceptions; I did not happen to see them. On the other hand, I did see poor beasts that offered not the slightest resistance, and whose angelic gentleness should have disarmed the executioner. It appears that when this performance has been gone through five or six times the colt surrenders unconditionally. In the days when horses were wild upon the prairies these practices might have had some excuse. Nowadays we have different ideas.

All these branches of work require, as may be supposed, a fairly complete set of buildings. Consequently, around the farmer's house there are outbuildings of every style of architecture which make the *estancia* a sort of small village, whence radiates the work undertaken on the Pampas. Thus ordered and thus spent, life in the fields is a "solitude" broken every moment by great herds and *gauchos* ever on the march. It has nothing to daunt even a man who is anxious not to lose touch with his fellow-creatures in these days of extreme civilisation. Therefore it is not surprising that a stay of some months at the *estancia* forms an agreeable part of the programme which the daily life of the Argentine landholder forces on all his family. The railway is never far off, since it brings colonists and is responsible for the whole agricultural movement. Railway construction proceeds at the normal rate of about five hundred kilometres per annum. The provinces of Buenos Ayres, of Cordoba, of Santa Fé, which alone furnish eighty per cent. of the agricultural exports, are naturally the most favoured; and also, naturally, it is on the Pampas, the immense reservoir of fertilising energy, that is concentrated the maximum of labour for the extension of the means of communication that are so swiftly and richly remunerative.

Thus it is not too difficult to move about in the *Campo*. Moreover, the motor-car—running now on a road, now on the great green carpet where movable gates provide a passage through the wire fencing—facilitates a pleasant interchange of neighbourly relations. I have said that absenteeism is unknown in the *estancia*. Often the head of the family, when kept for some reason in the city, confides the management of the estate to one of his sons, who in this way turns to magnificent account the grand energy of youth and manhood in intensely interesting work. What more natural than for the family to gather in the fine summer months beneath the shade of the farms, amid its herds so full of life, to enjoy the beauty of the harvest ripened with the warm kisses of the sun? The rides are unending beneath the pure sky of the long mornings, in the strengthening breeze which sets the blood coursing through the pulses with renewed force. In Brazil I heard people pity the Argentinos because they lacked the resource of the mountains in the great heat of summer. The Andes are, indeed, too far distant even with the railway that now crosses them. (The Transandine line is now working between the Argentine and Chile—forty hours' run from Buenos Ayres to Valparaiso or Santiago.) But the costly pleasures of a sojourn at Mar del Plata are quickly exhausted. The *estancia* offers a beautiful retreat of active and fruitful peace. There are visits to the farmers who, little by little, are coming to reside on the domain of the *estancia* (purchasing the ground originally taken on lease, and grouping themselves in such-wise that villages are in process of formation), or the continual inspection of the herds (*rodeo*).

Another occupation is watching over the harvest which spreads across the Pampas. There are daily pretexts for trips that combine pleasure with usefulness. The tall ricks grow in numbers, the grain falls to the snorting measure of smoking engines, the lean native cattle of the Pampas yield their place to monstrous Durhams, to Herefords, with their handsome white heads, to Percherons, to Boulonnais, to Lincoln sheep, with their heavy fleeces. It is by no means certain that the amusements of Trouville or Vichy are superior to those of the *estancia*. We may be allowed to think that the "gentleman-farmer" has chosen the better part.

I have said nothing of game-shooting. We must admit that in this respect the resources of the Pampas are greater than those of France. Hares and partridges are on the programme, as they are with us. M. Py told me he had tried to acclimatise the quail—in vain. Some thousands of birds were let loose in a selected part of the Pampas and disappeared for good. The history of the hare is very different. About fifty years ago some Germans liberated a few couples at various points of the Pampas, and the same animal which at home produces only one or two young each year began to swarm like the rabbit. Several families every year—and what families! The result, disastrous for farming, is that from eighty to a hundred hares may be reckoned to every hectare, and you cannot walk on the Pampas without perceiving a pair of long ears that spring up out of the grass every moment. The flesh has a poor reputation, perhaps for the reason that here they neglect that elementary operation which follows immediately on the death of the animal in our country. The partridge, smaller than ours, is a solitary creature. Its flesh is white and rather insipid. The martinette (*tinamou*), a sort of intermediary between the partridge and the pheasant, is the best of the Pampas game. One may hunt it without turning to right or to left—certain always of not returning with empty hands. The favourite amusement is the *rabat*, or the "rope," and shooting from the motor-car.

For the *rabat* horsemen are needed. A dozen or two of peons ride off at a gallop in no matter what direction, since the game is everywhere, to meet at a point out of sight and return at the top of their speed to the sportsmen.

Then, long before you hear their shouts or see their outlines on the horizon, there suddenly appears along the uncertain line at which earth and sky meet a swarm of creatures which rush and cross each other in every direction. Whether the mass is near or far off it is impossible to say, since there are no objects to measure by. If far, all these black spots on the luminous background may be horns. To our inexperienced eye they give the illusion of a herd of oxen. Then suddenly the truth becomes manifest. You have before you some hundreds of hares, which will quickly be within gunshot. But the animal is sharp to discern the danger, and, in less time than it takes to write it, the troop that was heading in a mass straight for the line of fire melts away until only the foolish ones at the back are left to continue their course with the acquired momentum. In this way the carnage, which promised to be terrible, resolves itself into ten or twelve more or less lucky shots apiece. This is inevitable, since the wire fence which effectually stops horses and cattle is powerless against running game. The day when the destruction of the hare is decided upon, which is certainly desirable, it will only be necessary to fence in three sides of an enclosure and drive the game towards the opening. In the present state of affairs the mere sight of three or four hundred hares running straight towards the guns, even though they make a right-about turn just in time, is an entertainment much appreciated by Europeans.

Shooting *à la corde* has a different aspect. The mounted peons form up to make a line of beaters a hundred yards apart. But, unlike our own *battues*, the beater precedes the shooter, instead of walking towards him. The reason is that every peon is attached to his comrade to right and to left by a rope of twisted wires, which sweeps the ground and puts up every living creature to the guns, which follow behind at the pace of a horse's walk. The hare does not wait till the rope reaches him. Often he gets away out of reach. But there is such an abundance of game that none misses the animal that may escape. The important point is for the peons to keep well in line, else huntsmen and horsemen are likely to get a charge of lead. At the Eldorado, M. Villanueva's place, this happened twice or three times in the same day. The partridge (always flying singly) and the martinette are never weary of marking time. They run before one without haste, and apparently determined not to fly away.

It occasionally happens that a sportsman tires of his game and wants to end it. Several times I left the line of guns and ran upon the enemy, which, without any excitement, still kept its distance and never gave its pursuer the satisfaction of seeing it even hasten its step. You look around for a stone, a bit of wood, or a lump of earth, which should have the effect of driving off the creature. On the Pampas is neither pebble, nor stick, nor clod of earth. You have no resource but to swear and make violent gestures that have no effect at all. The martinette, too, has a way of glancing sideways at you which expresses a profound contempt for the entire human race. All generous minds are sensitive to rudeness and feel a just vexation when thus treated. The rapid chase is the more painful that you have very soon before you several martinettes and as many partridges which fly backwards and forwards, leaving you in doubt at which to point your weapon, while, at the same time, you know that in leaving the line of fire you expose yourself to all the guns which may be tempted, by fur or feather, to aim in your direction. There is only one way out of this critical situation that I know of. It is to fling your cap at the running bird. He will fly off then and keep his distance.

The victory would be yours afterwards were it not that the chase under a sun that would seem hot even in summer has left you out of breath. To take aim while struggling for breath is to risk missing the bird. Happily, both partridge and martinette have a straight, low, and heavy flight, which permits you to return to the *estancia* without dishonour. Such are the peripatetics of this amusing form of sport, in which, all along the line, firing is incessant. The steady walk of the guns is only checked by the rope getting caught occasionally on some tuft of grass, or by an encounter, not at all rare, with the carcass of horse or ox in process of decomposition. Having left on his own initiative, he at least escapes from man's ferocity. You pass without even having to hold your nose, so thoroughly does the strong, purifying air of the Pampas carry away in its boundless currents every germ that cannot be returned to the soil to perform the eternal labour of fertilisation. On all sides the last vestiges of clean and fretted bones tell us how lives now ended are taking on new forms of life, and in the gentle murmur of the grass that bends to the breeze the huge white skeletons that brave the blue of heaven have all the eloquence of philosophy in their tale of the supreme defeat of living matter beneath the irresistible triumph of fatality.

With no other break in the horizon but the distant *ombu*, a group of *paraisos*, a ranch, or travelling herd, the murderous band pursues its way. The walking is good, and the motor-car, which follows slowly in the rear, is at hand to pick up the weary sportsman. But before that point is reached one is tempted to cast off, little by little, articles of clothing which rapidly become a burden under the sun's rays. A shirt and trousers are already much. Even so, a rest becomes necessary, and those who have any acquaintance with M. Villanueva will guess that there was present a cart laden with refreshments. Halts like these, in the precious shade of the car, are not without charm, if you have taken the wise precaution to put on something warm. When the incidents of the day have been thoroughly discussed the chase is resumed, but if you are really done up do not imagine your fun is over. The auto will take your place in the line of march behind the rope of peons, and, apart from the game of running after martinettes, nothing is changed. The endless prairie is so truly a billiard-table of turf that not a jolt need be felt, and, after a few attempts, one gets the knack of firing from the car with a good average of successful shots. The hare suffers most; martinette and partridge get off more easily. It must be admitted that the experienced chauffeur is a powerful auxiliary. In any case, if you are shooting the less brilliant, the pleasure of sport in repose, varied by all sorts of unforeseen circumstances, more than compensates for the misses and lends a flavour to the sport that is lacking in European shooting parties.

Better still—the day is slowly dying: soon the party will break up, but the shooting will go on all the same. The silent peons come up to say good-night. Dumbly, with courteous gestures, final greetings are exchanged, and then the order is given to set the helm for Eldorado. But there is still light enough to see by. So here we are zigzagging across the Pampas in complicated turns and twists, as one spot or another appears more favourable for game. And the slaughter is terrific, for hares abound. Martinette and partridge, with their dark plumage, have nothing to fear from us now. In the faint light of the setting sun the hare makes still an admirable target, and plover and falcon offer supplementary diversions. The gay little owl alone finds grace with the guns. And when the "dark light" of the poet left us no resource but to shoot at each other, pity or perhaps fear of the last agony sufficed to make us hold our hand. The gentle horned beasts moved out of our way, fixing on us their stupidly soft eyes, and leaving us wholly remorseless, while in the freshening breeze and empty blackness of sky and land we burst in upon the lights of hospitable Eldorado.

This simple tale of a day's sport in the Pampas has no other merit than that of being strictly accurate. The Argentinos might very well content themselves with the pleasures they have ready to their hand at all seasons of the year, for in these regions, half-way between barbarism and civilisation, the gamekeeper is unknown. But man can never be content with what is offered to him. Therefore the wealthy *estanciero* takes infinite trouble to get thousands of pheasants sent out to him from our coverts, so that he may breed them in his preserves. In districts that are not menaced by the locusts the birds will be let loose shortly in the woods, and the Argentine will then pride herself on shooting such as that of Saint-Germain. It is because of this approaching change that I have set down these impressions of a day's sport in conditions which will soon belong to a vanished age.

CHAPTER X
ROSARIO AND TUCUMAN

The traveller with only a few weeks at his disposal in this immense country of overflowing activity cannot pretend to make a very profound and detailed study of it. I am here setting down only those things that I saw, but, at the same time, I endeavour to show their significance, and to give some idea of their social import, while leaving my readers to judge for themselves. It is, of course, the subjective method, and is full of pitfalls, but it is, also, useful inasmuch as it sheds much light on the subject if used with discrimination. My friend Jules Huret, who has been inspired to reveal to the criminally incurious French public certain countries which they persistently ignore, takes all the time he needs to collect a voluminous amount of material, which he then proceeds to place before his readers in accordance with the strictest canons of the objective method. We know how successful he was with North America and Germany. He has marshalled before us so orderly a procession of men and things, that to my mind he has defeated his object, and left us no inducement to undertake the journey for ourselves and to obtain first-hand impressions by the direct contact which is worth all the books in the world. Huret is now publishing in the *Figaro* the result of a year's close study of the Argentine. He has taught and will still teach me much, no doubt, and I strongly recommend every one to read his admirable work. But in their way I still venture to claim for my unpretentious notes the virtue of creating in my readers a desire for further information, for the simple reason that they will assuredly want to test my views in the light of their own experience. Humanity, nowadays, is moving at high speed, and the chief interest that most men attach to each day's events is the opportunities they may afford for to-morrow's energy. But the real value of the "event of the moment," to which the Press attributes more and more importance, lies in the revelation it may bring of those general laws that we must all understand. Hence the living appeal made by cursory reflections, irrespective of what may be the verdict of the future thereupon, since our "truths" of to-day can never be more than successive eliminations of errors.

These generalities are intended to explain the spirit in which I prepared to leave Buenos Ayres, and drew up an itinerary that was necessarily curtailed by the limited time that remained to me. I had been told: "At Cordoba you will find a city of monks; Mendoza affords a charming picture of fine watercourses lined with poplars, vines in profusion, and a remarkable equipment for the wine industry; at Tucuman, there are fields of sugar-cane with dependent refineries and, also, the beginnings of an extensive forest." With irrigation-works, poplars, vines, monks even, I was already familiar: so without hesitation I headed for Tucuman, with a brief halt at Rosario, the second city of the Argentine Republic.

In its external aspect Rosario de Santa Fé differs but little from Buenos Ayres. There is the same florid architecture, the same desire to do things on a large scale, the same busy spirit, though naturally on a smaller scale. Rosario exists by reason of its port, which commands the Parana. The prodigious extension of the town is due to the building of numerous railway lines, which have produced an enormous development of agriculture in the provinces of Santa Fé, Cordoba, and Santiago del Estero. The cereals grown in these provinces, representing one half the total exported by the Argentine, are carried by these railways, whilst the Parana furnishes a waterway several thousands of kilometres in length for coasting vessels on the upper river and from Paraguay as far as the mouth of the Rio. A volume might be written of its docks, built by a French firm under the management of M. Flandrin, a compatriot and native of my own Vendean village. There is a peculiar charm about meetings of the sort. A journey of many days has brought you to the unknown land, where, with the help of some imagination, any strange event is possible. After sundry adventures, the curtain rises, and the first face that meets your eye, the first voice you hear, belong to your native place. Names, scenes, and memories rush in upon the mind with a train of unexpected impressions and emotions.

To think I had come all this way to be confronted with that special spot of earth to which through all travels and all life's changes we remain so firmly bound! Far away in the distant Brazilian mountains, I met a charming Vendean woman, whose tongue had kept that accent of the *langue d'oil* which belonged to Rabelais. When Sancho, from the height of his waggon, beheld the earth no larger than a grain of millet, his sense of proportion was truer than ours. Only, instead of being so many hazel-nuts upon the millet, as Sancho thought, men are, in reality, merely imperceptible particles in a restricted space, bound to collide at the least movement.

My philosophy did not prevent my feeling great pleasure at meeting M. Flandrin, who is as unpretentious as he is kind, and who is a credit to his native land. We made a tour of inspection of the docks, and the inevitable trip by boat round the harbour. All I can say of the port thus hastily seen and already described in many technical publications is that, in spite of tremendous natural difficulties, it has been satisfactorily accomplished, thanks to the tenacity of the engineers and the admirable method adopted. [29] Moored alongside the quays were a number of English and German cargo-boats (amongst which, I saw but one French, alas!) taking in grain at the rate of 800 tons per hour. The docks were begun in 1902. They were designed to cope with an average tonnage of 2,500,000, and it was at that time believed impossible to attain that figure before some thirty years at least. By 1909, however, it had been reached and passed, and a contract for their enlargement was immediately given to a French firm. Under these conditions, it is easy to understand how a town numbering 23,000 inhabitants in 1869 should, in 1910, contain nearly 200,000. This, also, explains a rivalry that exists between the second city of the Republic and Santa Fé, the historic capital of the province. Rosario complains, with some show of reason, that the enormous fiscal contribution paid by her to the national exchequer does not procure for her the advantages to which her population entitles her. The deplorable deficiency of schools in Rosario is more especially a subject of loud recrimination. I cannot but think that this claim will be before long admitted. As for the æsthetic future of the city, I can say nothing. When I saw it, it was disfigured in every direction by extensive road-making operations, thanks to which there will, in all probability, be open spaces enough, one day, to arouse the admiration of visitors. An excellent and modern hotel seems a good augury for the future. As usual, the welcome I received far exceeded anything I could have expected. But the municipal improvements scheme had occasioned a fever of speculation in land values, and the one subject of conversation was the fabulous fortunes to be realised in this way—so much so, indeed, that I was strongly tempted to spend a few *sous* on a plot of land which by now or a little later perhaps might be worth a hundred millions.

If Rosario has made a fortune out of the incredible increase of its corn harvests, it must not be supposed that cattle-rearing is neglected in the province of Santa Fé. By a fortunate coincidence, I arrived on the day of the opening of the great annual Cattle Show. The President of the Agricultural Society happens to be one of the most distinguished politicians, not only of the province but of the Republic, and, by his kindness, I was able to glean much information on general topics, and, at the same time, inspect some samples of agricultural produce that would not have been out of place in the first of our European shows. The surrounding provinces, including that of Buenos Ayres, had sent up some of their finest specimens of horses and horned cattle. As usual, there was a superabundance of British breeds to be seen; but our Norman horses were well represented, too. To tell the truth, the dual capacity of my guide, who was no less eminent as statesman than as cattle-breeder, caused politics to somewhat overshadow agriculture in our talk, and I found out that Señor Lisenadro de la Torre was the leader of a party that is aiming at the overthrow of the Cabinet now in power, whose majority, he informed me, was based on those very administrative abuses that I had already noted. The tendency is to use and even abuse authority to coerce the electors, who are unorganised for the defence of the public interests against private ambitions, [30] "an evil that spreads terror," as may truly be said, and one of which Rosario does not hold a monopoly. On this theme the clear-headed politician, with his concise manner of speech and decided tones, gave me a rapid sketch of the situation by a brief examination of the enemy's country. And I rejoiced to see that abuses common, more or less, in all old countries, and whose remedy lies only in private endeavour, have in this new community of the Argentine provoked the same keen intelligence and determination as others which I noted. Under whatever form of government, the worth of a country lies in its men —that is, in its sum total of disinterested activity. A race that can show the development of intelligence and character that have so struck me in the course of this journey can afford to await with tranquil courage the solutions of the future.

As it is my desire to leave no dark corners unexplored, I must make a reference to the strange hints of revolution that I heard at Rosario and, later, at Tucuman. "A certain military leader would be displeased if full satisfaction were not given him. There was every reason to fear a movement. Dispatches from the Government recommended a careful guard over rifle magazines," etc. I was, however, pretty soon convinced that all these rumours were but the expiring echo of a bygone condition with very little foundation in actual fact.

Here in Rosario we are not far removed from the life of Buenos Ayres. To-day the distance from one city to the other (300 kilometres) can be covered in five hours. The last part of the journey, which terminates at Tucuman (1100 kilometres from the capital), gives us the impression of a complete change of country. At daybreak, in full sunshine, the first discovery I made was that we were travelling through a cloud of dust that entirely concealed the landscape. With a kindness for which I can never be sufficiently grateful the President of the Republic, Señor Figueroa Alcorta, had lent me his own coach for the journey. I slept in an excellent bed, with windows carefully closed and blinds drawn. But the Argentine dust knows no obstacles. For this reason the prophecy in the Book that we shall all return to dust seems to me already fulfilled. My beautiful bedroom, my luxurious dressing-room, with its welcome douche, my clothes, my luggage, and my person, all were wrapped in a thick veil of fine red dust, ugly in appearance and dangerous to respiration. Yes, while I was sleeping in all confidence, the imperious dust had taken possession of train, passengers, and all that was visible to their dust-filled eyes. The stations: merely a stack of red dust; man: a vermilion-coloured walking pillar; the horseman, or vehicle: a whirlwind of dust. Horror! to my wrath a beautiful white shirt was discovered blushing rosy as a young girl surprised. I washed with red soap and dried with red towels my carmine-coloured face. Here is the explanation of the complexion of the Indian!

Tucuman is in sight—Tucuman, the land of Cacombo, the faithful servant of Candide. None can have forgotten that the Governor of Buenos Ayres, moved by the beauty of the lovely Cunégonde, was on the point of despatching Candide when he was saved by Cacombo. But what follows marks the difference between Candide's times and our own, for Candide and Cacombo in their flight paused in "a beautiful meadow traversed by streams of water," where befell the double adventure of the monkeys and the mumps, whereas for us meadow, rivulets, monkeys, and mumps all resolve themselves into universal dust. I strain my eyes to discern some features of the country: a dismantled forest is dying in the dust; some lean cattle are grazing, on clay apparently; enormous cactuses, like trees; flocks of small white birds with pink beaks, known as "widows" (*viudas*); and, from time to time, the beauty of a flight of cackling parrots, making in the sunlight flashes of emerald in the dusty air.

The *Marseillaise*! the Tricolor! the Governor, the French colony!—this is Tucuman's reception of me. Handshakes, salutes, welcoming words with affectionate references to the distant fatherland. An admirable official motor-car, but execrable roads where the best of *pneus* finds so many obstacles to jump that it becomes quite dizzy, as is shown by its continued stagger.

The first impression given by Tucuman after the jolting and shaking of the road is that of a colonial land. Everywhere the "half-house," hastily put up, but rendered charming by its *patio*, and comfortable by the disposition of its rooms to take advantage of the shade. The Indian half-caste is king in Tucuman, "the Garden of the Republic," whose women, they say, are more beautiful than flowers. Everywhere, in fact, one sees bronzed faces in which two impassive black eyes shine with the brilliance of the diamond. A long, lingering glance which says, I know not what, but something that is totally un-European. Simplicity, dignity, with few words, slow gestures, an imposing harmony of bearing. I know not whether one day the dominant race will succeed in modifying or effacing the native traits. At present, nothing seems to touch the indelible imprint of American blood. A few of the women are very handsome. The French colony in Tucuman is larger than I thought. I shall see it when I return from Santa Ana, where I am going to visit M. Hilleret's manor. As we pass, I notice broad avenues well laid out: the Place de l'Indépendance, on which there stands the statue of General Belgrano, in remembrance of the battle of Tucuman (1812), and the new palace of the Governor, which is impressive. From sixty to eighty thousand inhabitants. The town very commercial. The country broken, with high mountains. Fertile plain suitable for growing sugar-cane, tobacco, oranges, and the most beautiful flowers. Large and noble forests that are being ruthlessly devastated to supply fuel for factory furnaces. Uninterrupted cane-raising all the way to Santa Ana, where M. Hilleret, who came to the Argentine as a labourer on the railway, set up a sugar factory, [31] thanks to which—and to Protection—he was able, at his death, to leave a fortune of a hundred millions. We were magnificently received in a hospitable mansion that betrayed the taste of a Parisian architect. [32] A park and garden bearing traces of a recent attack from locusts. Specially beautiful were the tufts of bamboo, and the false cotton plants with their big balls of white down, amid which a tiny grey dove cooed softly like a wailing child.

What can I say of the factory that has not already been said? It is admirably managed. The cane is automatically flung on a slope down which it drops beneath heavy rollers. Two thousand workmen are employed, half-castes for the most part—a few are pure Indians,—and a small number of French foremen. There is a picturesque scene in the town of a morning, when troops of women, old and young, followed by a procession of children, come to market and fill their wooden or earthenware bowls with provisions, balancing them on their heads; their parti-coloured rags, gaily patched, add a piquant touch to the faces, whose firm lines seem set in bronze, all vitality and expression being concentrated in the dark fire of their eyes. The workmen's quarters are indescribable slums. On both sides of a wide avenue there are rows of tiny low houses from which the most rudimentary notions of hygiene or of comfort are, apparently, carefully banished—dens rather than dwellings, to speak accurately, so destitute are they of furniture. Women and old men sit immovable in the dust, the *bombilla* between their lips, in an ecstasy of *maté*. Children moving about on all fours are scarcely distinguishable from the little pigs which are grubbing in the rubbish-heaps. Ineffable smells issue from boiling cauldrons and stewpans, whilst in the darkness of the doorway the nobly draped figure of the guardian of the hearth stands, speechless and motionless, surveying the scene. According to European ideas, these folk are wretched indeed. Yet the climate renders existence easy and they appear to find quiet pleasure in it. We may be permitted to imagine for them a happier future and higher stage of civilisation, which they will achieve when they draw a larger share of remuneration from the monument of labour their hands have helped to put up. Laws for the protection of labour are unknown in the Argentine, which is explained by the backwardness of industry there. Although life beneath this beautiful sky must undoubtedly offer many conveniences, and although the mill-owners whom I met seemed to me both humanely and generously inclined, factories such as those I visited can scarcely exist much longer without the labour question being brought before the legislators. Members of Parliament with whom I discussed the point appeared favourably disposed, though inclined to defer remedies indefinitely.

The fields of sugar-cane can be visited without fatigue by train. We passed teams of six or nine mules—up to their knees in dust—on their way to the factory with loads of cane grown at a distance from the railway. The drivers, sitting postilion-wise on their leaders, raised their whips with threatening cries that made the lash unnecessary. But who could have imagined that it took so much dust to manufacture sugar! Out in the fields the peons, armed with the long knife that is always stuck in the back of their belts, cut the cane and with two dexterous turns of the blade divide it into lengths for the presses, leaving the foliage and part of the stalk for the cattle. At the wayside station there were five or six dilapidated cabins, in which the numerous progeny of the cane-cutters seemed to be thriving. In appearance they formed a temporary encampment, nothing more. The huts are made out of odds and ends picked up at haphazard, and follow a simple principle of architecture which requires a space of some twenty or thirty centimetres between the floor and the palisade—for it can scarcely be called a wall—to insure a circulation of air. Thus, one could, at a pinch, sleep in the place without arousing the smallest envy in the four-footed beasts that are happily slumbering under the starry heavens. Children, pigs, and donkeys live together in friendly promiscuity. Women, bearing in their arms their latest-born, appear on their threshold dumbfounded, apparently, at the sight of strangers. In my own language, I ask one of them for permission to glance at the interior of her hut. She stands aside, and I look in, not venturing more than a single step. The only attempt at furniture is planks laid across trestles, with rags of clothing (incredibly dirty) doing duty for mattress or blanket. A movable stove adapted to open-air cooking, and four stakes in the earth, on which are laid bits of anything that comes handy, with tree trunks for seats—this constitutes a rough-and-ready dining-room. Scattered about on the ground are different utensils for the use of man and beast. Then a commotion. A naked baby, who is sucking a sugar-cane, suddenly sees its treasure carried off by a lively little black pig. A fight and loud screams. Biped and quadruped come to blows, and the effect of excitement on the dormant functions of infant life is such that it is the child who succeeds in worsting the pig. The latter noisily protests. Then, there being no such thing as Justice on earth, it is the child who is carried off and set on the heap of rags whose odorous dampness will at nightfall soothe its sleep.

M. Edmond Hilleret, the eldest son of the founder of the factory of Santa Ana, had invited us to a tapir-hunt. To camp out in the forest for three days did not in the least daunt us, but a member of the Society for the Protection of Animals having urged upon me the shamefulness of letting dogs loose upon so inoffensive a beast, and Providence, with the same intention probably, having smitten our hunter-in-chief with appendicitis, followed by an operation, our shooting was directed humbly against the parrots. I speak for my companions; as for my own part, I announced the most pacific intentions towards the birds of the forest.

Peons on horseback and light carts start off in an ocean of dust. The only way is to get in front of the procession and leave to your friends the duty of swallowing your dust. As a lack of altruism on the part of my comrades had inflicted this experience on me as we went, I took care to return the compliment on the way back. The forest, which belongs to the factory, is generally denominated "virgin" for the sake of effect. But my regard for truth compels me to state that it was not even *demi-vierge*, for there are herds grazing in the clearings, peons keeping watch, and woodcutters and colonists unceasingly busy dragging away its veils with a brutality that is never slaked. Such as it is, however, with its inextricable wildnesses, through which only the axe can clear a way, with its tall, flowering groves, its ancient trees covered with a luxuriant parasite growth that flings downwards to earth and upwards to heaven its showers of lovely colour, it is marvellously beautiful. The wonder of it is this haze of parasites, so varied in species, in colour, and in growth, with their invincible determination to live at all costs, which wrap the giant tree from root to highest twig in a monstrous profusion of new forms of life. The dead branch on which we trample has preserved, even in decomposition, the frail yet tenacious creeper whose blossoms had crowned it high aloft. The tree is no longer a tree: it is a Laocoön twisted in a fury of rage beneath the onslaught of an ocean of lives whose torrents recognise no barriers. Whichever way one looks, hairy monsters are agonising in despairing contortions, victims of a drama of dumb violence; and the spectacle conveys a keen realisation of the eternal struggle for life that is going on all around us, from the summits of these verdant heights to the subterranean depths whence issues this living force. And, as episodes in the universal tragedy, the brilliant colouring of lovely birds lights up the gloomy enchantment of the silent tumult of anguished lives whose effort after mastery can only end in death. Having not yet learnt to know man's baseness, the royal magpies of Paraguay, with their startling plumage, pause on the branches close beside our path to gaze on us in, perhaps, the same astonishment as we on them. But already in the great clearing shots resound, betokening the salute of the first arrivals to the denizens of the forest. Now, my parrot friends, make for the fields as fast as you can, out of reach of the horde of enemies!

But it is precisely these clearings that the parrot loves, for here he, like us, can satisfy his appetite. When his tribe descends upon an orchard, good-bye to the fruit harvest. We were in a vast clearing, inhabited by a small colony of farmers, whose huts are built along a rivulet on the slope of a meadow. Here are fields of maize covered with dead stalks. The cattle wander freely where they will. In an orchard stands an orange-tree, the tallest I have seen, full of golden balls. Hard by a well, on a wooden post, there sits a green parrot, with red poll, his plumage ruffled, his eye full of contempt for the human race. Attracted by the noise, two women come out from a dark hut. Gossips probably, though what they can find to talk about in such a spot it would be hard to guess. One of them attracts attention by the beauty of her form, the nobility of her pose, and the warm, coppery tint of her face. She is a Creole equally removed from the two races. Her thick hair, intensely black, falls in a plait upon her shoulders. Instinctively she has twisted pink ribbon—found, probably, in a box of biscuits—in her hair, where it makes a line of light in the night of her tresses. Erect in the simplicity of the semi-savage, without a word, without the least acknowledgment of our presence, and without a trace of embarrassment or affectation, she stands looking at us, desiring, apparently, no better occupation. Her features are regular and delicate, according to the canons of European æsthetics. Two or three pock-marks make a startling patch. All the soul of the native race is visible in the dark light of her eyes, heavy with feelings that belong to an epoch too primitive to be comprehended, even dimly, by our aged and vulgar civilisation. That surprising pink ribbon and the shyness—like remorse for some unknown crime—expressed through the ingenuous and compelling eyes, are probably the secret of her charm. Whatever it springs from, the effect is the same. Whether girl or woman it would be hard to tell. This uncertainty often gives its brilliance to feminine power.

I tear myself from contemplation of the lady and wander into the forest in the wake of the chattering birds, carrying with me, by way of viaticum, an orange whose freshness and perfume have left me a souvenir no less delicious than that of the charm of the young beauty. I was slowly returning to the glaring sunshine of the clearing, absorbed in admiration of a flight of bright-plumaged parrots, when a vexatious gunshot brought me back to the realities of our sinful race. One of our party had concealed himself among the brushwood at the foot of the tree in which the birds were holding their parliament. The danger of the institution was instantly apparent, for five birds fell to the murderous lead. I still hold with parliaments, however, and with parrots which debate in the branches. I know not what they find to talk about, but, judged by the criterion of noise adopted at home, it must be of great importance. When we teach them to speak our language, I am aware they utter the words but attach no meaning to them. I have known humans to do the same without the birds' excuse. Moreover, a very remarkable trait in the parrot's character is that he is altruistic in the last degree, and will face any danger to assist a friend in distress by voice and gesture. When one is wounded, the rest, who have at first flown off in alarm, return with loud cries to the scene, abusing the sportsman and calling on deaf gods for justice. If further volleys make fresh victims, the flock will not give up its work of pity, thus exposing themselves to further slaughter.

All this is to explain how it was that, on my return to the place I started from, I saw on the ground a beautiful green parrot with a crimson head, lying now in the stillness of death, while two or three of his friends limped and fluttered round him, hurling maledictions at the human race. I fear they all figured later on the supper-table of the colony. The young woman with the pink ribbon, for whom the scene probably offered nothing new, stood and gazed at us as if we were the curiosity of the moment. One of the wounded birds had climbed a stump beside her, and, without any preliminaries, had nestled up against her like a child. The woman took no notice. Her questioning eyes seemed to be seeking forms in which to clothe her thoughts, but her tongue could give no assistance. I, too, would have liked to speak to her, to learn something of her story, of her notions about the world, and the ideas that influenced her actions. But I knew of no signs in which to clothe such questions, and not a word of either Spanish or *Guarani* (the name of a small tribe now applied to the relics of their language, which is that of the natives). With a rhythmic walk she returned to her hut, emerging once more to join our circle, with a tiny grey parrot perched on her shoulder, by way, perhaps, of a conversational opening. The bird, fluttering its wings, stepped down as far as her fingers, which were slim and coloured as though with henna, and I ventured to tease him. The long, red hand came slowly forward, accompanying the movements of the bird, without a shadow of a smile on her impassive face; and so, the time for our departure having come, we parted for ever with all our questions unasked.

On the following day we drove to the *Salto*, another clearing in the forest, enlivened by a waterfall. We fired at some hawks that we took for eagles. Large blue birds flew mocking above our heads, and our hunters ended by shooting at imaginary fish. They thought a walk in the forest absurd, so whilst I and two comrades ventured a little way, they chose the most natural occupation in the world for men who have come from the ends of the earth to see an almost virgin forest, and made up a game of poker. Oh, the joys of modern travelling, undreamed of by the early explorers!

Meantime, I wandered straight before me through the woods, at the risk of losing my way. Once I thought I was going to know the pleasures, which are not unmixed, of being hopelessly lost. Already I saw myself reduced to the necessity of hunting for an *ornero's* nest, the opening of which is always in the north side; but one of the party pointed out a line of bluish-grey lichen on every tree-trunk, which indicated clearly, without the help of the birds, from which direction blows the north—naturally the warm—wind. Finally, by way of putting a finishing touch to my education, he assumed that I was thirsty, and leading me to a creeper growing parasitically on a large branch at the height of a man above the ground, he dexterously inserted his knife into the joint of the leaves, and there burst forth a jet of water slightly aromatic in taste, like the fine juice of some grass. The traveller's sherbet! A few minutes later we came upon a peon mounted on his mule, who, more surely than either bird or lichen, set us on the right path.

The first sugar factory founded by M. Hilleret was at Lulès. There we found a fine forest, wilder still than that of Santa Ana, with gorgeous great trees bearing bouquets of flowers, some white, some pale violet, and some pink. Fine gardens, and a park where, under the management of a French gardener, every fruit-tree of the subtropical zone may be found, from the banana and coffee-plant to the mango and *chirimaya*, beside a thousand other strangely named growths better calculated to surprise the eyes than charm the palate. Of an evening there was dancing in the garden. Though national in character, dancing here is much what it is elsewhere, since there is but one way to move the arms and legs. The most striking part of the picture was the attitude of the dancers when resting. In our countries these assemblies of young people would have been the excuse for jokes and laughter, often, probably, carried to a riotous excess. Here the immovable gravity of the native does not lend itself to merriment. Young men and young women exchange, now and then, a few words uttered in a low voice with the utmost composure. On the invitation of her partner, the young girl rises in exactly the same way that she would move to perform some household duty, and goes through the rites of the dance with its rhythmic measures without the vestige of a smile or a ripple of gaiety on her expressionless face. It is not, however, for lack of enjoyment, for no opportunity is missed of dancing, and the balls are prolonged indefinitely into the night. We must only see in this deportment a conception of dignity and of conduct that is not our own.

On my return to Tucuman a great reception was given by the French colony in my honour. I went to call—as, indeed, it behoved me—at the House of Independence, more modest but no less glorious than that of Philadelphia. It was here that the first national Congress was held, and here that the Oath of Independence was taken (July 9, 1816). In order to preserve the humble house, now an object of public veneration, it has been built into a large edifice, which will preserve it from decay in the future. There is no decoration—some commemorative tablets only—but it is enough. When the heart responds readily to the call of duty, an unobtrusive reminder is all that is necessary.

I was infinitely touched by the grandiose reception given me by the French colony. In a fine theatre, which is their own property, the Frenchmen of Tucuman extended the warmest of welcomes to their fellow-countryman. I found a surprise in store for me. It was arranged that I should lay the foundation-stone of the new French school of Tucuman, and, if I am to believe the inscription on the silver trowel that remains in my possession, given me for the purpose of spreading the cement, the school will bear the name of him who was thus its first mason. This honour, which is wholly unmerited, sprang, of course, from the natural longing to attach themselves in any way to France. Not a word was spoken that was not an invocation of our country, of its fight against ignorance, source of all human woes. There was a numerous and fashionable company present, whose large befeathered hats proved that Tucuman is not so very far from Paris after all. The ceremony was concluded by a pretty march-past of small boys and girls carrying the Argentine and French flags, and singing the national hymn, the *Marseillaise*. The little people put a world of spirit into their song. One little girl, about two feet high and gaily beribboned, was very determined to vanquish "tyranny." How congratulate her? I tried to express the very sincere pleasure the scene had given me, and remarked that these little Argentine tongues had a slightly Argentine accent in the *Marseillaise*.

"That is not surprising," said their proud master. "They do not know a word of French."

Then what about that charming baby's loudly expressed hatred of tyranny? It is true the significance of the hymn lies rather in the music than in its phraseology, now a century old. Children, begin by learning French, and do not wait for the opening of the school whose first stone I have just laid. All things shall be added unto you.

CHAPTER XI
URUGUAY AND URUGUAYANS

Montevideo, at first sight, had given me so favourable an impression that I was anxious not to lose an opportunity of seeing more of it. But I had begun with the Argentine, and in such a country the more you see the more you want to see. I tore myself away from it with great regret, conscious that I was leaving much undone. Time had passed all too quickly. I had now only three weeks left for Brazil, where long months ought, rather, to be spent. Small as it is, Uruguay is for many reasons one of the most interesting of the South American republics. How far could a few days be made to go there? In its general features the country is not very different from the Argentine Pampas. There are the same alluvial soil, the same *estancias*, the same system of agriculture and cattle rearing. For me the principal interest lay in the Uruguay character. Three visits of one day each furnished me with an occasion to converse with some of their most distinguished statesmen, but is this sufficient ground on which to form an opinion of a race whose superabundant activity is directed towards every department of knowledge, as of labour, now the first essential in any civilisation? I do not pretend that it is. Still, I consider that even a brief investigation, if perfectly disinterested and unprejudiced, can and should furnish elements of sound information that are not to be despised. But perhaps I shall be excused if, instead of making affirmations that are open to challenge, I give myself the pleasure of dwelling on the splendid qualities of these courageous and modest men who are engaged in building up a social structure that is worthy of all our admiration.

Uruguay, once the "Oriental Band" of the Argentine, lies between that Republic and Brazil, forming thus a buffer State which, in the event of war between Rio de Janeiro and Buenos Ayres (which the gods forfend!), would make it somewhat difficult for the two hostile armies to get at each other. If for this reason alone, I am disposed to think the constitution of an independent State between the River Uruguay and the sea a very wise provision. I am aware, however, that peace between the Argentine, Brazil, and Chile is the accepted maxim of South American foreign policy; and it is very sound doctrine, the triple hegemony offering a fairly solid guarantee against usurpation by one. Notwithstanding its diminutive size, as compared with its gigantic neighbours, Uruguay appears well fitted morally to fulfil the conditions of an independent State. There is a marked development of national spirit among its population, whose most striking feature is a mental activity that is sometimes carried to excess. Brazil has laid out immense sums of money in the purchase of *Dreadnoughts* (not always perfect), and the Argentine felt, consequently, in duty bound to burden herself also with some of these sea monsters. Against whom are the Argentine and Brazil thus arming? They would both find it hard to say, since they have plenty to do at home without directing their creative energy in European fashion to the business of destruction, unless absolutely forced thereto. Let me tell them that it is but vain bravado that has urged them on the dangerous, downward path of armament. Where will they stop? When you have a population as large in proportion as that of the United States, it will be time enough, alas! to claim your share in the great international concert of extermination. Begin by giving life, oh, happy folk, who have been robbed by none and who have nothing to recover!

I have already spoken of the appearance of Montevideo. A broad bay, commanding the entrance of the Rio de la Plata, magnificently situated for a commercial port, the Government has not overlooked its advantages. In 1901 tenders were invited, and a French syndicate was granted the contract for the construction of the docks. There are important quarries in all parts of Uruguay, which is more favoured than the Argentine in this respect; and the builders found all the stone they needed close to hand. The colossal work is now nearly ended. In 1909 two of our armoured cruisers, the *Gloire* and the *Marseillaise,* visited the port of Montevideo. The comfortable boats of the Mihanowitch Company, which run daily between Buenos Ayres and Montevideo, moor alongside the quays. Why the large European vessels should be forced to remain outside in the roads is a puzzle; the only explanation seems to be a quarrel between the different governing bodies, to which, I trust, the Uruguay Government will speedily put an end. As things are, the building of the docks is but a sorry farce, and the more regrettable because one of the features of the handsome harbour is a simplification of the harbour dues, which entails the least delay on the vessels calling there. [33] M. Sillard, who has been in charge of the works from the beginning, took us to various places on the bay; and, in his motor-car, we climbed half-way up the famous Cerro, so that we might have the pleasure of walking a short distance over a road now under construction, which was spoilt for us by the disagreeable *saladeros*. [34] If I may say so without hurting the feelings of my friends, the Cerro fort is not, I believe, impregnable. Its demolition has, it is said, been decided upon. If an hotel or casino were built on its site, the Montevideans would have a pleasant object for excursion, for from the top of the hill there is a grand view over the town and estuary to the ocean and the River Uruguay.

The Lieutenant of the city—an American of European education, with five years spent in the Diplomatic Service at Rome behind him—kindly offered to do the honours of the town for us. Under the guidance of M. Daniel Muñoz, [35] who is as well known at Buenos Ayres as at Montevideo, we saw every part of his domain, from the business quarter to the luxurious suburban villas, the well-planted public squares, and large parks that are growing rapidly, to say nothing of a handsome promenade along the sea-front, and the unpleasant smelling *saladeros* of some of the environs.

A short halt at the Prefect's private house gave us an opportunity of judging of the comfort and luxury of the big Montevidean dwellings. As for the city itself, there is little to remark beyond the curious contrast offered by the tall, handsome, modern buildings and the singular little "colonial houses" so popular in Montevideo, which look as if some sprite had cut them off short at the first story for the fun of whisking the rest out of sight. As the town of Montevideo can boast, and must obviously preserve, the aspects of the capital city, these over-ornamented "half-houses" and the clumps of green trees scattered everywhere lend it a youthful charm which I hope it will not soon lose. As a matter of fact, these houses are charming in effect—in the eyes, at least, of those who do not walk about with their heads too high in the air—a pose that is not to be recommended. They not only constitute a very agreeable *façade*, taken all together, but their *patio* is so designed as to be admirably adapted to the special needs of the climate. If I were going to live in Montevideo, it would certainly be in one of these little houses. They have another virtue also, since they illustrate the necessity of experiment in building before one is committed to the settled plan. If the Town Council insists on constructing houses of several stories in some of the avenues, the measure may have its justification in the interest of the æsthetic and the useful. But before they trouble about the effect which their streets may produce as photographs, the Montevideans will, I hope, devote attention to comfort. Let the town spread freely, since there is plenty of space available. Is it not the curse of all our large European cities to be cramped and confined? New York, between two arms of the sea, has been obliged to invent its hideous "skyscrapers." One must encourage expansion to get all the air and light necessary to health. The population of Montevideo must be nearly a million now. [36] It has many a fine beach on its coast. A rich vegetation exists in all parts. Let no childish vanity induce it to attempt too soon to vie with Europe! Its friends can wish it nothing better.

I have said nothing of the public buildings, because they are everywhere the same, except, perhaps, in those European countries where the masses have taken possession of the palaces of their former masters. To me they were less interesting than their inmates—that is, the members of the Government. Of the three Presidents who did me the honour to receive me in the course of my journey, each has now, in the normal course of events, yielded his place to a successor. Señor Williman, who left the presidential chair on the 1st of March, had the keenest possible sense of his responsibility to his country. He was the son of an Americanised Alsatian, and seems to have imported into his exercise of authority that valuable quality of well-reasoned idealism which has made his race one of the most precious constituent parts of the French nation. It must not be forgotten that an American President is first and foremost a man of action, exactly the reverse of the chief of the State in our European democracies; and a turbulent Opposition, ever ready to rush to extremes, makes the task of government every day more difficult. Señor Williman gave me the impression of being somewhat reserved, but the genuinely democratic simplicity of his welcome and the slow gravity of his speech betokened a man whose convictions would be deliberate but profound. We touched on the political questions now engrossing Europe, and I found he had long been familiar with all the problems that are keeping us so busy.

It is not easy for me to give a personal opinion about the parliamentary world. The Senate organised a friendly reception in my honour at which we exchanged cordial toasts. But what can a Frenchman do when he knows not a word of Spanish, unless his Spanish hosts can speak French? There were only two or three members of Senate or Chamber with whom I could talk.

Smiles and gestures of good-will, as we clinked our glasses of champagne, were all that was left to us. The eyes asked questions that could be but imperfectly answered. Amongst graver politicians were many young men eager for reforms. One of the "youngsters"—in this fortunate land even the senators are scarcely out of their teens—observed to me, with gently emphasised irony, that Uruguay had travelled farther along the road marked out by the French Revolution than our own present Republic.

"The pain of death has been abolished in Uruguay. It has been retained by the Argentine and...."

"And in France, I acknowledge. We are, moreover, confronted with a strong retrogressive movement in favour of the right of society to take life."

"We have divorce by mutual consent. The Argentine has nothing even approaching it. The question of divorce has been raised there. The influence of the clergy prevented all discussion. As for the French Republic...."

"We have still retained the traditional system," I confess.

"And then our code grants the same rights to the illegitimate child, when recognised, as to those born in wedlock—this is common equity."

"I do not deny it. But the prejudice that exists in our public mind on this subject appears to me so deeply rooted that, without venturing on risky predictions, I think we shall not obtain the solution of the problem that your democracy has accepted without encountering the keenest resistance."

None will be surprised to hear that the conversation drifted quickly towards the Uruguay revolutions. Here the thread of our talk was picked up by a young journalist—a Deputy—who has spent a long time in Paris and is generally considered to be a coming man. In witty and picturesque language, he explained that Uruguay's revolutions had no more importance than a fit of hysterics. One is Red; another is White. A tie or a bit of stuff sewn on the hat serves as a badge. [37] The cradle supplies the bit of stuff; in a moment of popular excitement it is adopted, and becomes at once a point of honour. Then some little thing happens which, for one reason or another, leads to a heated discussion, and immediately there follows a general conflagration. The only fixed idea left in you is that you are a Red and the Whites must be exterminated, or *vice versa*, according to the camp in which you may be enrolled. There is nothing for it, then, but to let the effervescence escape.

But when I remarked that the life of a man counted for nothing when Uruguayan effervescence was escaping, the ready assent they gave me showed that on this point no discussion was possible.

"But I understood you had abolished the death sentence."

"It is legally abolished, but illegally...."

"Just so. Modern law, but ancient—very ancient—practice."

As may have been noticed, there is a general tendency towards comparisons—I ought, perhaps, rather to call it jealousy—of the relative progress in Argentine and Uruguay. The "Oriental Band" is, in Buenos Ayres, talked of with affectionate good nature, as if it were a sulky member of the family. You cannot praise Uruguay without winning universal approval, accompanied by a smiling reserve that seems to say, "The Orientals are worthy to be Argentinos." At Montevideo you are more likely to be asked frankly which country you consider foremost; and if you reply that you are quite incompetent to judge, be sure that your answer will be interpreted according to the inclination of the party interested. This often happened to me—annoyingly enough. Every nation has its strong and weak points, which must be judged according to the form they take and the times in which we are moving. I certainly did not go to the South Americans for a classification of the different States of Europe. Why should I have been expected to draw up a scale of civilisation for them? The Argentine, Uruguay, and Brazil are, each in their way, grand social structures, having their defects, like the countries of Europe. I am telling what I saw, leaving to all the liberty of replying that I was mistaken in what I saw. That is sufficient. But one of the best ways of moving ahead of one's fellows is to acquire the capacity of self-judgment and self-reformation.

Amongst so many kindly hosts I may pick out the youthful Minister of Foreign Affairs, Señor Emilio Barbatoux, whose polished Parisianism made him the mark for all the questions dictated by my ignorance. With unwearying courtesy the statesman, who is perfectly conversant with the French point of view, succeeded in adapting himself to my particular line of vision, and greatly facilitated the too superficial examination I was making by the clearness of his information.

I was invited to a very French dinner at the Uruguay Club, where I found the greatest comfort combined with Franco-American luxury; and I was able to study at my ease the pure Latinity of the Uruguay politician. If I had foreseen these "Travel Notes" I should have jotted down on paper some of the speeches to which I listened on my travels, when French culture was eulogised in the highest terms by the natives of these countries, whose future is of such interest to us. It was not till I had left it all behind me that I became conscious of the omission. I can only say that in the Uruguay Club, and again in Mme. Sillard's charming home, I found France again, as also in the *salons* of the French Minister at Montevideo. [38]

There was something of France, too, in the editorial offices of *La Razon* and of *El Dia*—for, of course, an old journalist could not resist the temptation of calling at a newspaper office. [39] Having gone there intending to interview the editor in my own way, the tables were turned on me and a volley of questions fired off at me. Next morning there appeared the very interview I had been avoiding, and all my "Ah's!" and "Oh's!" were cunningly interpreted to make up a tale. Consequently, all I can report of Uruguay journalism is that my *confrères* of Montevideo excel in the art of the Abbé de l'Epée, who managed to make the dumb talk. I trust this remark will be taken as praise.

The few occasions I had for talking with my *confrères* have left a very pleasant recollection. I can truthfully proclaim them all Latins of the purest water—Latins by their vivacity, by the warmth of their temperament, by the trend of their mind towards general truths, by every sign of their predilection for wrestling with ideas. In this respect it was impossible to think them otherwise than youthful and delightful. The estimable Renan, who was indulgence itself, gently reproached me once with a lack of leniency. Alas! Time, the mother of Experience, brings to us all in the end the faculty of appreciation in the sense in which the philosopher meant it, and he himself never consented to sacrifice one of his early opinions unless he could at least preserve its terminology.

Still, it is a serious question, not only which is the better, but which has wrought the more good in the world—youth, with its presumptuous eagerness, or weary wisdom.

Now, is it possible to deduce any definite ideas of the special features of the people of Uruguay from these faithfully reported but necessarily diffuse notes, culled in chance encounters? If I had not just come from the Argentine I should have plenty of material. But as it is, consider, pray, that I have only to modify some epithets in consideration of the smaller proportions of the subject and all I might tell you of the aspect of town or country, as also of the mind and character of its inhabitants, would, to all intents and purposes, sound in your ears like a twice-told tale. [40] Then, you will say, the Argentine and Uruguay are practically one and the same. That I cannot admit. As well might one confound Marseillais and Brestois, who, however, are of the same country. I prefer not to pronounce an opinion that might foment the never-slumbering rivalry that exists between the two Hispano-American peoples of La Plata. But as the common-sense of Governments and peoples generally prevails over public excitement, and as the paramount interest of both countries is the same in economic matters as well as in the more or less clearly defined field of American politics, there is, I think, no reason to fear that either can take offence at an opinion inspired by equal respect for both parties.

What more shall I say? A country of 1,400,000 inhabitants; a town of 400,000 souls. If Buenos Ayres is the second Latin city in the world, Montevideo follows—at some little distance, perhaps, but with a creditable total. The soil is no less well worked, cattle-rearing is equally successful, while the *saladeros* and large factories, like those of the Liebig Company at Fray Bentos, provide a market as good as the freezing-machines for Buenos Ayres. The political and social institutions are much alike, both inspired by the same regard for equality as proclaimed by the French Revolution, and permeated by our own doctrines of justice and liberty. And if the Uruguayans have ventured to carry purely logical solutions farther than we have done, the reason is probably that the democratic Governments of these new countries have not had to contend with the same atavistic resistance that must be reckoned with in older lands, where men's minds have been moulded by long history. A cheap criticism might here be made by considering only such and such an aspect of these young communities. We lay great stress on their revolutions, and whilst it is to be hoped that violence will before long be laid aside, I have unreservedly set down all I learned about these movements. Nevertheless, we must admit that Uruguay is not without a show of reason when she replies by throwing up at us the floods of blood that we have shed in the course of our civil wars, and that down to our most recent history. Let the sinless throw the first stone.

The ardent nationalism of Uruguay has nothing to fear from that of the Argentine. There are advantages and disadvantages in importing too great sensitiveness into every question. As a contribution to the International Exhibition in honour of the Argentine centenary, Uruguay published a very handsome volume, in which there was set forth in pictures and figures the entire history of their national development, the text being given in French and Spanish. The title was *Uruguay Through One Century*. The evolution of the Oriental Republic is therein set forth. Of course, the weak spot of such works is that they gloss over the deficiencies; and thus, though hiding nothing, there is always the risk of discomfiture when they are subjected to the brilliant light.

It remains none the less true that the economic growth of Uruguay is in no whit inferior to that of the Argentine in these last few years, and the promise of the future justifies the highest hopes. It is possible that on either side of the estuary the heat of political and social verbiage is not always in accordance with cold reality. This is a criticism that might be made of any land, and I could apply it easily to those I know best.

When all defects and excellences are taken into account, I should say the Uruguayan is distinguished from the Argentino by his impulsive idealism. Less sober-minded and less attached to novelty of doctrine—these are the two points that struck me first in his character. For this very reason he is more prone to argue about theories, and more expansive about himself and others. It may be that French is less current at Montevideo than at Buenos Ayres, though it seemed to me that, intellectually, French influence, if less profound, is more patent on the surface. The mixture of European races is about the same in the two countries. How is it that the first impression is one of greater Latinity?—Latinity of feeling, which lends a charm to social relations; Latinity of thought and action, with all the advantages of spontaneity, all the defects of method, its alternations of enthusiasm and hesitation in fulfilling its plans. The Latin conceived and created this modern civilisation, which the Northerner has appropriated to his own solid and empiric structures; but he has only succeeded in giving them their present universal application by renewed contact with the ideal in which the descendant of the Roman conquest too readily found consolation for his own desultory practice. South American Latinity has allowed itself to be left far behind by the great Anglo-Saxon Republic of the North, just as European Latinity has suffered its fiercest attacks from those who were designated the "Barbarians" by ancient Rome. Yet how great would be the darkness if the light of Latinity, as it survives even in its enemies, were suddenly to go out! If man could always measure the obstacle, he would frequently lack courage for the leap. It was the force of Latin impetus that sent modern humanity forth to besiege the fortresses of oppression, and it is the task of the experimental method to convert them by patience and perseverance into asylums of liberty; we know that to accomplish the miracle it will be necessary for the citizen to be made anew by the exercise of self-control and a primitive respect for the liberty of his neighbour. Considering all the feats that have been accomplished by the Latin races, I see nothing before them but this last and crowning marvel to complete their amazing history.

In Uruguay the first indication of this new order of things will be the suppression of revolution. Before this comes to pass there will be great changes on both sides of the ocean, in the reflex action of humanity and, in a less degree, in its reasoning consciousness. Here is an educational work which offers a vast field for future effort.

The Government of Uruguay is well aware that the greatest difficulty in the way of self-government is to establish the relation between principle and practice. It seeks, therefore, to implant in the young those broad general principles by which our private and public life must be regulated. [41] I lacked time to visit the schools, which are the most unmistakable thermometer of any social structure. A glance at the catalogue sent by the Primary Schools Council to the Third Congress of School Hygiene, held in Paris, August 2 to 7, 1910, will give us some light on the subject. This is not the place in which to describe the admirable organisation of obligatory primary teaching in Uruguay and the remarkable development of the primary schools under Señor Williman's presidency. The syllabus for a period of school life from the sixth to the fourteenth years is, I think, most interesting. In all the schools which are ranked as of first, second, or third degree, and in the country schools, the characteristic of the course is the revival of the object-lesson, still too often sacrificed in our European schools to the subjective teaching of olden days. In the very first year's work I note that the following subjects are included (to be carried farther in later years): geometry, notions of locality, the human body, animals, plants, minerals, weights and colour, demonstration lessons, etc.

It is obvious that the first notions of such matters must, if they are to reach the minds of infants of six years, be of the most rudimentary character. But is not this the right age at which to begin to give a bias to the child's mind? In successive years it will be taught to observe and make simple experiments, so that it is progressively prepared for contact with the world in which it will be called to live, in a way that has little in common with the absorption of general rules which, until very recently, constituted the bulk of what we call education. The very fact that they have evolved this system of education, and that they have put their theories into practice, proves that the Latins of Uruguay are on the right road to succeed in the realisation of their hopes. For if they claim to impart to budding intelligence a solid base of observation and experience, or, in other words, to teach them the sensations that different phenomena give to us, and offer such explanations as we can supply, they will surely not be checked by the higher generalisations which are the natural outcome of scientific study and also its crown. Thus, in the catalogue of the school libraries for the use of pupils and professors I find such French works as these: Le Bon—*Psychologie de l'Éducation, L'Évolution de la matière*; Le Dantec—*Les Influences Ancestrales, De l'homme à la Science*; Henri Poincaré—*La Valeur de la Science, La Science et l'Hypothèse*. If we are not careful these "savages" will outstrip the "civilised." I shall make no bold predictions. There is, as I hinted just now, so wide a margin between understanding and the act that should result from it that the magnificent progress made in words is out of proportion to the slow evolution of action. It remains for our Uruguayan friends, as for their European judges, to surprise the world by a new history of human society.

Whatever this history may hold in store for us, I am glad to think that our Latin republics of South America—and Uruguay amongst the first—will offer the spectacle of a splendid effort of high achievement. I will not seek to hide the great pleasure it gives me to record the fact, because, in the first place, the sight of man labouring to raise himself is always suggestive; and, secondly, because for a critical mind there is no better complement than the need of hope.

FOOTNOTES:

[33] The docks were built by the State alone without the help of a loan. In 1906 the tonnage of vessels entered and cleared in the port was fourteen millions.

[34] Meat drying and salting is the principal industry of the country. In the *saladero* the animal is killed and cut up, and the flesh dried and salted by a process analogous to that used with cod. Uruguay possesses thirty of these *saladeros* (as against fifty in the Argentine and Brazil), with Brazil and Cuba for its chief markets. This article of food is now much esteemed in both countries, though formerly it was reserved for slaves. At Fray Bentos there are the large establishments of Liebig that must be mentioned to complete the list.

[35] Señor Daniel Muñoz is now Minister of Uruguay at Buenos Ayres.

[36] Of these, 100,000 are foreigners.

[37] The Reds are the advanced party, the Whites the conservative. It was from the Reds that Garibaldi borrowed the famous red shirt that he brought back from Montevideo.

[38] I should have liked to thank M. and Mme. Carteron for their kindness. Alas! Mme. Carteron's sudden death has left a blank in her home.

[39] The papers are distributed in the streets of Montevideo by children on horseback. They fling the sheets skilfully into the doorways, where they frequently remain, respected by all passers-by.

[40] There is only one point that it is only just to repeat: it is that the women of Uruguay are very beautiful. More or less so than the Argentinos? In the Pan-American Congress the ladies of Buenos Ayres gave the palm to a celebrated beauty of Montevideo, in an outburst of hospitable chivalry. I would not have the bad taste to say a word either way. The two banks of La Plata appear to me equally propitious for the development of feminine æsthetics, and for the foreigner who loves art the handsomest model is ever that which is before his eyes.

[41] On the initiative of Señor Claude Williman, the late President, 360 country schools have been opened in Uruguay, so that the total number of primary public schools supported by the State reaches at the end of 1910, 1000, and gives us a ratio of one public school per 1095 of the population.

CHAPTER XII
RIO DE JANEIRO

The *Orissa* is an old coasting steamer of the Pacific Line, which calls at the western ports of South America, beginning at Callao, and passing through the Straits of Magellan, pushes as far as Montevideo, whence Santos and Rio de Janeiro are reached on the way to Southampton, the end of the journey, with a halt at La Palice. The *Orissa* is not a rapid boat, but she is very staunch, and if her internal arrangements, of the oldest description, be not more than rudimentary, the voyage I made in her was very agreeable, thanks to the company of the captain, who I found knew India well. A heavy sea and a head wind made us a day late—a fair record in a journey only supposed to cover three days. The greatest trial on board was the music that played at mealtimes, when, without any provocation, three old salts, of pacific aspect as befitted servants of their Company, made daily distracting attempts to draw piercing discords from instruments which proved a cruel test of the harmony of our constitutions. One blew wildly into the little hole of a metal rod which shrieked in response; the second scraped furious sounds from his strings; while a piano, built probably about the time of Columbus, vainly endeavoured to bring the others into tune. It took an alarming quantity of ginger and Worcester sauce to settle the nerve-cells so cruelly exasperated by the rapid absorption of food in the discordant tumult of this orchestra. We know the ancients believed in the soothing influence of divine harmony. I wondered whether the *Orissa's* fife might not have had something to do with the saraband of the wild waves we encountered. I lay the doubt before the directors of the Company.

One thing is certain; at dawn, with no music at all, and (remarkable coincidence) with a sea that had suddenly calmed down, we entered the Santos River. A long arm of the sea between low-lying shores ending in a vast bay framed in high mountains; marshy plains covered with a tangle of tropical vegetation, or a low line of hill buttresses; all that is visible of the land seems to be sending upwards to the blue sky its tall shoots of foliage, which testify to the effect of the vivifying orb on the quivering sap of the tropics. On all sides, under the swaying lacework of green leaves, there appeared brightly painted cabins, which set a note of bold colour in the sea of verdure. [42] *Pirogues* made from the hollowed trunks of trees and painted in the crude tones beloved of savages glide up and down the transparent waters. Nothing here that recalls Europe. This is where the curtain rises on the New World. Shadowy forms, in strange draperies, pass to and fro before the little cabins whose colouring gives them a strong resemblance to children's toys, and then suddenly disappear as though swallowed up in the luminous mystery of all this foliage. The relative proportions of all things are new here. Nature has broken her usual limit in these countries and developed immoderately, leaving man, by comparison, dwarfed and insignificant. Too small, he appears in a world too large. But already he is engaged in taking a revenge, as is shown by the disappearance of the yellow fever from the marshes of Santos. We know that no other town has been more cruelly tried. The simple fact of drying up the marshes when the harbour was building sufficed to destroy the scourge. The low shores of Santos Bay are still covered with salt marshes where little scarlet crabs clamber amongst the brushwood, but every trace of fresh water has disappeared, and we know that it is only in fresh water that the dangerous mosquito can live.

The *Orissa* moored alongside the quay, amongst the large cargo-boats down whose yawning holds long lines of porters were flinging bags of coffee. Each in turn advanced with alert step along the swinging plank, and as soon as the man in front of him had deposited his sack the same movement of the shoulders, repeated immediately after by the man behind, gave an uninterrupted cascade of yellow bags, [43] falling from the docks, where were heaped the mountains of berries, to the vast bosom of the ship. You, who, like me, have heard Creole laziness abused a thousand times, learn that the "lazy" Brazilian only relaxes this hard labour for the period strictly necessary for rest; and not even in the hottest part of the summer, when the sun is at its fiercest, does he indulge in so much as a *siesta*. In Brazil, indeed, the *siesta* is unknown. I do not mention the fact in order to reproach Europeans. My only intention is to do justice to the toilers whose reputation has suffered at the hands of the ignorant and foolish.

To return to Santos. We are impelled towards the quay in the first place by a strong desire to penetrate to the very heart of the marvellous landscape, and scarcely taking the time to shake the French hands outstretched to us on the landing-stage, we set out for the beach of Saint Vincent. Oh, surprise! A French hotel, all white, and redolent of the modern watering-place, where there awaits us a table decorated with orchids. But behold a tramway that runs to the end of the beach! In these countries to be in a tramcar is to be in the open air. So we follow the wide curve of silvery sand, bordered with villas whose gardens are enchanting with flowers and unexpected plants, whilst on the rocks of the small wooded islets, a cable's length from the shore, high waves are breaking stormily to melt softly away at our feet. The first impression is one of vigorous vegetation. In my first delightful surprise it seemed this could never be surpassed. We stop at Saint Vincent, and then return.

According to the legend, it was in the little Bay of Saint Vincent that Calval with his warriors and monks first landed on these shores, thus discovering Brazil, which it only remained to conquer and convert. Naturally the event has been commemorated in stone and bronze. But Calval himself has reminded us that, if we would land in time, we must first catch our boat. A hasty lunch, and we are again on board the *Orissa*, which to-morrow at sunrise will enter the bewitching Bay of Rio.

The entry is triumphal in this inland sea encircled by high mountains, with bristling summits like rocks in battle array, but relieved by sunny shores, with flowery and mysterious islands, where the dazzling lights of sky and sea are blended under the sensuous sunlight in the clear shade of lofty leafage. At four o'clock I was already on deck. Haze, a fine rain—there will be nothing visible at all. Jagged rocks emerge from the mists, which all at once conceal them from view. We are moving through a cloud. Two forts, the São João and the Santa Cruz, guard the entrance for the sake of appearances. In one of the recent revolutions they bombarded each other for a whole month for the entertainment of the inhabitants of Rio, who used to come out to the quays of an afternoon to criticise the firing. At the moment they are in a spasm of peace. Farther away, we are shown the soft outline of the *Minas-Geraes*, the redoubtable *Dreadnought* which—but we must not anticipate the story. Then come the hideous steeples of Gothic sugar-icing which the Emperor Dom Pedro II. felt himself called to place on the most ridiculous palace that ever disgraced a small island. We stop here, for the quays are not sufficiently extensive for us to draw up alongside. Now we can see the town, with its spots of bright colour on the misty background of swelling green hills. We have reached Rio de Janeiro—the January River—so called by the first comers from Portugal, who took the bay for a river as the Spaniards had done for the La Plata estuary. Perhaps in January—that is, in the height of the summer—these explorers had like us the excuse of a fog, for tropical vegetation is only possible when there are alternations of rain and sunshine such as the climate of Rio abundantly supplies. It is the rarest of phenomena to see the horizon perfectly clear. The distance is invariably wreathed with a light haze which softens the violence of the colours. After the fierce sun, a refreshing rain; after the shower, the joy of warm light. For the moment we are enjoying a fog. A bark hails us, the national flag flying at her bows. She brings a delegation from the Senate, with their Speaker at their head, come to offer a brotherly welcome to their French colleague. Next arrived the brother of the President of the Republic, who acts as his chief Secretary, and who was accompanied by an officer of the military household of the Minister of the Marine. Many complimentary speeches were made as usual, and a handful of brother journalists followed, having among them M. Guanabara, editor of the *Imprensa*. What touched me most was the way in which they all spoke of France and her *rôle* of high civilisation which she plays in the world. The President of the Senate, M. Bocayuva, whose son is just now Brazilian *chargé d'affaires* in Paris, is a Republican of the old school and unanimously respected by all parties. One realised as one listened to the heartiness with which he called up a picture of the moral authority of France that he was in close harmony with the traditions of the French Revolution. In this way are we in full communion of mind and heart with the main currents of thought and feeling which are carrying the nations of the world towards the better forms of justice and liberty. Here in Brazil, too, I shall find once more my country, as I quickly discovered in the course of the conversation I had with Señor Bocayuva during our drive from the Farou Quay to the handsome house which the Government has done me the honour to place at my disposal.

The sun had scattered some of the fog by the time we reached the Avenida Central, a magnificent highway which would be the pride of any capital city, [44] and as the motor-car sped swiftly down it or along that equally fine promenade above the quays jutting into the bay, whose features now grew gradually visible, and the gay villas with their frame of gorgeous foliage, we got a highly attractive view of the town, softly caressed on one hand by the luminous waters with their ever-changing horizons, and on the other, ever threatened by invasion of the tropical forest, struggling with the eagerness of the builder, whose efforts are ever hemmed in by parks and gardens and trees of all sorts that spring up from the soil at haphazard, evidences of the irresistible force of life that is here in Nature. Since the day when the sea brought man to the country, the struggle for existence has continued between the encampment of the budding city and the impenetrable thickets that ever repelled the invader. On the spurs, the ledges of the round green hills, everywhere the painted cabin has obtained a footing facing the bay, cutting out for itself with the axe openings through which may enter the daylight. Below, the town, which spreads out to the beach, would appear to be cut up by the farthest buttresses of the mountain range, and, pending the time when they will be tunnelled, the *Flumineuse* [45] will still be obliged to make many a long *détour* to reach any given point. But why linger in the city, except to mention the Municipal Theatre, which cost far too many millions, and the pleasing Monroe Palace built for the Pan-American Congress? Even the parks, whose extraordinary trees draw loud exclamations of surprise from us every minute, cannot compete in interest with the forest. We can never get tired, however, of the wondrous promenade on the quays, seven kilometres in length, and presently to be doubled. Following the graceful lines of the sea front, with its array of flowers, whence at every moment we get a new view of the bay, we drink in the ineffable light that makes the sea palpitate and the mountain leap in a single voluptuous rhythm. In the distance a white line, Nicterchy, the capital of the State of Rio (40,000 inhabitants); at the entrance of the bay the tall cone of granite known as the "sugar-loaf"; then the green islets, the rocks, the mountains that melt in the blue gauze of the horizon, and if you turn round, the high "Corcovado," hovering over the city, from whose summit the whole expanse of the bay will be revealed to us—rapidly changing scenery whose excess of living quality defies pen or pencil. The infinite variety of the Rio Bay (140 kilometres in extent [46]) with all its hidden indentations in which lie screened from view so many richly wooded shores, where new forests are in process of formation, is beyond all possibility of description. I have said enough: I have seen it, and my dazzled eyes will not soon forget the picture.

My first visit was, of course, to the President of the Republic, who was about to yield his place to Marshal Hermès da Fonseca, whose visit to Lisbon, planned in all ignorance, was destined to coincide with the Portuguese Revolution. A warm reception from Señor Nilo Peçanha, who showed me round his fine park, where royal palms which are one of the glories of Rio de Janeiro form a gorgeous avenue down to the very shores of the bay. The Baron de Rio Branco (a family ennobled under the Empire), [47] Minister of Foreign Affairs since 1902, was at one time Consul-General in Paris. He knew many of our public men and received me with the cordial simplicity of a friend. "The Baron," as he is commonly designated, enjoys sovereign authority in all matters pertaining to the external policy of the country. Friends and foes unite to leave him a free field in this respect, and all unite, too, in praise of his remarkable talents as diplomat. He does not conceal the fact that his sympathies are with France, though his admiration is reserved for Germany. The German Military Mission to Brazil was his idea, but it came to nothing. Some one in his immediate entourage told me he considers the German instructor to be specially capable of instilling into Brazilian troops the sense of military duty. Too many instances of insubordination—some very serious—have indeed shown the urgent necessity for such teaching. But can Señor de Rio Branco really think it possible to instil into the mind and manners of a democracy the doctrine of absolutism in military duty such as William II. has laid it down in repeated public utterances? If such absurd stress had not been laid upon the supposed rivalry between the States of Saint Paul and Rio de Janeiro, I believe that Baron de Rio Branco must have admitted like every one else the merits of our admirable French Military Mission to Saint Paul, of which I shall have occasion presently to speak again. If I may speak freely, I do not consider it diplomatic for France to leave so important a post as Rio for more than one year in the hands of a simple *chargé d'affaires,* no matter how experienced.

Whatever happens, two features in the Brazilian character will to my thinking remain predominant. They are democratic idealism and a consequent innate taste for French culture. This was brought powerfully home to me at the official reception with which I was honoured by the Senate. This demonstration was carried by a vote that was almost unanimous, there being only one against. [48] In a public sitting, the speaker chosen for the occasion seated me on his right hand and then made in

French a noble speech, in which after the usual compliments he declared that his country also upheld the glorious traditions of the French Revolution. Then a senator from the Amazon, Señor Georges de Moraès, got up to speak, and, also in French, delivered an admirable harangue on the *rôle* of French culture in the general evolution of civilised society towards social justice and liberty. This oratorical effort was frequently interrupted by the unanimous applause of an audience quick to grasp the crisp outlines of our splendid dogmas of Latin idealism. This magnificent homage to my great country, coming from the highest representatives of the noble Brazilian democracy, itself invariably attuned to the realisation of humanitarian justice, touched me profoundly, and I could but say how great was my joy to hear my nation spoken of with the respect and gratitude due to the grandeur of its action on the world. I wished I had at my disposal the same eloquence to express, in my turn, the deep gratitude I felt for this movement towards France, whose history has, by some fate, been so grievously checkered by many painful conflicts. What encouragement there is for us in this brilliant demonstration of disinterested cordiality! What hopes for the future may be founded on this bond of union between peoples working equally in the cause of democracy, and towards a great and universal peace based on the rights of man in all civilised continents! I endeavoured to make this clear, and the simple words of brotherly friendliness that sprang to my lips roused unanimous applause from the benches of the august assembly. I wish I could have done better. I trust my good intentions will speak for me. Never did I feel so strongly the influence of the loftiness of human nobility and its power to raise our minds to the highest aspirations after justice and liberty. Before bringing the sitting to an end the President called for three cheers for France, for President Fallières, and for the guest of the Senate. And all the assembly on their feet, with the gravity of suppressed emotion, gave three times the cry of "*Vive la France!*" amid the applause of the spectators.

I am sorry to say I cannot speak of Brazil in the way I should like. I was there only three weeks, just long enough to recognise how great an interest is attached to all the developments of this marvellous land in the different departments of human intellectual and physical activity, but far too short a time to warrant any opinion of the prominent men I met there, or on the multiple questions which are raised by the political and social progress of this democracy. I was able to converse with only a few politicians, and in my anxiety to see everything, I touched on too many subjects in too brief a space to have succeeded in assimilating the very complex impressions which might have enabled me to speak with some degree of authority. I can therefore only offer to the public a few rapid impressions for which I claim only the merit of sincerity.

When I said that the ancestor of my friend Señor Acines de Mello had given a performance of Voltaire's tragedies in his home, 1400 kilometres from the coast, in 1780, it sufficed to show that neither general civilisation nor French culture is a new thing in Brazil. The Republic of Brazil is an "ancient" Latin community which can show titles of intellectual nobility and lofty social ambitions. Its economic development, if less sudden in origin than that of the Argentine, is none the less remarkable in all respects and holds out no less hopes for the future. Coffee, india-rubber, timber, sugar, cotton, rice, and mines are a source of wealth that the future will reveal. There are immense stretches of country that are and must long remain unexplored. The effort of a fine race has too long been held in check by slavery, but its incessant activity has already produced astonishing results. For numerous reasons, one of the principal being the domination of theocracy, neither Spain nor Portugal has up to the present been able to give in modern Europe the full measure of their force. In South America they are making ready a magnificent revenge, which, however, will not, I hope, prevent their taking and keeping in Europe the position that is their due. If I may venture to make a hasty judgment from what I was able to see, the distinctive traits in this people would appear to be an irresistible force of impetuosity in an invariably gracious guise, and every talent necessary to insure the fulfilment of their destiny. I have spoken of the crossing of the race in the Argentine, where the black element has been re-absorbed. It is not the same in Brazil, where at every step one comes across the African half-breed amongst the masses. The Portuguese woman and the negro seem to get on well together, as is evidenced by the innumerable young half-breeds to be seen in their serene bronze nudity at the doors of the cabins. It is difficult to estimate the general results of this mixture. The negro has the reputation of being idle, childlike, and kind except in his outbursts of rage. As I have said before, the vice of laziness cannot be imputed to the Brazilian. It may be that African blood is partly responsible for the demonstrations of emotional impressionability and unexpected violence that sometimes take hold of the populace. I dare not carry this argument too far.

Yet, to my mind, the mutiny of the crews of the *Saint Paul* and *Minas-Geraes*, as of the troops of marines in barracks in the island of Las Cobras, was largely due to the excitable African blood. The "governing classes" seem untouched by this infusion of blood. But for some reason or other, their virtues and their defects seem remarkably well adapted to the corresponding characteristics of the masses. Idealists with a cult for intellectuality, equally ready for higher culture as for the hard labour without which nothing is ever achieved, gentle and violent by turns, or even simultaneously—the variable sons of this soil, less disunited, however, than one might suppose, may invoke in their favour with a just pride a work already grandiose though but a feeble embryo by comparison with what it must in time become.

In every department of modern activity Brazil need have no fear of the criticism of Europe, for she possesses men comparable with any of our chiefs of industry. Even a short visit suffices to show that there is no lack of either intellectual quality or business method. But the field is so vast that it would need innumerable legions to fully occupy it. Considered in this light, every effort appears totally inadequate in comparison with its immense possibilities. Admirable labourers they are, none the less, hard at work, in their modesty and perseverance, with no wish to spare themselves, and asking nothing from the struggle with inanimate Nature but ground for fresh hope. Does this imply that in certain directions of public action there is no wavering visible? How happy would modern society be if this could be said only of Brazil! Politicians are never in very high favour with the intellectuals of a country. I will say nothing against either the one or the other. The celebrated retort: "'Nothing' is a wide field: reign there!" may with some slight modification be applied to the most gifted of men when they persist in riding the eternal hobby of the ideal heedless of earthly conditions. Some of the problems with which humanity has wrestled for centuries have been solved by a single illuminating word uttered in calm authority by men who would not have shone in *rôles* that call for a gradual development of character. Politicians, on the other hand, whatever their shortcomings—and I must acknowledge that, in a moment of trial, they are frequently disappointing—have yet this merit, that they play the labourer's part. They have to handle every kind of problem, not to find a graceful solution that will delight the intellectuals, but to extract therefrom certain conditions of private and public life which according to events may make the fortune or misfortune of the public. It may be that in Brazil they are too much attached to the higher culture always to give sufficient consideration to the common necessities of our daily life. It may be that they are too intrinsically Latin always to be able to resist the temptation of rushing events. These defects, if they really exist, are being cured. The politicians with whom I had an opportunity of exchanging views, both at Saint Paul and at Rio de Janeiro, would bear comparison, whether as regards culture or systematic firmness in action, with any in the world. An aristocracy had grown up around the person of the Emperor, the last remnants of which are now being fast submerged in the current of democracy. I shall mention no names, for I do not want these hasty notes to bear the smallest resemblance to a distribution of prizes. Let me only mention one case—a very rare one in Latin nations—of a leader who is universally obeyed. I have no doubt that Señor Pinhero Machado possesses all the qualities of a leader deft in handling men, but it is less his talents that astonish me than his self-abnegation, which has brought into line so many politicians of Latin temperament.

The more momentous political questions of the day relate to organisation, there being no room for any serious attacks on principles that have been proclaimed and incorporated in the Constitution of the Republic. It is in practice that difficulties are apt to occur. The Empire showed a marked tendency towards centralisation. [49] The Republic, being, like the United States, a federation of States, is based on the theory of pure autonomy. But if the autonomy of these States is to be more than a vain word, some way must be found of constituting in each province of a territory which is eighteen times as large as France, and contains twenty millions of inhabitants unequally scattered over it, a sufficient force of intelligent determination to create a select governing body which will express the intellectual and moral capacity in the masses; otherwise democracy becomes only tyranny disguised. In some States, notably in that of Saint Paul, there is obviously a superabundance of energy. In others there is not enough. Time and community of effort can alone remedy this condition of affairs. Meantime, the balance is destroyed, and the Constitution enjoys principally a theoretic authority. It is inevitable that the result should be some confusion in Press [50] and Parliament, although the strife is rather one of dogma than of action, and lies principally between Federals and Unionists.

Religious questions are practically outside the public domain. The separation of Church and State in Brazil goes with a papal nuncio, by means of whom South American innocence supposes the fact adds a distinction which should dazzle the outer world. I fancied that some of the public men viewed the activity of the religious Orders with apprehension, but I will say nothing further on the point.

Laws for the protection of agricultural and industrial workers are here unknown. The Brazilian Republic will want to place itself on an equality with other civilised countries on this head as soon as possible, for already a number of colonists in lands where the administration has shown itself slow to take action have protested so loudly against the grave abuses that result that some Latin countries have been obliged to forbid emigration to Brazil. Take heed lest the States invoke their sovereign rights, which would be tantamount to declaring the central authority void. This throws light on the obstacle which now confronts progress on these vital questions—namely, the lack of an adequate Constitution in some of the States for the work of self-government, and of balance between those which have already a highly perfected civilisation and the districts theoretically on a footing of equality, but whose black or Indian population can only permit of a nominal democracy stained by those irresponsible outbursts which characterise primitive humanity.

As might be expected, the same remarks could apply to public instruction. There is in certain States—as, for instance, Saint Paul—a magnificent group of schools which respond to the general consciousness of a pressing need for the spread of higher education; in other parts there is a lamentable deficiency. [51]

It was, moreover, inevitable that the Federal Government itself should suffer from the unequal distribution of its military effectives. The State of Saint Paul is justly proud of an armed force which it owes to French instructors. I need not criticise the Federal army, which is officered by men of fine public spirit; but all agree that the force needs reorganising. There is no question, of course, of preparing for war; but the public interest requires that a military force should be at the disposal of the Government, capable of enforcing obedience to the laws. To me it seems more urgent than the acquisition of *Dreadnoughts*, which swallowed up millions of money and gave nothing but mutiny in return. Naval discipline necessarily suffered by the amnesty imposed by men who had just massacred their officers. As we know, this deplorable incident was followed by a mutiny amongst the marines stationed in the island of Las Cobras, which, however, for once, was severely put down. I inspected this body of troops at the manœuvres arranged for my visit. The young officers gave me an excellent impression, and the barracks certainly left nothing to be desired; but there were far too many coloured men in the ranks. Who can tell the effect produced on these impulsive natures by the capitulation of the public governing body before a military rebellion? The rebels cruelly expiated the faults of others by adding thereto their own.

As regards municipal administration, the greatest services have been rendered to the city by the Prefect, who interests himself especially in his schools amongst a long list of other duties. But the man who deserves the most from his country is Dr. Oswaldo Cruz, who has devoted himself to the improvement of the sanitary condition of the city and has instituted a service of sanitary police stationed at every point of contamination, and who, by dint of unwearying labour, has freed Rio of yellow fever. The Government has lent him generous pecuniary assistance in his work, but what is money without the man's perseverance and zeal? As we know, the disease is propagated by the sting of the female mosquito (the *Stegomya calopus*) just before the egg-laying season. In 1903 Dr. Oswaldo Cruz, having obtained from Congress all the necessary powers, began his fight with the fearful scourge. A body of sanitary police, organised by himself, was charged with the mission of getting rid of all stagnant water in the streets, houses, courtyards, gardens, roofs, gutters, and sewers, and from all other spots where the larvæ of the *stegomya* could exist. In this he found material assistance in the scheme of public improvements then being carried out in the city—the building of the quays, [52] the drainage of marshy land, destruction of insanitary houses, cutting of new avenues, etc. In the course of the first year of these sanitary works there were 550 deaths from yellow fever; in the following year the number fell to forty-eight, and for the last three years not a single case has been recorded. Needless to say, the sanitary police brigade are continuing their duties, and in all parts of the city and in all the houses every trace of standing water is swept away. This constitutes a never-ending tyranny; but the result is the complete purification of a city which was once a den of pestilence, and is now one of the loveliest ornaments of the planet!

Dr. Oswaldo Cruz was making ready to go to the Amazon, which is in a specially wholesome condition; he had already fulfilled a mission there last year. He will now complete the task of general sanitation already started, for which the Congress has furnished the necessary funds. This, perhaps, is the most important part of his project, for it will throw open an immense region of unlimited productiveness to every sort of civilised activity.

Such a work would suffice to the glory of any one life, but Dr. Oswaldo Cruz is one of those men who are capable of continuing indefinitely their labours. The ex-pupil of the Pasteur Institute was anxious to endow his country with a similar school of therapeutics and prophylaxy. In a picturesque loop of the bay there stood a small building which was used by the engineer of the prefecture in the burning of rubbish. Dr. Oswaldo Cruz has transformed it into the *Institut Manguinhos* (Institute of Experimental Medicine), with the special mission to study infectious and parasitic diseases in men and animals, as well as hygiene, and to prepare the different serums which modern therapeutics has adopted. It was hardly necessary, perhaps, to add all the *fioritura* of Moorish architecture to a building intended for studies that call for no flourish of trumpets; still, there is something about these fanciful lines which harmonises agreeably enough with the natural arabesques of the prodigal learage. The institute aims at supreme perfection, and supplies having been furnished without stint, the results place it beyond comparison. Vast laboratories, comfortable studies, fitted up with all the latest appliances; operating-rooms for animals, with the most complete surgical outfits, disinfecting-rooms, vacuum machinery; lifts everywhere, gas, electricity, pipes for water and for compressed air; library and magazine-room, with all foreign periodicals properly classified; separate buildings for the study of infectious diseases and the preparation of the corresponding serum. Each building has its own stable, so constructed as to be readily sterilised, with boxes permitting a close watch over the animal as well as feeding him without opening the door; and its own hall for experiments and laboratory, a furnace to destroy all refuse, electric generating engines, etc.

A group of young Brazilian *savants* were at work under the guidance of Dr. Oswaldo Cruz and two German bacteriologists. One of them, Dr. Chagas, a Brazilian, is well known in the world of science for his studies in bacteriology and parasitology. There is an immense field open, for tropical diseases are still uncharted, whilst in the field of marasitic diseases of men and animals there is fully as much to learn.

The *Mémoires de l'Institut de Manguinhos* are published in Portuguese and in German. I was struck by the effort that the Germans are making to draw towards themselves the medical corps of the country. The heads of the laboratories and their assistants had all been brought from Germany, and their scientific method had been cordially accepted. At the Berlin Exhibition a first prize had justly been awarded to the Manguinhos Institute. Of late years two French *savants*, MM. Marchoux and Salimboni, of the Pasteur Institute, have been charged by the Brazilian Government with a mission to study yellow fever. To-day two of our army veterinaries are investigating the *morve* at Rio.

But it is time to leave the abode of the Mosquito Killer (*mata mosquitos*), as Dr. Cruz is nicknamed. The sun is mounting above the horizon. In the enchanting light of the bay there are now revealed to our gaze the serrated outlines of the soft shores where the intensely profuse vegetation runs riot, the glowing masses of bare rock which rise high above the water to meet the sun against the filmy background of the distant mountains, and, lastly, the islands with their rippling masses of rich verdure, which spring skywards like an offering from the sea.

Impossible to pass the Island Viana by in silence. On the neighbouring island Señor L———, the descendant of a French family, has set up his dockyards for naval construction, which he took us to see with a modesty that was not without a point of legitimate pride. I shall not describe what is well known. There was a surprise in store for us, however, in the form of a colony of Japanese labourers working in wood and metal, and learning in this distant land a trade to be practised later in their own. Most diligent of workmen, remarkable by their gravity and steady application. Amongst them, tool in hand, one of those small boys whose oblique eyes we have learned to know by heart through the picture-albums of Nippon; dumb, motionless, the whole of his mind concentrated with intense force on the work in hand, this child of some ten years is taking a demonstration lesson in technical work that, as you see by his attitude, he is determined to profit by. I would rather have seen these little chaps playing at ball. I seem to see them as they show themselves to us, gathering up all their powers, even at the threshold of life, in order to take possession of the future. I was told that in the evening schools they accomplish wonders.

The day's work ended, Señor L—— crossed a short arm of the sea and landed in his own island of Viana, where he has laid out a large park which at the same time satisfies his love of the beautiful and of comfort. Each member of the family has a house to him- or herself—and what a house!—English, or perhaps American in style, with the finest supply of light and air provided by great bay windows opening upon that immense expanse of sea framed in beflowered shores and broken by high blue peaks which lose themselves in the sky. Kitchen-gardens, flowery meadows, lawns, groves, woods—there is nothing wanting, and each in turn is planted in the best possible way to take advantage of the splendours of the views. And to make Viana a world in itself, all the loveliest birds of Brazil are to be found in this earthly paradise; and the supreme magnificence of the Brazilian types of winged and feathered creatures repays in beauty what man's munificent generosity daily distributes. Here within reach of my hand a large yellow bird is pouring out its mad and merry song, while two toucans, with their exaggerated beaks, light up with gold and clear sapphire hues the sober green of the thicket. I pretend to try to catch them; they barely feign a retreat. Eden before the Fall! I congratulate Señor L—— on the artistic way in which he spends the money he succeeded in making in business—two talents that are seldom found together.

"It is all very well," he murmured in reply, "but you see what happens. My wife prefers Paris, and my children, who might have found here, at twenty minutes' run from Rio, a worthy occupation for their time, have elected to try their fate in the unknown. My eldest son is in New York. *Ma parole!* I believe he sells seltzer-water there, or something of the sort. What do you think of that?"

I said nothing. But I thought to myself that in the pursuit of happiness not even the most favoured escape some setbacks.

FOOTNOTES:

[42] In Brazil there are none of the half-houses of the Argentine and Uruguay. The Brazilian eye loves, on the other hand, bright colours. The houses are therefore daubed with blue, yellow, and red, which harmonise as they may with the green background.

[43] A sack contains 60 kilogrammes.

[44] Like Florida in Buenos Ayres, Ouvidor in Old Rio still remains, notwithstanding its inadequate dimensions, the principal business thoroughfare of the town.

[45] The *Flumineuse* is the native of Rio. There is no excuse for people who, knowing that there is no river in Rio, yet insist on being named after a stream (*flumen*) that is non-existent.

[46] The Rio harbour, built by the English for a French company, represented in 1907 eight millions tonnage entered and cleared.

[47] The father of Baron de Rio Branco, Minister under the Emperor Dom Pedro II., is the author of the Law of the *Ventre Libre*, which emancipated all slaves to be born in the future. In remembrance of this measure, which preceded the abolition of slavery, a statue has been raised to him in one of the Rio parks.

[48] The vote of a senator belonging to the Church party.

[49] The Emperor Dom Pedro II. is kindly remembered. Every one speaks of him with respectful sympathy.

[50] The Rio press is not so fully equipped for news items as the European or American papers, but it is literary in tone and occupies a worthy place in the Corporation. The largest circulation is claimed by *El Commercio*. The *Imprenso*, whose editor is Alcindo Guanabara, Member of the Brazilian Academy and deputy, is, with *El Pais*, one of the most important party sheets.

[51] We must do justice to the effort made by the Brazilian Government to extend education. According to an article in their Constitution, the "unlettered cannot vote," but I will not swear that the rule is severely applied. In each State the primary schools are supported by the municipalities and States themselves, as are also the training colleges. There are too many calls on the strength of the youth of a new country for secondary education to be very enthusiastically welcomed. On the other hand, the different institutions of higher education attract the rising talent of the land.

[52] At Santos, one of the most severely tried, yellow fever was entirely stamped out by the building of the quays, which drained off the marshes.

CHAPTER XIII
BRAZILIAN SOCIETY AND SCENERY

I have already jotted down a few characteristics that struck me in the people of Brazil, and these will form a sort of prelude to what I am now about to say. For a traveller who claims to convey only first-hand information, the difficulty, of course, is to make any definite statements when aware that his observations were all too hasty and brief to warrant generalities.

Brazilian society is very different from that of the Argentine, its elements being more distinct and more complex, while equally European in trend, and with the same immutably American base; the strain of French culture is more attenuated, the impulsive temperament more apparent, but for steady perseverance and capacity for hard work the Brazilians cannot be surpassed. In criticising the social conditions in Brazil, it must be borne in mind that the abolition of slavery dates only twenty years back. I do not think the slave-owner was systematically cruel, but slavery does not precisely rest on any inducement to kindliness. Certain buildings that I came across and the explanation of their use that was given to me showed plainly enough, what we already knew, that the blacks were treated like cattle, with just as much consideration as was dictated by self-interest. Since man is almost as humane as he is cruel, no doubt the masters had their benevolent moments, but the institution was, nevertheless, fully as demoralising for owners as owned. The blacks multiplied, however, [53] and if the abolition of slavery was not accompanied here as in the United States by acts of violence, the reason is that, to the everlasting honour of the white man, the institution had been universally condemned before emancipation was proclaimed.

It has been said that in Brazil slavery was buried beneath flowers. The fact is it had become practically impossible when its disappearance was publicly and officially acknowledged. And as, happily, there was no race hatred between whites and blacks, these two elements of the population were able to continue to live peaceably side by side in a necessary collaboration. They went farther than this, as a matter of fact, and the races mixed with a freedom that I noticed everywhere. From the point of view of social concord, this is cause for rejoicing, while it must be left to time to correct any lowering of the intellectual standard. Every one knows that the principal feature of a slave-owning community is the absence of a middle class whose mission it must be to hold the balance in an oligarchy and prepare the way for the emancipation of the oppressed.

When the principle of democracy was proclaimed by the "big whites" of Brazil, they could rely for support only on the leading intellectuals of sound general education, and on the inorganic masses of the population formed or deformed morally by slavery, and its attendant evils, with an incoherent admixture supplied by immigration. This, necessarily, was the situation that had to be faced on the morrow of the decree of emancipation. By degrees this state of affairs has been and is still being improved. The substratum of the community remains, however, such as I have shown it. I am aware, of course, that in this immense territory there are vast districts of varying soil and climate where Indians and blacks are very unequally divided. For the purposes of this brief summary, I am naturally only taking into account representative centres of population. In some parts the negroes have deserted the plantations for the towns to which they were attracted by the opportunities for employment, and their place has been taken by Italian colonies who have established themselves as small farmers. Elsewhere the ex-slaves remained in their cabins and continued their accustomed tasks with more or less zeal, content if thus enabled to live as they liked. They appear to work and live in perfect harmony with their former owners.

As regards the social *élite*, it is less easy to pick out its general features here than it is in the Argentine, where on every hand there are visible points of comparison with Europe. We are constantly obliged to revert to our starting-point, which is a feudal oligarchy, the centre of culture and refinement, which by a voluntary act is in process of formation into a single heterogeneous mass without any jarring of racial relations. For a long time the Empire preserved a nucleus of aristocracy of which only a vestige remains to-day. There might now be a danger of submersion beneath an inferior intellectual element which lacks the powerful bias towards higher education peculiar to the Brazilian mind. It is necessarily this element which will prove the salvation of the country. It is on his plantation (*fazenda*), in the centre of his influence, that we must seek the planter (*fazendero*). Of a highly refined theoretical feudalism, deeply imbued with

European ways of thinking, and with the generous social standards that distinguished, at one time, our own eighteenth-century aristocracy, sublimely unconscious—and destined probably to remain so—of the first spasmodic movements of forces whose evolution towards a new order implies confusion at the outset, he is infinitely superior to the generality of his kind in Europe, who are either the product of tradition or the outcome of democratic circumstance. He leads the broad and simple life of the large landowner in a land whose soil offers every inducement to try fresh experiments. Everywhere within you will notice evidences of his search for the Beautiful and his thirst for knowledge. And everywhere without you will see the convincing proofs of his endless activity. In Paris one of these influential men may pass unnoticed, so little does he resemble his prototype as invented by satirists, with his modesty of speech and simplicity of bearing. He would, however, repay a closer study, and when he comes among us to obtain fresh force for his strenuous task, I should like to see some of our young men seize the opportunity to improve themselves by paying him a visit.

All these social forces have a natural tendency to form themselves into groups. But the Brazilian planter, like other feudal survivals in Europe, is exposed to the attack of every modern commercial and industrial force that is tempted to wield some sort of social authority. This is now the base of all communities—in Rio, in Saint Paul, or in any other city of the world. A reception on extremely Parisian lines given by Senator Azeredo, assisted by Señora Azeredo, proved once again how strong is the likeness between circles that believe themselves to be utterly different. A single telegram suffices to give uniformity to the toilettes of all the women in the world, and if those to be seen in Señora Azeredo's *salons* were less extravagant than some Parisian examples, Rio struck me as being quite as eager as Paris in its pursuit of beauty's adornments. Shall I mention that Brazilian women have large black eyes, which seem to ask a thousand questions, usually pale complexions, sometimes of a golden bronze tint, that they are vivacious in speech and take a delight in conversational tourneys?

Señores Pinhero Machada and Guanabara were kind enough to give me an invitation that enabled me to see a little more of some of their politicians. Señor Pinhero Machada has a house that is built among the palm-trees on a height that commands the whole of the bay. I confess that in this enchanting place I was more tempted to open my eyes than my ears; still, in spite of the counter-attractions of the lovely landscape, I managed to study the mysteries of Brazilian politics a little more closely, and, as I had begun to do at Señor Guanabara's, to realise that reasons for union are and will remain predominant providing that the question of personalities does not obtrude.

How shall I fail to speak of the ball given in commemoration of the Independence of Chile, where I had the pleasure of meeting the flower of Rio society together with the representatives of all the foreign Powers? I should only give it a passing mention were it not that the President of the Republic, who opened the ball in person, had conceived the idea of inviting me to form one of the official quadrille, with the thought, of course, of paying a compliment to my country. When the excellent Prefect of Rio announced this decree of public authority, I believed a catastrophe was imminent, and did not hesitate to impart my fears to his charming wife, who declared herself ready to go under fire by my side. The worst of it was that I had before me the mocking eyes of the papal nuncio with whom I had just shaken hands, and I could see that he was far from wishing me success in the perilous career on which I was about to embark. Timidly, I broke it to my partner that it was over fifty years since I had danced a quadrille, and she returned my confidence by acknowledging that her education as regards the art of dancing had been totally neglected. The great fat man in scarlet, whose ring was large enough to boil an egg in, found our predicament vastly amusing. I saw myself about to become the scandal of Christianity. Uniting our ignorance, my partner and I took up our positions and arranged to imitate to the best of our ability the movement that might be suggested by the music to the youthful couple that formed our *vis-à-vis*. Thereupon, the orchestra, a piano and some other instrument, began to play, and we saw that the charming young couple on whom we relied were obviously waiting for us to set the example. What was to be done? I looked at my neighbours. They could not agree. One advanced, the other retired. The President of the Republic tried to encourage the rest of us by getting himself into hopeless muddles. I soon saw that all we needed to do was to tread on the toes of our neighbours and then bow our apologies, to begin again immediately the same manœuvre. This I accomplished, to the great disappointment of the scarlet man, who was obliged to give a wry smile at the spectacle of the grace I managed to display in the service of my country.

I should have liked to see the theatres. Time was lacking. I saw only a performance of *The Daughter of the Regiment*, given in Italian at the Lyric Theatre, formerly the principal play-house of Rio under the Empire. The Imperial box was placed at my disposal and proved to be a veritable apartment, furnished in the style of Louis Philippe. I was told it had been kept unchanged.

The Municipal Theatre, practically a copy of our own opera-house, is one of the finest buildings in the Brazilian capital, its only fault being that it swallowed up too many of the public millions. On the ground floor there is a very luxurious restaurant containing a faithful copy in glazed bricks of the frieze *The Immortals,* brought by M. and Mme. Dieulafoy from Suez and now in the Louvre. Here the French colony gave a dinner in my honour. A certain number of statesmen accepted the invitation of my compatriots, and thus I had the great pleasure of assuring myself by my own ears of the friendly relations that exist between French and Brazilians. At one time we had a very important colony in Rio. For reasons that are not too clear to me, it has dwindled away of late. I found, however, at the reception held by the French Chamber of Commerce that if lacking in quantity, the quality of these French representatives left nothing to be desired. The natural affinity between the two peoples is so obvious that the multiple attractions of this great and beautiful country are for French people enhanced by the joy of a genuine communion of thought and feeling which links their hopes and aims. To my intense satisfaction, I had a proof of this at my first contact with the public of Rio, and the same experience was pleasantly renewed later at Saint Paul; I found that I could speak with the utmost freedom as a Frenchman to Frenchmen, for there was not the smallest suggestion of a foreign element in the mind of my audience to remind me to adapt myself to new susceptibilities. I know not how adequately to thank my audiences for what in French eyes appeared the supreme gift of a spontaneous manifestation of French mentality. The Academy of Medicine were good enough to invite me to pay them a visit, and I will freely confess that a consciousness of my unworthiness made me hesitate to face this learned assembly. On this point they reassured me by declaring that the meeting would be merely in honour of French culture. I went accordingly, and scarcely had we exchanged our first greetings when I already felt myself at home in a French atmosphere. Medical science being out of the question, the delicate fare offered to me was some reflections on the general philosophy of science, as developed by the magnificent intellectual labour of France, and on the powerful lead given to the activities of civilisation by our country. Could anything be more encouraging than this disinterested acceptance of the testimony of history, considering how many there be who would exalt themselves at the expense of France?

A very different atmosphere awaited me at the Bangu factories, where are admirable spinning and weaving mills; here the raw Brazilian cotton is transformed into those printed stuffs of vivid colourings in which the working classes love to drape themselves and thus supply a feast for our eyes. Here there were fewer abstract terms employed to declare the esteem so freely accorded to France. But here, as in other parts of the great Republic, I found the few brief words uttered in private encounters still more convincing than the noisier demonstrations. Wherever the work of social evolution is being carried on, wherever there is seen a fine promise for the future, their it is a joy for the French to find the name of their country associated with the forward movement. The splendid industrial development of Bangu among many other similar centres shows what is being done in Brazil in this direction. I have seen nothing more striking in Europe. The Brazilians possess in an equal degree with the Argentinos the capacity of bringing to the highest possible perfection any work to which they set their hand.

I have already said that in Brazil our laws for the protection of industrial and agricultural labourers are unknown. Not but what politicians have studied the matter. But in the imperfectly centralised organisation of all these floating authorities, it is difficult to see how such laws, if voted, could be effectually applied. All the more credit is therefore due to the large employers of Brazilian labour who have done their best to improve the material condition of their hands without waiting to be compelled to do so. The working population of Bangu is scattered about the country in *chalets* that appear to be admirably hygienic, and all wear the aspect of the finest of physical and moral well-being. A large building has been provided for meetings of all kinds and a theatre in which the hands may amuse themselves with theatricals and concerts. It is unnecessary to state that we were received to the strains of the *Marseillaise* and that the French Republic was vigorously cheered. I do not go so far as to say that there were no dark sides here or elsewhere to the picture. I have not concealed the fact that immigrants complain loudly of the want of supervision from which they suffer in some regions. It seems fair to infer from what has already been accomplished that more is being attempted. It is naturally the farmer on the *fazendas* who receives the most attention because he is the deep and almost inexhaustible source of the national wealth.

It would appear that there are no limits to the productiveness of this soil, whose fertility has been developed and renewed during so many centuries by the combined action of sun and rain. Side by side with the barbarism of slavery there has been a barbarous system applied to the land, which has resulted in its impoverishment. Now the relation between production and fertilisation has come prominently forward. There is still, however, much virgin land that awaits the farmer. The real problem of a rational system of agriculture to be applied in Brazil will be left for a future generation. Meantime, their finest forests are burning and filling the horizon with smoke. This represents what the Brazilians call "clearing" the land. But the Brazilian forests deserve a volume, not a paragraph, or chapter—and its writer should be both learned and a poet. I did not visit the fairylike regions of the Amazon, but however amazing they may be, I think they could scarcely surpass the powerful impression made on me by the forests of Saint Paul. There is a limit to our nervous receptivity, beyond which point we become insensible to sensation. We in Europe have dwelt amid a beautiful harmony of the forces of Nature which have moulded all our impressions in a certain form of beauty; to find fault with them would be sacrilege, since the highest inspirations of art have been drawn from this source. Thus, consciously or not, we have lived in an equilibrium of pleasing emotions, that imposes on us certain limitations of sensation to be derived from the spectacle that Nature provides. Therefore, when we are suddenly confronted with an unknown Nature, whose power and vigour shatter all our preconceived notions, and alter the whole focus of our organs, the only possible effect at first is one of complete bewilderment. We must take time to get used to this new order of sensations before we expose ourselves to another and get back again to the standpoint of a corresponding sense of æsthetics. I had to endure several headaches before I could rise to the level of the genius of Berlioz or Wagner. What if we compared our own landscape with the music of Gluck or Mozart? Then you may grasp the Wagnerian fury of the virgin forests which produce a stupefaction that leaves you incapable of analysis and a prey to a tumult of superlatives. And all this happens simply because we have been exposed to the shock of a higher manifestation of the terrestrial forces of the world.

The Botanical Gardens of Rio are famous the world over. The astounding forms of foliage, the bold growth of ancient tree and young shoot, the illimitably dense profusion of every form of vegetable life, recalling what must have been the earliest stage of the life of our planet, reduced me to a state of speechless surprise. I promised myself a second visit to its marvels, but never accomplished this, for spectacles of even greater magic detained me elsewhere.

"Bon Vista," the Emperor's country house in a suburb of Rio, is surrounded by a fine park which is going to be turned into a public garden. The *Flumineuses* make frequent pilgrimages thither, with their families, to spend a day in the shade of its trees during the hot season. But, to tell the truth, while they in this way enjoy Europeanising themselves in artificially made gardens, I took a delight in drinking in the Americanisation that awaits you in the outposts of the young Corcovado forest, which seems to be advancing to the attack of urban civilisation and pursues man even in the very streets of Rio.

This urban forest is one of the charms of the Brazilian capital. It clasps the city in its powerful embrace and seems determined to drive back the population into the sea, whence it sprang, creeping insidiously into every open space, blending with the avenues, spreading over squares and parks, and everywhere declaring the triumph and victory of the first force of Nature over the belated but redoubtable energy of humanity. Trees, creepers, ferns, shrubs—all these forms seem to be mounting to the heights that crown the bay in order to draw from the sunshine a renewal of their vigour. The high peak of the Corcovado (over 2000 feet) that broods over the city, looms large on the horizon, and one can readily believe that the first thought of the invader was to climb that height and survey the marvellous panorama before him. Unlike the Galilean, he needed no tempter to sow in his mind the desire of possession. But, alas! the task of appropriation is not accomplished without encountering some obstacles, and the would-be mountain climber is forced to concentrate his attention on one spot of the planet that holds him in the grip of an irresistible attraction. A funicular railway performs this office for him; and with no more trouble than that of letting yourself be drawn up under the branches, you suddenly emerge on a height whence you get a magic vision of Rio, with her bay, her islets, and a mass of mountains heaped one upon the other, until they are finally swallowed up in the sea. A new world is here revealed to your gaze—a world in which the whole miracle of the earth's multiple aspects is epitomised, where the eternal play of light and shade constitutes an ever-changing picture that creates a world-drama in inanimate Nature. Are you surprised to meet some Parisians up here? No, not much. The first result of our industrial equipment is to diminish the proportions of the globe. It is easier to-day to go from one continent to another than it used to be to go from one village to the next. I am personally glad of this, for nothing could be better for us French people than to travel in foreign countries, since in this way we get a standard of comparison that we badly need.

Coming down from the Corcovado, you must stop at "Silvestre," whence a shady path cut in the mountainside will bring you back to the city, through a wilderness of wood where a profusion of parasitic growth covers the boughs, tying them up in a mad confusion of tendrils.

Next after the Corcovado the Tijuca will attract you, and, like the former, it ends in wondrous points of view. In this case the pleasure is in getting there. You pass now through lines of tall bamboos, whose light foliage meets overhead; now you follow the course of a noisy waterfall that seethes amid the verdure of the forest; anon you descend into a valley that is shaded by the fresh and delicate foliage of the banana-trees, or rise to the top of a hill from which all the indentations of the great bay are plainly visible, and a small gulf hidden in an avalanche of rocks and boulders lies revealed, where the mysterious waters sob and vanish on a bed of flowers. Ever onward, the motor-car pursues its headlong way at a speed one longs to check. Often we stop to prolong the pleasure of a moment, but if one did not take care one might stop for ever. The pen is powerless to convey what, perhaps, the brush might reveal—the joy of life that swells to bursting the sap of every twig and leaf, every flower and fruit, from the humblest blade of grass to the loftiest extremity of the tallest trees, and renders so impressively active every organ of the vegetable world. I remember pausing before a simple creeper which had produced some billions of blossoms, and had imprisoned a whole tree in a kind of tent of blue flames. This example alone will serve to give the measure of the tropical fecundity. The object of our drive was the "Emperor's Table" and "China Street." After the view from the Corcovado this seemed less grandiose, but in any other country of the world it would arouse a rapture of admiration. We returned to the city by another route, traversing a part of the mountain where rows of villas embowered in flowers seemed hung up half-way between sky and sea. You are back in Rio before you realise that you have left the forest.

It is impossible to speak of Rio without mentioning Petropolis, which owes its success to the yellow-fever mosquito. The *Flumineuses* formed the habit of migrating to this mountain station in order to escape from the attacks of the plague-carrying mosquito, which is so active after sunset. A well-founded fear of the scourge drove all those who could afford it out of Rio, and at their head were the Emperor—later the President of the Republic, the Ministers, and diplomatists, with their families. Thus Petropolis, an hour's journey from Rio, became in some sort a fashionable watering-place, whose charming villas stand in a forest of tropical gardens. It is a delightful spot for all who can turn their back on the business of the outside world, which seems, indeed, far enough away. For this reason the European diplomatists spend long days here, filled with visiting, excursions (there are many charming ones to be made from this centre), or the idle gossip that constitutes that work is lacking; but we know that everywhere custom is stronger than utility, and custom is very exacting. Now that the mosquito has deserted Rio the Government has settled in the capital, leaving the mountain station to the diplomats and their papers. How can diplomacy exist without a Government round which to "circumlocutionise"? For the smallest formality one must take the train. Coming back in the evening is fatiguing. One goes to the hotel for the night. Your friends take possession of you, and while you are dawdling in Rio all your correspondence is lying unanswered at Petropolis. There is, in consequence, a strong feeling now that "the diplomats ought to settle at Rio," near to the Baron de Rio Branco, who somehow invariably manages to be at Rio when they are at Petropolis and *vice versa*, just to upset our worthy "plenipotentiaries." All this is not done without a certain expenditure of money. Budget commissioners, beware!

Theresopolis is another mountain station, three hours from Rio. On the opposite shore of the bay a railway climbs or winds round the lower slopes, cutting its way through the forest as far as a vast plateau, whence radiates a number of paths that invite you to wander amongst the astonishing phenomena of this fiercely abundant vegetation. A "circus" of bare rocks bristles with pointed peaks, one of which, bearing some resemblance to the forefinger of a human hand, is known as "the Finger of God." Whichever way you bend your steps this formidable and imperious finger lifts itself against the horizon, as if tracing the path of the planets through the heavens. The beauty of Theresopolis lies in its madly bounding torrents, which leap the giant boulders heaped up in its course, ruthlessly destroying the green growths that make a daily struggle for life. For me this giant strife provides an incomparable spectacle. I confess that the series of forest panoramas that open out on either side of the railway, from Rio Bay to Theresopolis, give a magic charm to the day's excursion. Tall ferns raised against the sky the transparent lacework of a light parasol, monstrous bamboos threw into the mêlée their long shoots, shaped like green javelins; shrubs, both slender and stout, and of every kind of leafy growth, encroach upon the heavy branches, worn out with the weight of parasites; the creepers twined like boas round their supports, flinging back from the crest of the highest trees a wealth of fine tendrils that, on reaching once again their native earth, will there take fresh root and draw renewed force for the future fight with fresh resistances, a single one of the family, with leaves like a young bamboo, so fine that the stalk is well-nigh invisible, entirely shrouding a whole tree in its frail yet stubborn network, transforming it into a green arbour that would put to shame any to be found in our ancient and classic gardens—all these and many other aspects of the marvellous forest arouse an unwearying and never-ending admiration, mingled with wonder at the blows dealt on a battlefield of opposing forces where the weapons are none the less deadly for being immovable.

There is no forest to be seen on the road from Rio to Saint Paul. Here man has passed. On all sides are visible the signs of destruction wrought by systematic fires. Thanks to Señor Paul de Frontin, the Company's manager, and two friends of whom I shall have occasion to speak again later—Señores Teixera Soarès and Augusto Ramos—I made the journey under the best possible conditions. The great point was to see the country as we passed. Could any better way be imagined than that of placing the locomotive behind the coach, which was arranged like a *salon*, its front wall being taken away and replaced by a simple balcony? With rugs to guard against the freshness of the breeze, you find yourself comfortably installed in the very centre of a landscape whence you may see mountains, rivers, valleys, fleeing before you in the course of a run of five hundred kilometres. For the whole of the day I was able to drink in the fresh air and strong lights, as I looked out eagerly to discover new beauties. As a matter of fact, I saw nothing but mountains and hillsides that had been wantonly despoiled of their native vegetation. Here and there a small banana-wood growing in a crevice showed the proximity of the cabins of negro colonists and their offspring, who displayed in the sunlight the unashamed bronze nakedness for which none could blush. They were leading the nonchalant life of the farmer who expects to draw from the earth the maximum of harvest for the minimum of trouble. Whether under cultivation or lying waste, at this time of the year the land presented the same appearance of bare wildness. Sometimes on the top of a hill there would be seen one of the old plantations surrounded by walls built to imprison the slaves, or coffee-gardens, now abandoned because the soil was worn out for want of dressing, or long stretches of pale green denoting young rice crops, watercourses dashing over rocks and gliding through brushwood—the last resort of the birds,—vestiges of calcined forests where the new growth of vegetation eager to reach the sun was ever cut back and repressed; and everywhere flashes of red light that resolve themselves into birds, shuddering palpitations of blue flames that become butterflies, or the bronzed reflections of phosphorescent light that reveals a dancing cloud of hummingbirds. On the horizon spots of black smoke, betokening forests that are blazing in all parts to make way for future harvests—a melancholy spectacle of a wanton destruction of natural beauties that has not even the excuse of necessity, since the splendid forests are only attacked to save the trouble of fertilising the land exhausted by cultivation. I was told that at the first outbreak of fire the great birds of carrion come up in flocks to cut off the retreat of the monkeys and serpents that flee in terror. I did not witness this part of the tragedy, but I was near enough to see all the horror of the fearful flare. In the crackling of the burning palms, in the whirling clouds of blinding smoke furrowed with a sinister glow, boughs and branches lay heaped up on the ground in immense flaming piles, through which the charred stumps of boles, brought low by fire, crashed noisily to earth, where their corpses lay and slowly smouldered to ashes on the morrow's coffee plantation in accordance with the law of Nature, which builds fresh forms of life out of the decomposed elements of death.

At nightfall, we entered the station of Saint Paul, where the cheers of the students, loudly acclaiming the French Republic, made us a joyous welcome. A few minutes later we found ourselves at a banquet attended apparently by representatives of every country of the world, and Brazilians and Frenchmen here united to express their brotherly aspirations in words of lofty idealism.

The city of Saint Paul (350,000 inhabitants) is so curiously French in some of its aspects and customs that for a whole week I had not once the feeling of being abroad. The feature of Saint Paul is that French is the universal language. Saint Paul's society is supposed to be more markedly individual than any other community in the Republic, and it offers this double phenomenon of being strongly imbued with the French spirit, and, at the same time, of having developed those personal traits that go to make up its determining characteristics. You may take it for granted that the Paulist is Paulist to the very marrow of his bones—Paulist in Brazil as well as in France or any other land; and then tell me if there was ever a man more French in courtesy, more nimble in conversation in his aristocratic guise, or more amiable in common intercourse, than this Paulist business man, at once so prudent and so daring, who has given to coffee a new valuation. Talk a little while with Señor Antonio Prado, Prefect of Saint Paul, and one of the leading citizens, whose mansion, set in the frame of a marvellous park of tropical vegetation, would be a thing of beauty in any country, and tell me whether such elegant simplicity of speech could imaginably express any but a French soul. The same might be said of his nephew, Señor Arinos de Mello, of whom I have already spoken, a clever man of letters who divides his life between the virgin forest and the boulevard, and who might easily be taken for a Parisian but for a soft Creole accent. Frenchmen basking in Brazilian suns, or Brazilians drinking deep of Latin springs—what matter by which name we know them, so that their pulses beat with the same fraternal blood!

The fact that the Paulist character has been strongly developed along lines of its own and that the autonomy of Brazilian States permits of the fullest independence of productive energy within the limits of federal freedom has led some to draw the hasty conclusion that there is a keen rivalry between the different provinces, and to see separatist tendencies where there exists nothing but a very legitimate ambition to forward a free evolution under the protection of confederated interests.

The States of Saint Paul and Rio stand at the head of the confederation, both by reason of their intellectual superiority and by their economic expansion, and the steady increase of their personal weight in the federation is naturally in proportion to the influence they have succeeded in acquiring in the exercise of their right to self-government. As no one seeks to infringe any of their prerogatives, and as the only criticism one might make would be that certain States are at present unfit to fulfil all the duties of government, while any attempt at separatism must tend to weaken each and all, no serious party, either at Saint Paul or Rio, or, indeed, in any other province, would even consent to discuss the eventuality of a slackening of the federal tie. The Paulists are and will ever remain Paulists, but Brazilian Paulists.

My first visit was paid to the head of the government of Saint Paul, who extended to me the most generous of hospitality. Señor Albuquerque Lins, President of the State, received me in the presence of his Ministers—Señor Olavo Egydio de Souza, Minister of Finance; Señor Carlos Guimaraès, Minister of the Interior; Señor Washington Luis, Minister of War; and Señor Jorge Tibiriça, who had just vacated the Presidential Chair, and was one of the most distinguished statesmen of Saint Paul. Señor Augusto Ramos and our Vice-Consul, M. Delage, whose tact, intelligence, and wide understanding of his duties are above all praise, were also present on the occasion. The President, who had an exaggerated opinion of the defects of his French, managed to convey to me in excellently worded phrases his warm sympathy for France, which, indeed, he proved by his cordial reception of us. I, in my turn, assured him of the fraternal sentiments of France for Brazil and Brazilian interests in general, as also for Saint Paul and Paulist society in particular. And then, as though to prove that our compliments were not merely those demanded by etiquette, the conversation turned upon matters in which Saint Paul and France were so mixed that the Paulist seemed to take as much pleasure in acclaiming France as did the Frenchman in expressing his admiration for the stupendous work carried out by the Paulists with such giddy rapidity, in developing a modern State that founds its hopes for the future on the miracles accomplished in the past.

It was a joy to me to run about the city at haphazard. You do not ask from Saint Paul the stage-setting furnished by Rio; yet there is no lack of the picturesque. The suburbs of Saint Paul, where costly villas make bright spots of colour in the gorgeously beflowered gardens, can offer some fine points of view. At the end of an esplanade bordered with trees the plateau suddenly falls away into a gentle valley which would seem admirably designed for the site of a park, worthy the ambitions of Saint Paul if the authorities would but set about it while the price of land is still moderate. The only public garden at present owned by the town is a pretty promenade that can scarcely be considered as more than a pleasant witness to a modest past.

In the course of our walk we came upon the museum, which stands on the hill, from which the independence of Brazil was proclaimed. It contains fine zoölogical, botanical, and paleontological collections. I was shown moths of more than thirty centimetres in breadth of wing, and hummingbirds considerably smaller than cockchafers. I paused for an instant before the cases containing relics of prehistoric America, with utensils, ornaments, and barbaric dresses of the aboriginal Indians who to-day are sadly travestied in abbreviated breeches and remnants of hard felt hats.

There was no time to visit the schools, to whose improvement the Paulist Government attaches high importance. I promised, however, to call at the Training College, and, indeed, could scarcely have done less, since this marvellous institution would be a model in any country of Europe. I can but regret that I am unable to lead the reader through the building to see it in all its details—its rooms for study, its gardens, its workshops. The young Headmaster, Señor Ruy de Paula Souza, who was a pupil at our Auteuil College, does his professors the greatest credit and does not conceal his ambition to surpass them. A much too flattering reception was given me, in the course of which I had the surprise of hearing quotations from some of my own writings introduced into a speech made by one of the professors. France and French culture received a hearty ovation. The warmth of the welcome given me at Saint Paul could only be outdone by Rio. The charm of a hearty expansion of fraternal feeling was added to the cordiality of the demonstrations in honour of our country. The pleasure felt when members of the same family meet after separation, and find their mutual affection has been generously developed in the course of life's experience—this was the impression made on me by the greeting of the students both at the Training College and at the Law Schools, where one of the young men delivered a speech in excellent French that formed the best of introductions to the lecture that followed. In the evening the same young men organised a torchlight procession. I stood at a window with a French officer on either side of me. A moving speech was made to me by a student who stood on the balcony of the house opposite. The procession passed by to the strains of the *Marseillaise*, amid a tumult of hurrahs, in honour of France.

I mentioned two French officers. There is here now a French Military Mission, to whom has been entrusted the training of the police force, whose duty it will be to ensure order in the State of Saint Paul. Colonel Balagny, who is in command, was away on furlough. Lieutenant-Colonel Gattelet, who takes his place, is a highly deserving soldier, who appears to combine strict discipline with the national urbanity.

I observed with satisfaction that the Mission was very popular at Saint Paul. When the march of the *Sambre-et-Meuse* rang out a crowd assembled to watch the passing of the troops with their French officers at their head. Intensely proud of this force, the public takes a delight in cheering them. I was present at a fine review held on the field of manœuvres at Varzea de Corma. The soldier of Saint Paul would figure creditably at Longchamp, for in precision and regularity of movement he can bear comparison with any. I must add that the Brazilian officers who second the efforts of the Mission are actuated by a zeal that merits a large share of the credit of the results.

When I congratulated Colonel Gattelet I felt I ought to inquire whether he had been obliged to have frequent recourse to punishment in order to bring the men to the point at which I saw them.

"Punishment!" he said. "I have never had to administer any. I have no right, for one thing; and if I wanted to punish I should have to ask the permission of the Minister of War. But I have never had occasion even to think of such a thing, for all my men are as docile as they are alert and good-tempered."

I could only admire. It is true we were discussing a select troop, who enjoy not only special pecuniary advantages but also quarters called by the vulgar name of barracks, but which, for conveniences, hygiene, and comfort, far surpass anything that our wretched budgets ever allow us to offer to the French recruits.

CHAPTER XIV
BRAZILIAN COFFEE

It is not possible to speak of Brazil, still less of Saint Paul, without the coffee question cropping up. The fabulous extension in recent years of the coffee plantations and the crops that have permitted the present extraordinary accumulation of wealth have drawn the attention of the whole world to the Brazilian *fazendas*.

Big volumes have been written on the subject, and I gladly refer my readers to them. There they will find all the figures that I as well as another might quote, but I adhere to my intention of leaving to statistics their own special eloquence, and of giving here an account of only such things as my eyes have seen.

If you want to inspect the Brazilian coffee plantations you have only to look around you. I can show you the coffee-plant, a shrub between three and five yards in height, which, for foliage and manner of growth, bears a strong resemblance to box. The flower is very like that of the orange-tree, but with a more subtle scent. The fruit, or "cherry," red at first, then of a brownish colour, contains two kernels. The characteristic feature of the coffee-plant is to bear flowers and fruit at the same time, in all stages of maturity, when once the first flowering is over, providing a spectacle that interested me greatly. But under these conditions it follows that at whatever season the harvesting may be carried out the crop is bound to be very unequal in quality. The only rational way to meet the case would be to have several harvests each year, but the cost of the proceeding would not be covered by the difference in the quality obtained. For this reason the *fazendero* generally makes but one harvest a year, plucking at the same time berries of varying quality, from the small rolled *moka*, which is found on all plants, to the more or less perfect berries destined for the average consumer. Not that the *fazendero* makes the mistake of placing on the market a mixture of coffee of all qualities. When the berries have been dried in the open air on asphalt floors they are sorted by machinery, and thus seven different kinds are obtained, whose value naturally depends on their quality.

But, unhappily, the canny dealers who buy the Brazilian product classified in this way have nothing more pressing to do than to invent fresh combinations, tending to increase their own profits but, at the same time, to ruin our palates. Here we have the Bercy mysteries of wine adulteration imported into the coffee market! We need not be surprised, therefore, to learn that to some palates coffee is only drinkable when mixed with chicory, with burnt fig, or roasted oats—the last more especially appreciated by the North American public. The best of it is that at home with us Brazilian coffee bears but an indifferent reputation among the epicures who like only the *moka* of Santos. I confess that one of the surprises awaiting me in Brazil was to find their common coffee infinitely superior to any we get in our best houses. It is a light beverage, with a subtle, soft scent; and, being easily digested, it does not produce the usual nervous tension that causes insomnia. In the hotels and railway-stations of Brazil a cup of coffee is a perfect joy, not only for its delicacy of flavour but also for its immediate tonic effect, and cannot be compared with the article offered in similar places at home. The cups certainly are smaller than ours, but I fancy the average Brazilian drinks quite five or six in a day. It is true I did hear "Brazilian excitability" put down to coffee intoxication, but one would like to know just what this "excitability" amounts to, and, besides, I am not clear that alcoholic countries have a right to take up a critical attitude towards coffee-drinkers. Man in all parts of the world seeks to stimulate his powers, and only succeeds in obtaining temporary results—which have to be paid for later on in one way or another, either by a reaction of debility or by hypersthenic disorders.

No one needs to be astonished, then, to find coffee in every mouth, both as a drink and as a topic of daily conversation. If it be true that coffee has made Saint Paul, I can testify that Saint Paul has repaid the debt. The muscles and the brains of the entire population are devoted to the same object. Enormous sums of money are invested in it, large fortunes have been made in it; and when the famous "valorisation" was operated, it looked as if a fearful catastrophe were preparing. This is not the moment to dwell upon the economic conditions of coffee-growing in the States of Saint Paul, Rio, and Minas-Geraes. I shall confine myself to recommending the reader to refer to the excellent book that M. Pierre Denis has published on the subject. [54] As for the "valorisation," a stroke of unparalleled audacity, it consisted in forbidding the laying out of new plantations at a moment when the market was menaced with a glut that seemed likely to bring about a "slump," and in forcing the State of Saint Paul to purchase the whole of the surplus stock—some eight million bags—and hold it until prices had recovered their tone, when the article could be placed gradually on the market at a remunerative figure, the scheme to be executed by means of a financial operation the details of which need not be gone into here. This is a piece of advanced State Socialism which looks like succeeding, contrary to the expectations of the economists, but which it would be highly imprudent to repeat on any pretext. As may be imagined, the scheme aroused the keenest opposition, for in case of failure the risks might have amounted to some hundreds of millions; but it sufficiently denotes the extraordinary mixture of audacity and foresight that belongs to

Brazilian statesmen. The perilous honours belong more especially to the President of the State of Saint Paul, M. Tibiriça, and to Señor Augusto Ramos, a planter of the Rio State.

As I took a keen interest in the peripatetics of this social drama that threatened to swallow up both public and private fortunes, I naturally desired to visit the great laboratory of the *fazendas*, where modern alchemy transmutes into gold the red earth that contains the mysterious *diabase* which is the essential element in coffee-growing.

A member of the Prado family kindly offered to show us his *fazenda* at Santa Cruz. The beauties of the landscape were, unhappily, concealed beneath a haze of fine rain, but man, alas! had done worse—for it is a disastrous introduction to the glories of the *fazenda* to cross smoking tracts of forest on fire. In the distance huge trees were still blazing, around us was a waste of ashes and of half-consumed boughs, and the falling rain seemed only to quicken the dying conflagration. In some of the great green holes were fearful gaping wounds through which the sap was oozing, while some tall trees still stretched to heaven their triumphant crown of foliage above a trunk all charred that would never sprout again. The Brazilians contemplate spectacles such as this with a wholly indifferent eye, and, indeed, even with satisfaction, for they see in the ruin only a promise of future harvests. To me the scene possessed only the horror of a slaughter-house. At least we have the grace to hide ourselves when we massacre innocent beasts, since an implacable law of Nature has decreed that life can only be supported on life. Why can we not hide in the same way the savage destruction of the beauties of the forest?

Between two harvests the *fazenda* is a scene of quiet repose. We witnessed all the different operations—from the drying to the sorting, and to the final departure of the bags to the Santos warehouses. Although our tour of inspection was arranged by the proprietor himself, he was only present on our account. The imposing mansion, the splendid gardens—all were deserted. The Italian colonist has taken the place of the slave. The former master, now the employer, is no doubt attracted towards the city. The overseer looks after the colonists, who are collected into a village, and the labour is organised as it might be in a factory. The families seemed prosperous enough beneath their coating of original dirt. Only babies and pigs were to be seen—scarcely distinguishable the ones from the others, except that the pigs occasionally wallowed in a chance pool. This was risky, however, for the terrible jaws of the crocodile lie in wait on the banks of the neighbouring pond.

The coffee plantation furnishes occupation for entire families. Men, women, and children bring equal zeal to bear upon the task of weeding, which has to be repeated five or six times a year. The prolific Italian reaps an advantage from the size of his family. Moreover, plots of land are set apart for him, on which he raises forage for his cattle and the maize, manioc, and black beans on which he lives. Often, too, he gets permission to raise his private crops in the open spaces between the coffee-plants. All the colony is afoot when the time comes to pluck the berries. The Saint Paul growers claim that they have only a single crop, all the berries ripening at the same time. I saw them full of blossom, covered thickly with bouquets of white flowers. But I noticed also in the sorting-rooms a great irregularity in the grains.

We walked out to the plantations—vast stretches of red earth in which the shrubs are planted at irregular intervals. Beside the path and amongst the young plants there were great charred branches rotting in the sun, the melancholy remains of forest monarchs laid low a dozen years ago and awaiting final decomposition. Here and there colossal tree-trunks were still erect, though hemmed in on all sides by the green bushes whose monotonous uniformity triumphs over the dethroned sylvan power. Occasionally some forest giant that has escaped by miracle from the flames raises to the sky its splendid stature, sole evidence of past splendours. In the bare flatness of the immense plain covered with the low coffee-plants, where no outstanding feature provides a scale of measurement, it is difficult to realise the real dimensions of these relics. It is only when standing actually beneath a bole that you can estimate its proportions, and a series of "Oh's!" and "Ah's!" of amazement burst from all lips. One of these trees, whose trunk was no less than seventy metres in height, had a girth so immense that eleven men stretching their arms in a circle round it could not entirely span it. I was told that it was worth from two to three thousand francs. There would be some expense attached to getting it to the place where it was wanted.

Still, under a gentle sprinkle of rain, that fell like drops of clear light, we proceeded towards the great forest, across which a fair carriage-road has been made. This is not the decaying forest whose timber feeds the factory furnaces, such as that of Santa Ana or of Lulès. This was the forest that had stood for countless centuries, as is shown by Titanesque survivals of those unknown ages, but it remains the forest eternally young, its vital force still unimpaired by time. The grand architectural lines of trunks and boughs, where the sunlight plays tenderly in an unending scale of changing tones upon its depths, offer a feast for the eyes. Creepers entwine themselves among the branches, making a thousand fantastic turns and twists, while slender stems spring like fireworks heavenwards, there to burst into bouquets of rich blossom. Part only of the monstrous tree-trunks are left visible. Beneath its inextricable tangle of boughs the *jequiticaba*, all in white, its spurs and ramparts high enough to conceal a man, rises high above the rest—a Tower of Babel that has escaped the destruction of the others.

Yet at our feet there lay a colossus that fell only three days ago, and seemed to point to the final destiny of all earthly glory. It was no tempest that had thus laid it low. Healthy, straight, and tall, it had fallen before it could be weakened by age, simply because the fatality of the action of underground forces crowding upon it from all sides had decreed that it should end then and there. We felt it, measured it, and examined every part of the gigantic corpse, and not one was inclined to quote the assassin of the Duc de Guise—"I thought it larger." No. Lying here at our feet it was no less amazing in its might than it had been in its ephemeral glory. Even in the beauty of death the splendour of life is impressive. In the clearings, where the slender stems of tall palms sway their parasol tops in the wind, flocks of large parrots were busy exchanging opinions as to the reason of our presence; and, if one may judge by the inflections of their cries, they thought it an ill omen. In the patches of blue sky visible between the branches we could see them swirling overhead, uttering loud curses. I had been promised a glimpse of monkeys, but it appears that our cousins retreat before the sound of wheels, and only tolerate—at a safe distance—the company of pedestrians. I thought if I separated from my fellows I might happen on the sight of one or two. Failing a specimen of the *Pithecanthropus erectus* any little chap on four legs would have found a brotherly welcome. Since none came, why not go after them? But walking is a dangerous pastime, since at every moment one stands a risk of treading on a *trigonocephalus* concealed in the brushwood, here as high as a man's waist, to say nothing of the fact that there are no landmarks, and that before I had taken a hundred steps I should have hopelessly lost my way. I walked about twenty yards, and that calmed my ardour. I saw neither monkey nor snake. I was not inconsolable, however, for the Brazilian snakes had no mystery for me.

I saw them in all their forms collected in a charming little garden which Dr. Vital Brazil has laid out expressly for them at Butantan. The coral serpent, the *trigonocephalus*, the rattlesnake, glide about the grass, climb the bushes whose branches effectually conceal them, or seek the shelter prepared for them in solitary corners. But for the absence of Mother Eve one might fancy oneself in Eden. I must add that a moat full of water, with a wall above, renders impossible the machinations of the Evil One; but I confess I did not go near them, even under these conditions. Dr. Brazil showed them to me in his laboratory, preserved in transparent jars, where the aggressive force of the creeping beast is revealed by means of sectional surgery, and again in the narrow yard of his menagerie; here one alarming-looking reptile after another was fished out of its prison on the end of a stick, and then seized by the throat and forced to choke up its venom into a small glass.

You may suppose that in all this Dr. Brazil has some plan. You are right, and it is worth explaining. He is engaged in a quest after a cure for snake-bites, or even perhaps for some way of rendering humanity immune. Brazil and India have a specialty of the most venomous of snakes. Dr. Brazil, who spends his life in their company, declares that even the most deadly species is without hostile feeling for man. No one has ever been attacked by a snake. His poison (I refer to the snake) permits him to paralyse instantaneously the prey destined for his food. But if by mistake you walk on his tail he is carried away by a desire for reprisals. I do not want to argue about it. It is sufficient to state that some hundreds of Brazilians and some thousands of Indians whose pleasure it is to walk barefoot in the forests die annually from the deadly sting of this philanthropist whom they have unwittingly annoyed, notwithstanding the humanitarian opinions of snakes in general. This is the evil for which Dr. Brazil is trying to find a remedy.

The Butantan Institute, half an hour distant from Saint Paul, prepares antidiphtheric and antitetantic serums, but its specialty is the antiophidic serum. Dr. Calmette was the first to discover a method of procuring immunity, but the serum of the Lille Institute, prepared from the poison of Indian cobras, proved, in the hands of Dr. Brazil, powerless against the Brazilian rattlesnake. In this way Dr. Brazil made the discovery that each South American species had a special poison, the serum of which took no effect on other poisons. Accordingly, at Butantan three different serums are prepared—two act on special species, and the third, called "polyvalent," is used in cases where the owner of the poison has omitted when stinging his victim to leave his visiting-card and thus establish his identity—the most common case. [55] But Dr. Brazil is not satisfied to cure or render immune those who seek ophidic inoculation. He has discovered a superprovidential serpent, which, having no poison of its own and being invulnerable to the stings of its kind, renders them all innocuous to humanity by eating them. This is the friendly *mussurana*. They offered him to me for inspection, and he looked neither better nor worse than the *trigonocephalus*—I should not at all like to find him in my bed. I tried to coax him, however, to munch a poisonous comrade. He had just breakfasted, and wanted only to sleep. Dr. Pozzi, luckier than myself, had the pleasure of seeing him swallow a certain *jaracaca*, whose slightest caress is deadly. The story has been published in the *Figaro*. How must we regard this phenomenon unless as a freak of Nature? To try to multiply the *mussurana* in order to exterminate rattlesnakes seems to me a dangerous experiment. Dr. Brazil has not yet succeeded in obtaining a single young one, and for my part I cannot yet see man and the *mussurana* living in harmony together.

As a final surprise, we were informed that Dr. Bettencourt Rodriguez had obtained some excellent results by treating yellow fever with antitoxic serum. The most certain method seems, however, to suppress the mosquito, the propagator of the disease, as Rio and Santos have done.

Santos, now a healthy city, is an agreeable place whose only mission is to receive the coffee from Saint Paul and export it to all the continents of the world. We had a brief look at it as we passed, and saw enough to wish to return there. But this time, instead of approaching by sea, we descended upon it from the plateau, 2500 feet in altitude, which shuts the city in with its salt marshes, bounded by mountain and sea, using the famous electric railway which is celebrated throughout the world for the picturesque moving panorama it offers to travellers. From an industrial point of view the port is not equipped to cope with the present traffic, statistics for 1908 showing that 109 ships left its quays, carrying 50 millions of kilogrammes of coffee—three quarters of the total output of the world. As for the Brazilian *floresta*, it is difficult to judge of it at a distance. I was placed on a little balcony in front of the motor, between the Minister of the Interior of Saint Paul and Señor Augusto Ramos, and thus enjoyed an unrivalled point of view, while, at the same time, I was relieved from feeling any excess of heat. Mountains, valleys, forest-clad slopes—it might have been Switzerland or the Pyrenees, and I have assuredly no inclination to belittle either. Yet what a difference from the impression produced by a walk in any part of the forest, where every step lifts you to an ecstasy of admiration. Shall I confess it? The railway stations, melancholy halting-places on the mountain, have left the best souvenir in my mind. In the first place, there were rows of cups of coffee awaiting us there—coffee which revives and refreshes a traveller and perfumes the air with an aroma unknown in Europe. Then, and still better, there were delicate orchids climbing over the verandas, irradiating showers of warm light, and left there out of respect for one of Nature's *chefs d'œuvre*, for they ill support the fatigue of railway travelling. The orchid season was just beginning when I left Brazil. What I could see of it in the forest, where the earth was piled up with all kinds of decaying vegetation which the marvellous harvest was already preparing, delighted me, for such beauty gains much from being viewed in its natural setting. And in the desolate railway stations, from all these wood chips, there spring sheaves of vivid colours transforming everything, as if the yawning rags of some beggar revealed a fabulously rich treasure.

For the Brazilian flora has extraordinary resources. When I crossed the Bay of Santos to take the tramway, which runs in twenty minutes to Guaruja beach, I had no idea that the pleasure of the journey could excel that of my first arrival. The Guaruja beach is extremely fine. It lies in a frame of rocks and forests, and in its fine sands it filters the high waves that rush in from the open sea in magnificent cascades of fury, which suddenly melt away into great rings of pacified foam. But how find words to express the enchantment of the road! The low shores of Santos Bay are but a broad marsh, where a frail vegetation rejected by the forest has full sway. On both sides of the road there is an ever-changing sorcery of leaf and blossom in the most lurid of hues. Not an inch of space between two boughs but is promptly filled by stem, bud, creeper, parasite, and some kind of growth, large or small. Trees that are wasting beneath the cruel tendrils eating into their flesh don a robe of orchids. Cannas make patches of flaming scarlet in the thickest part of the brushwood, and the wild banana-palm lifts a tall head from above the two-cornered spirals of saffron-coloured flowers, which gives an effect like monstrous crustaceans warring with the branches—a wild scene, in which it looks as if all the forces of terrestrial fecundity were convulsed in one impudent spasm.

Just as I was closing my visit to Brazil, with great regret at leaving so much unseen, I had accepted an invitation from Señor Teixeria Soarès, the owner of a *fazenda* in the State of Minas Geraes. Señor Soarès is the manager of a railway company besides being devoted to land and its fruitful joys. Modest and quiet, he tries to efface himself socially, but his methodical and clear mind is attracted by every big problem, and forces him into the front rank of all the different enterprises which are an honour to his country. I was greatly impressed by the way he spoke of his *fazenda,* the management of which he has confided to his son. It was easy to see that he had centred there, if not the best of his energy, at least the highest pleasure that can be derived from the collaboration of man with the soil. When I inquired of one of the *fazenderos* whether it was true, as Señor Soarès boasted, that he grew the best coffee in Brazil, and obtained for it the highest market prices, I was told that the fact could not be disputed, but that Señor Soarès had the reputation of spending more on his coffee than it could bring in. I could not help fancying the words covered an acknowledgment of inferiority. Idealism, in agriculture as elsewhere, is apt to be costly. It may not, however, exclude the active qualities that make for success. Señor Soarès devotes himself more particularly to the improvement of coffee-plants and the raising of new species. Now it was said that he had got from an horticulturist (of Montmartre) a certain plant with whose fame the world would shortly ring. He wanted me to open the new plantation, and as an ex-Montmartrois, I certainly could not refuse the invitation.

I shall say nothing of the journey. As usual, there were miles of forest destroyed by fire. In the villages cabins and colonial houses were scattered about on the river banks amongst great groves of trees. The Parahyba made amends for the melancholy waste of the land by its innumerable rocky headlands, its tree-stems, its islets where a note of beauty was lent by the brilliant plumage of birds.

Small, impatient horses were waiting for us at the station, and seated in "*boggies*" that bounded over the deep ruts of the road, we passed through woods where large-leaved creepers made a magnificent stage-setting which only ended in the acropolis of Santa Alda. This rustic baronial hall, that belongs to days of slavery, is set on the summit of an eminence which commands a tangle of valleys, and it offers a comfortable simplicity of arrangement clothed in an avalanche of flowers. Wide verandas, colonnades, arches, are all overgrown with multi-coloured bouquets that are perpetually in flower, and under the rays of the sun distil a delicate ambiance of scented prisms. The impression is one of charm as well as of force, and when the young planter, accompanied by the pleasant queen of the domain with her group of small children, is seen in this background of rustic nobility, you are conscious of a fine harmony between man and Nature. The strains of the *Marseillaise* burst out, as we crossed the threshold, from instruments concealed in the plantation. It was a greeting to France that was touching enough from these Africans, but yesterday ground down in an odious slavery and to-day the free and light-hearted comrades of a man who by his kindly ways has retained the little colony in a place where the associations must be painful enough.

The attraction of the gardens is too strong to be resisted, and we wander out, strolling amidst the clumps of tall, brilliantly coloured plants, anon gazing in rapt admiration at the warm line of the distant hills which hold up against the gorgeous crimson of the sunset a delicate fringe of palm foliage, or watching the hummingbirds which chase each other in the branches and form a dancing cohort of glowing brands. When night fell a golden light pervaded the atmosphere. We did not go in until we had taken a look at the stud, which boasts some of the finest English sires, and we wound up the evening by an amusing performance by an agreeable African conjurer, who gave an explanation in French of all his tricks and was clad in gentlemanly attire—frock-coat, white tie, tan shoes, all the latest style of the *Floresta*.

To-morrow, a good hour before sunrise, we are to start for a last visit to the Brazilian forest, and although a heartless doctor has forbidden me riding exercise, I have not the strength of mind to refuse the expedition. They set me accordingly upon a plank, having a high wheel on either side, and soon I taste the joys of football, not as player, but as ball, leaping with its round elasticity heavenwards after a vigorous kick. And the pleasure of bounding upwards is as nothing to the austere sensation of falling back again on the implacable boot sole. In this fashion I was rolled through a series of black holes which I was told would appear in the sunlight to be valleys. As luck would have it, we presently came upon a hill that had to be climbed, and my courser dropped to a footpace. The violent shocks of the earlier part of the journey now gave place to a comparatively simple sensation that suggested an anvil beneath the blows of a hammer. Then the day broke. Señor Soarès, junior, who watched my progress from the back of a tall steed, pointed out his first experiments with rubber-plants and with cocoa, and described his coffee-gardens, of which I had already seen some specimens. The sufferings of the lower part of my person now gave way to the admiration of the higher as I mentally compared the wretched, stunted lives in our cities with the wide freedom of existence led by this high-spirited youth who was wrestling out here in the glorious sunshine with the exuberant forces of a fruitful Nature which he is certain to master in time. O you, my French brethren who in alpaca coats sit eternally on your stools, bent over useless documents, know that the earth has not yet exhausted her gifts, learn that there is another life, free from the anæmic, cramping condition which you know! This thought was still in my mind when we turned our reins across the moors that led to the coffee plantations, where dried palm-leaves protect the young shoots from the heat of the sun, and where the new species derived from a plant grown on the sacred hill of Montmartre-en-Paris is being carefully cultivated. Come out here, young men in shiny threadbare sleeves who make your way homewards nightly to the close dens around the Sacré Cœur; come and see these black coffee-planters—men, women, and children—living close to Nature on the outskirts of civilisation, and compare your own wretched quarters furnished by Dufayel on the "hire" system, that has cost you such anxious moments, with the blissful nudity of these cabins, and tell me where you see the worst form of slavery, here amongst the newly emancipated Africans or at home under your own roofs.

The forest! the forest! I have seen it once and again, but I could never tire of it, and my great regret is that I cannot come back again to it. The sun has made its sudden appearance on the scene, glowing like a violent conflagration, and a thousand voices from the winged population of the woods have greeted him, singing the joy of light returned. Everywhere is the same eternal hymn to life. I was shown a small bird whose female dances round her spouse as soon as he begins to pour forth his love serenade in joyous notes. Blue and yellow toucans dazzle us with their splendour. Valleys filled with colossal ferns open out in the daylight their unexpected vistas of a delirious vegetation. I ask after the monkeys. Alas! they do not leave their retreats before two o'clock in the afternoon. They only arrive for five o'clock tea! But for no inducement would they leave their dressing-rooms until the sun has gone down to the horizon. When you have once seen the heart of the forest wilderness, where the same luxuriant life in manifold manifestations is to be seen at your feet and in the high tree and hilltops, where profusely flowering creepers wind themselves around every twig and bough, placing these forest kings in tender bondage, you will not blame the monkeys for being content to remain in their sumptuous domain. I was shown fruit half eaten, the refuse of a monkeys' restaurant. I can well believe it. A wood-cutter told me he was attacked yesterday by a dozen, who were so pertinacious that he had to defend himself with his stick. Thus, though I never saw a monkey, I did see a man who had seen one.

At last we reached a waterfall which was, it appears, the limit of our excursion. On our way back we came to a difficult crossing, and as my horse was even more exhausted than myself by the rough treatment he had given me, he was taken out of the shafts, and a swarm of some eleven negroes pulled and pushed me along, with bursts of laughter at their performance. But for their chuckles, I might have fancied myself some Roman victor arriving in triumph. It lasted only ten minutes, but I should have been covered with confusion had some chance cinematograph been on the spot to reproduce the scene. This misfortune was spared me. Thanks to the fact, I take the pleasure of holding myself up to ridicule.

The ceremony of inaugurating the Montmartre coffee-plant took place half-way. The operation is less difficult than might be thought. I climbed up a slope from whose top I could see rows of holes, with heaps of coffee-plants, their roots carefully wrapped up, and each in a small basket by itself, lying at intervals over the prepared ground. One of these baskets with its young green stem was offered to me, I stuck it in the first hole that came handy, and thus the glory of Montmartre, like that of Brazil, reached its apogee.

I do not know what will become of *my* coffee enterprise at Santa Alda. It is more certain that Señor Soarès has begun to manure his land instead of merely scattering the shells of the berries over it. It is possible that the Brazilian *fazenderos* will be a little worried by this example, seeing in it only a way of increasing expenses. But the established fact that Señor Soarès's coffees are in great demand seems a curious coincidence, for no one can suppose he amuses himself in this way for the fun of losing his money. When I left Santa Alda, I carried with me a pretty collection of canes made from the finest woods produced on the *fazenda*, and on board the *Principe Umberto*, which brought me back to Europe, I discovered a chest of coffee, which enabled me to give my kind hosts the authentic testimony of a consumer.

The *Principe Umberto* is in every way like the *Regina Elena*, as indeed she ought to be considering her origin. There are the same comfortable arrangements, the same excellent service, the same Latin courtesy from the officers. We had two adventures on the voyage. A madman threw himself into the sea one night. The siren shrieked the alarm. A boat put off but returned after a fruitless search. I was told that this was a typical "return" case. On the way out Hope holds us by the hand. To make one's way back, after disappointments, is for human weakness perhaps a sore trial. We do not all get to Corinth. Let us pity those who make this an excuse for never setting out. The commissary told me the story of one third-class passenger, all in rags, who deposited with him when he came on board the sum of 150,000 francs. There are evidently compensations.

The second adventure was more general in interest. It took the form of a strike among the coal-heavers of St. Vincent. The harbour, with its border of bare rock, lay still and deserted. A few saucy niggers dived for our edification after coins flung from the ship. But that was all, neither white nor black man appeared, for the order had been given that no one should come off to meet us and we on our side were forbidden to land. We need not be astonished if the first lesson learnt by the blacks from their white "superiors" is that of violence preached by grandiloquent politicians, trembling inwardly with fear, but, none the less, tenacious in their inglorious arguments. The negroes have the excuse of having reached our civilisation late in the day. Are we too exigent when we implore the whites to preach by example?

We coal at Las Palmas, the capital of the Grand Canary. As other boats are there ahead of us, we are obliged to spend an entire day in harbour. We land, therefore. The "Happy Isles" have inherited from the ancients such a reputation that some disappointment is inevitable. Seen from the sea, the Canaries show only a cluster of arid rocks devoid of vegetation. Las Palmas is a picturesque town whose palms can but inspire an amiable benevolence in people who have seen Brazil. The country is purely African in character. Square white houses without windows, banana-groves down in the valleys, hills of calcined stones. After an hour or two along a road that is thick with dust, you reach a pretty restaurant standing in a garden whose exotic vegetation would be charming if one had never seen the Riviera. The canary of the islands that is said to abound revealed itself to me in the guise of a vulgar chattering sparrow. Yet the boatmen who boarded our ship offered authentic canaries in cages hung from a long rod, but I was told they had been procured from Holland. These birds have a particularly sweet song, and they sing to order, oddly enough. It is enough to shout to the seller, "Your canary does not sing," for the birds to burst into a flood of trills and turns. It is the triumph of a songster with the imitative faculty. Buyer and seller both are taken in and the greatest *serin* (canary, also used to mean "duffer") is not the one you might think.

Before I take my leave of the reader, I want to say a word for the creation of a line of fast ships making the journey between France and South America. So little space remains to me that I cannot treat the subject as I should like. The case is simple; formerly the French line was very popular, but it has allowed itself to be entirely outdistanced by other companies who have built more rapid boats while we continue to send our old vessels over the sea. The contract held by the Messageries Maritimes expires in 1912. By some culpable negligence no steps have been taken to improve the service or even to continue it. The matter cannot rest there. If we are to enlarge our dealings with South America, it is of capital importance to France to have a service of rapid boats fitted up on the most comfortable of modern lines.

I shall venture to make a brief extract here from a report that I got my friend Edmond Théry to make out for me, since his authority in matters economic is universally known.

For the last twenty years there has been a prodigious increase of production and public wealth in the two Americas. This fact accounts for the enormously increased proportion of travellers to Europe drawn from North America, Mexico, Brazil, the Argentine, etc. The proof is that the luxurious hotels springing up anew almost daily in Paris and on the Riviera to cater for this class of customer are always crowded.

Brazil and the Argentine Republic have more especially profited by the rise in value of their land. In the course of the last ten years, from 1900 to 1909, their working railways have gone up from 14,027 kilometres to 19,080 in Brazil, and from 16,563 to 25,508 kilometres in the Argentine Republic.

These 13,998 kilometres of new lines (46 per cent. increase since 1900) have opened the door to agriculture, cattle-breeding, forestry, in immense and hitherto desert regions, and the results of this may be traced in the increase of their foreign trade:

Foreign Trade of Brazil and the Argentine Republic in Ten Years.

	1900	1909	Total increase in 1909.	
	Millions of Francs.	Millions of Francs.	Millions of Francs.	Per Cent.
Brazil— Imports............	634	935	301	47

Exports..........	836	1,606	770	92
Total........	1,470	2,541	1,071	73
Argentine Republic				
Imports..........	567	1,514	947	167
Exports..........	773	1,987	1,214	157
Total........	1,340	3,501	2,161	161

Thus during a short period of ten years the exports—*i. e.*, the surplus of home-grown articles after supplying the needs of the country—have increased in value by 770 millions of francs, 90 per cent., for Brazil, and 1214 millions, or 157 per cent., for the Argentine Republic. As for the total value of the foreign trade of the two countries, it has risen 1071 millions of francs for the former and 2161 millions for the latter: in other words, an average of 107 millions of francs per annum for Brazil and 216 millions for the Argentine.

These startling figures show clearly enough the importance of the economic advance the two countries are making, and we may say that French capital has built up this prosperity.

We ought now to seek to retain the advantages to be drawn from our financial intervention in the new Brazilian and Argentine undertakings, and one of the best ways to attain this end is to make sure of rapid means of communication between France and the two great South American Republics, which shall be up-to-date in every way and luxurious enough to induce Brazilians and Argentinos to come to Europe and return to their own country in French boats rather than in English, German, or Italian vessels.

Such means of communication are already in existence between France and the United States, but are wholly lacking in the direction of Brazil and the Argentine Republic.

The French boats which call at these stations have been a long time in use, and their fittings are in no sense in conformity with modern ideas of luxury such as the class of travellers to which I have already alluded invariably expects. As for their average speed, it certainly never goes beyond fourteen knots, for they make the journey from Bordeaux to Rio de Janeiro, with the different scheduled stops by the way, in a minimum of seventeen days, and if they go on as far as Buenos Ayres, in twenty-two days.

The distance between Bordeaux and these two ports being 4901 and 5991 nautical miles respectively, it is only necessary to have boats capable of doing twenty knots as an average, or twenty-three miles an hour, for the journey to Rio de Janeiro to be performed in ten days and five hours, and that to Buenos Ayres in twelve days fifteen hours.

There is nothing to add to this clear statement of the case.

And now, how can I resist the temptation to draw some sort of conclusion from these rambling notes, made with the sole desire to make use of the knowledge acquired for the benefit of French extension, and this in the interest of humanity at large? In every calling there is but one road to success—work. When Candide returned from Buenos Ayres, he brought back from his travels the lesson that we must work in our gardens. Since his days our gardens have grown considerably, and since we are ourselves the first elemental instrument for all work, the first condition of improvement must be the improvement of the material. Therefore let us work.